NEVER A DISCONNECT

NEVER A DISCONNECT

SADHNA SHANKER

NIYOGI
BOOKS

Published by
NIYOGI BOOKS
D-78, Okhla Industrial Area, Phase-I
New Delhi-110 020, INDIA
Tel: 91-11-26816301, 26813350, 51, 52
Fax: 91-11-26810483, 26813830
email: niyogibooks@gmail.com
website: www.niyogibooks.com

Cover Design: artcreations

ISBN: 978-81-89738-66-2

Publication: 2010

All characters in the book are fictitious and any similarity to persons living or dead is purely coincidental.

Printed at: Niyogi Offset Pvt. Ltd., New Delhi, India

For my parents Malti and Gauri Shanker
and for those who love me.

One Thursday in May

What the Maths teacher is saying makes no sense to her. She looks around in a daze at the other girls sitting in the class. How normal everyone looks—Smriti is actually raising her hand to answer a question and Diya, as usual, is staring out of the window. Parul's mind is in a whirl. She wants to stand up and scream out to the world—my mother is getting married today. I am so angry, so mad … and so scared.

Instead, she feels a lump in her throat and blinks furiously. 'Parul, what do you think the correct answer should be?' Why is the teacher being so cruel to her? Ten-year-olds have many problems to tackle other than those mathematical! If only the teacher would leave her alone. If only she could share the overwhelming sense of despair with someone. She feels ashamed that her mother is getting married. Such things just never happened! *Never*! None of her classmates ever had such ignominy heaped on them. Tara's parents were divorced too, so at least she, Parul, was not the only one whose parents had divorced. But no one's mother had married again—it sounded kind of obscene!

Parul had lived with her Ma, Nana and Nani since she was about two years old. Ma told her about the divorce when Parul was six, after Ma returned from Japan. Parul understood that divorce meant that her father and mother did not live together as they were no longer married.

Ma taught her what to say unhesitatingly if anyone asked about her father. She had learnt to deal with the situation.

But now this! Mothers don't marry; it is unimaginable, unacceptable. The break is over. It is nearly ten-thirty. They must have already left for the court. In another two hours, just about the time she usually reaches home, it would all be over. Ma would be married. In court. Nobody marries in court—marriage is a colourful affair with new clothes and good food. Just two months ago, they had gone to attend Vidya Didi's wedding. What fun it had been. Running around in new clothes, tugging playfully at the strings of marigold and dancing with abandon to loud music.

But Vidya Didi was young. She did not have a ten-year-old daughter fighting her tears in school while her Ma got married.

Parul wished the day at school would never end. Worse still, her best friend Shipra has not turned up today. Some time ago, she had told Shipra what was happening in her life. Shipra had listened to her attentively, and then asked rather sweetly, 'Do you like your new Daddy?'

Does she like him? Her mind searches for an answer. At the moment, it is not important. What matters is not whether she likes who Ma is marrying, but that she is marrying.

The bell rings. School is over. Parul drags her feet towards the bus that takes her home. But outside the gate, Gaurav Bhaiyya is waiting with the driver in Nana's blue Maruti. So today she will not spend time in the bus. She will be whisked away home. Gaurav

Bhaiyya opens the car door for her. She steps in, shrugging off in a second the burden of her schoolbag, and stares at the rear-view mirror till her school is reduced to a speck.

Gaurav Bhaiyya holds her cold and clammy hand silently through the drive. As the car turns into the lane in the government colony in Pandara Road where they live, Parul notices the parking space left vacant by their red Maruti. So they have gone in Ma's car! Later, Reena Didi tells her that Ma actually drove to the court for the marriage.

Desultorily, Parul enters the empty house. Usually, it is empty when she returns home. But today it feels different. At that moment, she feels she hates her mother the most in the world.

The cast is very uncomfortable. It is extremely hot outside. In May, summer in Delhi can be quite killing. It does—every year many die as the relentless heat wave spreads its sway across North India.

Inside the dull and drab hospital room, the rickety air conditioner tries to win a losing battle against the heat creeping insidiously from every nook and corner. Aarti Devi mops her sweating forehead with the towel kept near the pillow. Why do we build houses with swanky tiled bathrooms when we are young? As we get on in years, we slip on those very tiles, and land up with casts in hospitals. One can never understand when young, how difficult old age can be—even mere physical balance becomes precarious with every passing year. Probably that is why Indians consider marriage essential—a *sanskar*—a cherished ritual, something that has to be done. To have children and a companion by your side in old age. Couples spend a lifetime in dreadful or indifferent marriages—just for this security.

But why is she thinking of these things? Aarti Devi tries to turn on her side, but cannot. The cast in her leg is too thick and stiff. She cannot turn over without help. However, today no one is around to help her. Everyone is busy with her daughter's wedding. Lying alone in the hospital room, Aarti Devi wants to be with her daughter in mind and spirit, but she finds her thoughts are more with her granddaughter. Ever since Parul, at the tender age of two, moved out from her father's house with her mother, Aarti Devi has thought of her as her third daughter.

'*Asal se sood pyara hota hai*' (The interest is more delectable than the principal)—an old saying flashes across her mind—Aarti Devi never understood how true this was until the small bundle called Parul came to live with them. The fun and frolic she never shared with her own daughters, was hers to have with this little one.

She feels the sweat inside the cast. She could never imagine herself in hospital, bound to the bed on the day when her daughter was getting married. But she slipped in the bathroom just a week before. Was it the tension of looking into the details of the upcoming marriage, or her inability to figure out whether it was a good thing for her daughter, or just that the tiles were too slippery—she cannot decide. The outcome, however, is that here she is with a big cast on her puny leg, all alone, with her thoughts for company while the marriage is taking place a mere two miles away.

It is nearly 2 pm. Parul must have come back from school. No one in the family had married in court till today. No one in the family had gone in for a second marriage either.

When Abha's marriage failed, Aarti Devi had felt very guilty and insufficient as a parent. Something must have been lacking in the way she had brought up her children, in the values she had instilled in them. Her daughter had not been able to adjust to her new surroundings and carry on living, as a married girl should have—even after Parul was born. Yet, when she had seen the resolve in her daughter's eyes, Aarti Devi had put all doubts resolutely behind her and stood by her side—through the courtroom drama, the custody battle and the tough years of single parenthood.

Why does the mobile not ring to confirm that the marriage has taken place? Court marriages hardly take time. She knows that. She wants someone to bring Parul to the hospital. She knows Parul is upset. There is no right or wrong in what is happening. It is simply to be accepted.

For all of them, it is a difficult day. Most of all, for her daughter, perhaps … .

Delhi, Growing Up

When Abha was born, she was dark, and a very ordinary looking child. Moreover, she was a second daughter. Aarti Devi had seen disappointment writ large on her husband's face—the newborn was not the son he had so desired. When she had come home from hospital, and enquired about the new pram, her husband had replied flatly, 'The old one will do'. That was the only vocal expression of disappointment from him.

Each time they travelled to his dusty ancestral village in the heart of Uttar Pradesh, the village women would surround her. 'Lali, when are you having the boy? Someone has to inherit the land here you know!' Not that there was much of it. However, a patch of land in the village was essential in their time. They were the eager generation of free India. Busy building the new country, while keeping their rural roots alive.

Employed with the railways, Aarti Devi's husband worked in different parts of India. Her father-in-law lived with them. The annual visits to the village continued till her father-in-law was alive. Each time they landed up with only Bina and Abha in tow, the loud advice would be dished out again—loud enough for Aarti Devi to eventually start hating the village.

Her health did not permit her to have any more children. She never asked herself if she wanted a son. The cacophony around her never gave her the space to understand her own desires. She immersed herself in bringing up her two daughters.

Whenever Aarti Devi saw them play, she was struck by the difference. Bina was fair and delicate looking; Abha was dark and had blunt features. Her only redeeming features were her eyes. Big, bright and intelligent.

But that was then. As the years went by, her dusky younger daughter grew into a charming young girl. She lost her dark hue and her razor-sharp mind reflected in her nicely rounded face. Aarti Devi's two daughters were beautiful, each in their own way. The house was full of the camaraderie and love only sisters could share.

Aarti Devi had completed her graduation, a rare feat for her times. It had come about because her father, a district judge from the British times, was a great believer in education. He had tried to find educated and professionally employed husbands for his four daughters. Aarti Devi was married to Abha's father. An engineer in the railways, he came from a humbler background. But that was not the only difference between them.

Aarti Devi and her husband had their differences, though none of the kind afflicting many modern marriages. There was no other person, no conflicting careers, no material clashes. Their difference was one of personality. In her time, women had to mould themselves to their husbands' wishes and demands. There was no scope to think or even dream of living a life of their own. Aarti Devi was educated in her father's house where a newspaper came everyday. Her alert and thinking mind nibbled at her soul and nebulous longings took root. Fortunately, with each new generation women change—maybe gradually and imperceptibly, but they do.

Aarti Devi's mother had been married off at twelve. She had borne her judge husband twelve children, nine of whom survived. She was barely literate. But she had disagreed with her husband regarding his views on the freedom struggle. When Mahatma Gandhi gave his clarion call for the boycott of mill-made and foreign goods as part of the non-cooperation movement, she had burnt her mill-made saris. She had gone a step further in the freedom struggle and given shelter in her government house to her husband's brother—a freedom fighter. Her anglicized husband, who dreamt of travelling to England one day, could do nothing about it.

For Aarti Devi, the need for her own space and aspirations did not need a freedom struggle to surface. It crept into her soul silently.

It was already 7.30 pm and there was no news as to when Aarti Devi's husband would return from office. In winter, the sun sets early in Delhi, and the dark cold evenings ensure that people remain huddled inside their homes. Located in an open area on the way to the airport, the railways had provided them with a double-storied house, with a big lawn and backyard, but only three rooms. As her father-in-law walked up and down the verandah upstairs, the constant tap of his walking stick grated on Aarti Devi's nerves. Both the girls were studying in their room upstairs. At least Bina was. Abha was in the room with her, so Aarti Devi hoped she too was studying. Apart from the sound of the stick striking the floor at regular intervals, there was only a deafening silence.

The quiet within the house and in the railway colony, with vast lawns separating houses, made Aarti Devi's sense of isolation even more acute. Her husband remained on tour nearly every week, and even when he was in town, he never came home until it was near dinner time. Aarti Devi would sit through long evenings, wrapped up in loneliness, waiting for her husband to come home.

On such evenings, the headlights of the car would light up the driveway, indicating that at last he was home. The bell would ring and the moment Sarbati, the maid, opened the door, he would go upstairs. After speaking to his father for five minutes, he would be back, but for Aarti Devi those five minutes would seem interminable. Their conversations would follow a similar pattern.

'Let us have dinner. Call the girls. Dadda must have had his food. Tomorrow I have to go on tour for two days.'

'We have a dinner invitation at the club for day after tomorrow.'

'Aarti you know that I hate wasting time at the club. I will not be in town either.'

'It is always like this. You have no time for me or for a life with me. You only think about work.'

'Don't start this again Aarti. You know that work is important. I just don't understand what you want.'

He was a man in the traditional mould. He gave his wife all material comfort, status, children—but he could never understand that there was, or could be, something more to share between a man and a woman. He was the husband of a beautiful and educated bride. He loved his job and was passionate about it. Aarti knew nothing about that part of his life, and he did not think it necessary to share with her what happened in his professional life. In his mind, home and work were two separate spheres with no congruence.

Bina would be able hear the voices upstairs. She would cringe. They were arguing again. She hated it. Abha would be busy reading a book. Bina often wondered how Abha managed to block their fights out of her system?

The club lawns were spic and span and the winter sun shone bright. The women were dressed in their finery. The swish of expensive saris mingled with the tinkle of jewellery and the whiff of exotic perfumes. It was the monthly meeting of the railway officers' wives in the colony. This was the favourite pastime of railway officers' wives. The Mahila Samiti meetings and activities kept most of them busy.

'Hello, I am Mrs. H.V. Saxena, Deputy Chief Engineer (Track). We are new to this colony.'

'I am Aarti. My husband is Deputy Chief Engineer (Construction). We have been here for a while now.'

Aarti Devi wondered why women completely submerged their identities into that of their husbands in this manner. She had come for a Mahila Samiti meeting after a long time, hoping that after a long gap the group would have something new and interesting to offer. The faces had changed, but not the topics of discussion—recipes, problems with servants, gossip about those not present. None of this engaged her mind. Each time she attended such meetings, she came away with the firm resolve that her daughters would not be doing this in the future. Not just this.

Like millions of mothers before her, she decided that her daughters would not live the life she did.

'How can you fail in Maths? Or any other subject for that matter!' Aarti Devi was aghast when she saw the red line in Abha's report card.

'I will clear the finals Mummy, don't worry,' said Abha, nonchalantly tossing the report card on the table. Then she scampered up the stairs to her room. Her ponytail bounced on her shoulders as she made her way.

How could two children born and brought up in the same household be so different? It was incomprehensible. Bina was always at the top of her grade; she was up-to-date with her homework, never chatted on the phone and rarely went out—the ideal daughter. Abha was the other extreme—casual about studies, innumerable friends, never at home. The difference was so stark that at times Aarti Devi wondered if they were both her own.

The phone started ringing.

'Aunty may I speak to Abha,'—a teenage boy whose voice must have recently begun cracking, tried to sound gruff.

Now boys had started calling her. No boy had ever called Bina in all these years. Her husband would be very angry if he knew of it. After enquiring from the young caller his identity, Aarti Devi called out to Abha. She came running down and spoke for a few minutes and then was off again.

It was all right. Aarti Devi told herself. They knew the parents of the young caller well. In the railway colony that provided some comfort at least. She picked up the report card and kept it on her husband's study table. She knew there would be another flare up at home when he got back from his tour to Allahabad.

Abha and her father were always at loggerheads. He did not want her to play or swim in the colony club everyday. He wanted her to be at home, study and be more like Bina. The eternal tension between the young and old constantly hung like a taut wire across the house.

Aarti Devi swung like a pendulum from one end of the wire to the other. As often happens, unhappy marriages tend to divide parents over children. Aarti Devi found herself unwittingly on Abha's side during the fierce arguments that often broke out at the dining table.

'Why should she not go to play at the club? All the officers' children go there. We don't go there because you don't like it, but why must that be a punishment for our children?' or 'Abha talks on the phone a lot, I know, but she also manages her studies well. We know all her friends—they are children of our colleagues. Even if they are boys.'

And now this. Aarti Devi's arguments seemed to have lost their basis. Abha had never brought home a red-marked reportcard before. Aarti Devi was disappointed and sad. Not only because Abha had failed, but also because she strongly felt that in the times to come, Maths was going to be essential for a bright future. And that is what she wanted for her daughters—a bright future, where they would be financially independent and secure.

Ever since Aarti Devi had decided to concentrate on her daughters, she had a one-point mission. To instil in her daughters the need to be financially independent. She was not going to do what other mothers did—groom daughters from the day they were born for a single goal—marriage to a suitable boy.

'Don't take up sports! Your husband's family may not like it.' 'Learn to cook well, it will stand you in good stead.' 'By the time they are nineteen or twenty we must find a good match for them.'

Everything in a girl's life was geared only towards a good marriage. Little surprise then that girls often grew up without any clear ambition, and without a keen desire to work. This was the cycle Aarti Devi wished to break. She wanted her daughters to think of a career first and marriage thereafter. Change had to touch the lives of her daughters at home for them to think differently.

She would neither dangle the option of marriage before them nor threaten them with it. First, they would have to become financially independent before marriage was even remotely considered.

This was Aarti Devi's legacy to her daughters. She thought about these things often in the lonely evenings. She spent them in dreaming about the future of her daughters.

It was a pleasant summer night. The moon was incandescent in the sky. On the terrace, the beds were neatly laid out. The white sheets were like extended rays of the moon above them. Cool and inviting.

In the late 1970s, Delhi was safe enough for families to sleep outside, especially when they were living in the protected environs of a railway colony. The Indian Railways owns some prime properties in each city. Delhi was no different. On the road to the airport, in front of the green belt of the Ridge, the houses of the colony gleamed in the moonlight.

Tucked into bed, Bina and Abha could see the eucalyptus tree bending and swaying in the wind above the wall of the terrace. The leaves of the old mango tree rustled in the garden below. Their parents had gone to sleep. Ensconced in the snug comfort of bed, the two of them held hands and talked.

'How come you failed in Maths?'

'Bina di, you know how I hate it. I hate all the subjects that require calculation—Physics, Chemistry. They are all trash. Once I finish the tenth Board exams, I will never look at them again.'

'But Papa will not let you drop Science in school. He thinks, and I think quite rightly, that Science in school opens up many options for you after the twelfth grade.'

'What Bina di? He didn't let you join IIT, even though you qualified. You ended up with Economics which you hate.'

Some silences just continue the conversation before words take on the relay once again.

'Abha, you must not fail in the finals. That would be disastrous. Remember as a student you are supposed to study—that is your primary work. If you excel in studies, you can get your way in other things far more easily.'

Bina could see Abha's face in the moonlight. The way her chin seemed to shrivel up when she was sticking stubbornly to her thoughts. As the elder child of the family, Bina felt she needed to take on the responsibilities a younger one could easily ignore. Perhaps, the price the first-born has to pay for the undivided love of parents till another child comes along. Perhaps …

If Mummy was tense, or there was a fight or an argument with Papa, Abha was out of the house. But Bina always stayed back, trying to calm things down. She listened to both of them—tried to understand both points of view calmly, in a non-judgmental manner and tried to soothe ruffled feathers. She tried to do things that would not upset either of her parents. She was the peacekeeper in that house. She was always there. Bina was home once back from college. Her friends rarely came over. She never went out to play either.

Abha was the one ready to fight out the smallest issue. Probably in the five years between the two girls, Mummy had managed to shed from her DNA the submission programmed into a woman's genes over centuries.

'That's right Bina di—it never struck me. If I do what I am supposed to be doing well, then the rest falls into place. Goodnight. Tomorrow I am going cycling with Simran in the morning. She will be here at 6.30 am.'

The moon seemed to smile. It was as if it could see what the lesson learnt on the terrace would yield in future.

Abha did not take Science after the tenth grade. A compromise was reached. For her part, she took Commerce to ensure that Maths remained part of her life while her father agreed on the stipulation that she would try to secure admission in the prestigious Shri Ram College of Commerce in Delhi University. At last, she was free of the drudgery of Physics and Chemistry.

The day it was finally decided, Abha rushed to Simran's house on her bicycle. Simran's house was smaller than her own, and full of people—Simran's parents, and their four children. Ravi Bhaiyya, the eldest brother, Simran, Shikha and then Seema. Their home was very different from Abha's. Simran's parents never fought. Her mother did all the housework with the girls pitching in. Ravi Bhaiyya was the pampered one. He had a room all to himself, while the girls shared one room. Being the eldest among the three, it was called Simran's room.

Soon Abha and Simran were out of the house and Abha was cycling around the colony with Simran sitting behind. Simran watched the wind cut through Abha's hair as she cycled around in the winter dusk. Why was Abha her only friend? Abha always had so many others—Ritu, Nisha and not to forget all the boys she played badminton with. However, over the years of a shared childhood, Simran knew she was Abha's closest friend. They had shared the pain and agony of the first period, the excitement and secrecy of the first crush and the consequent endless cycling around the boys' school bus-stop and not to forget, a glimpse of the forbidden the first time that they had stolen a book from Simran's brother's locked cupboard.

It was one of those rare days when no one was home except Simran. Ravi Bhaiyya had taken the family to their maternal uncle's home. Simran had stayed back due to housework. Abha was always keen to have a closer look into the forbidden arena of Ravi Bhaiyya's room. After much prodding Simran had agreed that day. They entered the room, which had been left open. His clothes were strewn on the bed awaiting Simran. A wooden cupboard stood in the corner with an imposing lock in the corner.

'That remains locked Abha. Let us go. There is nothing to interest you here.'

'Come on Simran let us see what he tries to hide in it.' Abha started looking around the room for the key. Maybe her enthusiasm was infectious, so Simran also began to search. They found the key in the most unimaginative place. On top of the cupboard.

They opened the cupboard with a sense of thrill. It was full of books, magazines, cigarettes and whisky bottles. The thrill of discovering the contents of the cupboard was overshadowed by the fear of being caught. Simran grabbed a book and a magazine and quickly shut the cupboard. Taking them to her room they hid them among a pile of books. Over time, they devoured them and when realization dawned that this is what men and women do—they were unable to look at each other for sometime. It was even difficult to imagine that one's own parents did 'that kind of thing'. But that was when they were eleven.

That had been a long time ago. Now in their teens, they felt they were well versed in the entire theory of sex—dirty jokes, dirty magazines and so on. Simran's brother had been a boon; his hidden treasures were a great storehouse of information for the two of them.

'Simran, let us go to CP tomorrow. I have been thinking. I want to get my nose pierced.'

Abha had stopped her cycle on the side. Whenever an idea struck her, she promptly pulled up.

'Have you asked your mum? It is a lifetime thing you know. And where do you plan to go?'

'I think it will look nice on me and by the way it's my nose you know. One of my cousins got her nose pierced at Bhimji Zaveri, you know, the jewellers. I have enough of my pocket money saved up.'

The next day they both took a Delhi Transport Corporation bus towards Connaught Place. The bus sped along the heavily wooded Wellington Crescent and turned the roundabout at Gol Daak Khana. Simran loved reading the thought put up on the notice board of a Church that was clearly visible as the bus passed by. In Connaught Place they got off the bus at Regal, and walked across to Janpath, to the jewellers. In a matter of ten minutes, without too much pain, Abha had a nose ring. She looked rather nice, thought Simran.

Once back in the colony, Simran went off to her own house, while Abha went home. Aarti Devi was shocked to see her pierced nose. She did not have a pierced nose, nor did Bina.

'You should have told me you were planning it. I would have taken you.'

Aarti Devi knew that Abha had this fiercely independent streak, and presently she could not be angry with her. Abha had done very well in the tenth Board exams and she deserved some kind of a gift. In her mind, Aarti Devi promised herself that she would buy Abha a nice nose stud soon.

The next evening, Abha was preening her new nose ring in the railway club. Again, Simran felt slightly out of sorts. She never understood how Abha sometimes made her feel so unnecessary. As if she did not matter in her life. Simran shook off the feeling. It was a heady time. All of them had cleared the first big hurdle of life, the last two years of school remained and then college beckoned around the corner.

Growing up in the railway colony together, most of the children had known each other over the years. There was always an opportunity to make new friends, as people moved in and out, as well as build lifelong relationships. Each of them, from their old group, had now a personality of their own. Ritu was slim and sexy, Nisha was a pain, Simran was homely and Abha was bright and beautiful.

'It's a deadly combination you know—a woman cannot and should not be both bright and beautiful. Makes a man feel inadequate.'

When Ravi Bhaiyya had rejected a wonderful girl for marriage, this was his explanation. Simran wondered if it was true. It did not matter to her much. At sixteen, all she wanted was to be beautiful and if possible do well in the forthcoming exams. Abha and Simran were lying on the bed in Simran's room, staring at the ceiling. Simran told Abha about Ravi Bhaiyya's reasoning. Outside, the lazy winter sun receded from the trees like a shawl dropping off a woman's shoulders. A Wills Navycut cigarette packet was lying unattended on the bed. Simran saw that Abha was eyeing it repeatedly.

'Don't even think about it. If my mother finds out that I tried it she will kill me.'

'How come your brother smokes then?'

'He is a man Abha. They can do all this. We are girls; we should not. It is not done.'

'Who wants to be a smoker? I want to try it. No one is at home. Get a light.'

Simran always found it difficult to resist Abha's suggestions. Bolting the room from inside, Abha lit the cigarette. The smoke was rancid; it made them cough and gasp. Three drags and the feeling had subsided. Then it hit them. The swirling sensation of tobacco inhaled for the first time. By the time the cigarette burnt out, the room was full of smoke. Simran opened all the windows in panic, put the fan on at top speed and lit *agarbattis* to get rid of the smell.

Why is there always such a thrill in breaking taboos? Each day as they inhaled, they knew smoking was not something to get into. But the kick of stealing cigarettes one by one from Ravi's packet, finding places to light them, feeling grown up while inhaling and never getting caught—the sensation was simply heady.

After a few weeks, Abha had declared one day, 'Simran, I think this is enough. We have spent the whole vacation puffing nearly everyday. I don't want to become a smoker you know. Now that I know what it is like.'

Simran was glad about this renunciation. She did not enjoy it much and was scared to death each time they hid and smoked, since it was mostly her house where they indulged.

The last two years of school began on a fresh slate and the potential smokers were lost in the pall of smoke that had disappeared from their lives.

Bina was getting married. At last, thought Bina. Although she agreed with Mummy that girls should be economically independent, she was keen to marry. Apart from the usual reasons, she wanted to be free of her peacekeeping role. Marriage seemed the only escape. When parents spend most of their married life arguing and fighting, it can be tiring and at times just overwhelming for the children.

Bina had completed her Master's from the prestigious Delhi School of Economics, and thereafter appeared for various competitive exams for government jobs or banks. Despite her father's insistence, for a change she had ruled out taking up teaching. The results of her efforts were awaited when Papa suggested the prospect of Kishore as a match. In the hallowed Indian Administrative Service, and of the same caste, Kishore was the ultimate suitable boy.

Kishore had come to see Bina with his family. She had liked his soft and courteous approach, but he was barely her height. Mummy and Papa had explained to her that in the long run it did not matter. As long as the family was good, the boy well placed and presentable, height was not a concern. Anyway, he was not shorter than she was. Both sides gave a yes.

Aarti Devi had agreed, despite her lifelong promise to herself that her daughter should be financially independent before marriage. The proposal had everything going for it. It would be foolish to ignore it. She was above all, a loving mother—wanting the best for her daughters. And in life many promises are meant to be broken.

Bina's marriage was solemnized in Lucknow where Kishore's family lived. It was a colourful and joyous affair. The swirl of relatives, colourful dresses, food, music and most of all Bina's radiant glowing face had given a feeling of fulfilment to Aarti Devi. The thought of her emotional sounding board going out of her life depressed her a little. However, she also knew in her heart that it was a good match for her loving, compassionate and considerate elder daughter.

Abha had worked hard for the marriage, although her twelfth Board exams were only two months away. The family had gathered in the verandah, near the car that would take Bina to her new home. Aarti Devi saw stress and pain writ large in her younger daughter's eyes. It was incredible that two such different individuals could be so closely bonded, but then that is love—it grows roots wherever there is fertile ground.

Bina, the responsible and caring daughter, was looking around for Abha. She saw her standing near a pillar looking forlorn and lost. For a moment, Bina was taken aback. She had never seen Abha look so defenceless. In her casual and 'couldn't care less' demeanour, one often forgot that Abha was a caring and loving person. She had her own way of expressing it. When Bina went and put her arms around her younger sister, Abha broke into a hungry sob. In the corner, Papa was crying away and Abha too was sobbing. Strangely, the two people in the house who remained fairly indifferent generally were overwhelmed by the marriage while Aarti Devi and Bina were very much in control.

'Abha, now that I won't be there, please try and stay home more often. Mummy needs company and you have to now broker peace between them.'

Bina had passed on the baton. The car drove off, and in a few days the remaining three had returned to Delhi. To home, to school, to exams and to greater intimacy between Mummy and Abha.

Aarti Devi noticed the change that came into Abha. She remained at home more often, tried not to argue with her father and spent more time with her mother. Her exams were on her head and Abha had definite plans. She wanted to join SRCC, and then she wanted to join the civil services. Her aims and targets were clear, and she worked towards them with determination.

Around the time Abha's exams were to begin, Bina gave them some good news. Not the one normally associated with newly-weds. She had qualified for a job as an economist in the government. Her in-laws and husband were also enthusiastic about it. Aarti Devi's dream had come true. Her elder daughter was now truly settled.

Aarti Devi then focused all her attention on Abha. She knew her two daughters were different, but siblings always were. In her mind, the pattern their lives would follow would be the same, maybe in a different order for Abha—job and then marriage.

'Simran, come over, I have something to tell you. It's important, in fact it's great.'

Simran groaned inwardly as she put the phone down. In the hallowed preparatory leave she was busy preparing for the forthcoming Board exam. But she knew that she would go, it must be something important for Abha to summon her immediately. Ten minutes later, Simran found herself in the room that Abha had all to herself since Bina di's marriage.

'Simran I got kissed today. You know, on the lips!'

'Who was it? How dare you? Aren't you scared if someone finds out? How was it?'

The questions poured out of Simran like the clatter of a machine gun. For an eager seventeen-year-old in the Delhi of the early 1980s, kissing was something that did not happen even in Hindi movies, and in real life was only found between the covers of a Mills & Boon romance.

'I had gone to get the English book from Sridhar, Sharma auntie's son. You know it just happened at his place. Actually, I let him because I wanted to know what it was like. It was just all right. Nothing really like what a Mills & Boon tell you.'

'Abha, you don't even have a crush on him.'

'Is that essential?'

They had discussed the process threadbare for quite sometime. Then, on Abha's insistence got down to the business of life—exams and studies. Sridhar had called up Abha a few times thereafter, but the exams were nearing and Abha was never in doubt where her priorities were.

Every time Abha would sit at the dining table, she heard the discourse on the importance of the twelfth Board in her life. 'Performance in the twelfth grade determines the course of life—entrance into a reputed college can change your life forever.' It was like the refrain of a song her father sang out everyday.

It did have an impact. The results were out. Both Simran and Abha had done well. The next stage of life had arrived.

In the month of June, Delhi is like a sweltering inferno. Despite that, Delhi University started its admission process in June. The days were hot and the sun was beating down mercilessly on the deserted streets. At times, a mirage would shimmer on the black tar roads. For admission hopefuls, this was the time to run around. Gathering forms from various colleges, filling them up within deadlines and then keeping track of the lists—first admission list, second and then the last and final. Scores of photocopying and attestation of school results, a scramble to prove that one is good at everything—studies, sports and dramatics and what not.

Abha and Simran stood at the Dhaula Kuan bus stop. They were headed towards Lady Shri Ram College in the South Campus of Delhi University. On their maiden trip to North Campus the earlier week, they had struggled to find routes to various colleges. Many of the other girls had fathers and brothers in tow. These two had each other only. They had discovered that St. Stephen's and Hindu were opposite each other, but Abha had to aim for SRCC and it was somewhere across the sprawling Arts Faculty.

'I will never join LSR Simran—it's a girls-only college. After a "girls only" school, I think it's about time we realized what the real world is like. We must join a co-ed college.'

Lurching along in a DTC bus, Abha had made this pronouncement. In a way, Simran agreed with her, but if they did not manage admission in a co-ed college as prestigious as LSR, no one would allow them to ignore LSR. They had become adept at travelling in DTC buses rather quickly. It was tough at times. Simran hated it when men pushed and fell all over. Once she got so angry, she had crushed the man's foot with her heels. He had quickly moved away. It was a blessing that at the time of the day they travelled, the buses were not usually packed. The wind coming in from the window was blowing Abha's ponytail. She looked quite pretty.

'Tell me Simran, why do you think only St. Stephen's has this interview business? No other college holds interviews. Admissions are just based on marks. It must be so that they can accommodate people with lesser marks, but higher contacts!'

'Abha, why are you bothered, you are bound to make it to the first list in SRCC. Are you going for the Stephen's interview?'

'Of course I will. It will be my first interview experience. I want to know what it feels like. The very thought of it makes me nervous.'

The application rush was over and the race to find one's name on the lists stuck on college notice boards had begun. Abha and Simran were hanging out in the St. Stephen's campus, as Abha had her interview that day. Abha's name had been called out. In Simran's view, it was an utter waste of time to appear for an interview with no intention of joining the college, but Abha had been adamant.

Abha came out of the interview room, and they moved towards the water cooler.

'The Principal simply asked how I could cope with Economics with only 62% in Maths. Nothing else. Then one of the other three on the panel said they could offer English or History.'

'What did you say?'

'Obviously I said no—who's interested in either?'

'If you have finished drinking water may I please step in?' —another candidate for the hallowed portals of the college asked Abha.

'Let's go and eat something in the canteen Simran, I am hungry,'—Abha said, as Simran drank water.

'You know in Stephen's it's not referred to as the "canteen" it is called the "college cafeteria".' The waiting candidate clarified for them.

'Are you a fresher or senior?'

'Like you I have come for the interview. Hi, my name is Ujjwal. Can you tell me a little about the interview?'

'Well you know there are three of them … .'

Abha's voice trailed off as they walked towards the 'cafeteria' and Simran followed them. There was no place to sit inside; they took their trays to the shade of the tree in the sprawling lawns of the college.

'Thanks for all the tips Abha. And best of luck for your admission to SRCC.'

'Thanks. See you around sometime. Best of luck to you too.'

It was a fortnight of stress and tension. Choices had to be made and decisions taken. The day the first list in SRCC was to come out

Abha was nervous and Simran knew that. The day before, Abha had refused admission in LSR because she did not want to submit her original mark sheets and miss the chance of joining SRCC. Simran actually admired Abha's courage for giving up something as prestigious as LSR for the unknown. Perhaps, Abha had taken as a challenge her father's statement that Abha should aim for SRCC. Simran had not got admission in the Economics course in LSR, and she had not thought of applying in any other stream.

Simran and Abha were standing at the bus stop for the 240 bus in the Central Secretariat. It would take them to North Campus. From Rakab Ganj Gurudwara nearby, the faint strains of devotional music floated in the air. A nice breeze was blowing across the street. The night before, after nearly a week of fierce heat, there had been a thundershower, bringing the temperature down. But the promise of heat was hidden in the breeze.

'Hi Abha. How are you? Made it to SRCC?'

Ujjwal had come to the bus stop with a few friends.

'Not yet. How about you? Made it to St. Stephen's?'

'Well as a matter of fact yes. I am going to deposit the fees today.'

'Congratulations. Today is my big day—the SRCC list will come out today.'

The bus came and they boarded it. Throughout the forty-minute drive, Simran watched as Abha and Ujjwal chatted continuously. He was not the type Abha liked. Dark, lean with a long and ordinary looking face, but he did have a nice, wide and infectious smile. At the Stephen's stop, the boys tumbled out.

'I am sure with your percentage you will make it to SRCC. See you around soon.'

Abha waved from the window as the group crossed the street to enter the red brick building of St. Stephen's. The bus carried on, and Abha and Simran got off next at SRCC. There were many students milling around. Simran thought she could hear Abha's heart thudding, but realized it was her own. Her own fate hinged on the Economics list in SRCC. Otherwise she would have to go to Miranda House, and Simran did not want that.

The crowd of students near the notice board where the lists were pasted was huge. They struggled to get closer and peered anxiously down the lists.

'I made it Simran. My name is there on the list. Oh God! I cannot believe it.' Abha sat down on the steps near the staircase where the lists had been pasted.

'Abha I also made it to the Economics course here.'

'That's just great. Now we will be together in college too. Let us see what the formalities are. I wish I could tell Ujjwal about this.'

Simran should have paid more attention to that wish expressed in the throes of ecstasy, but there was so much more to think about at that moment.

The next day armed with original mark sheets and paperwork, Simran and Abha were again at the 240 bus stop. What a difference twenty-four hours had made. Yesterday they were tense, unsure of their future. Now there was the confidence of a destination chartered, the next three years were on course. The thrill of leaving school and entering the portals of University was creeping in. The stuffy heat that enveloped the city did nothing to dampen the joy in their hearts.

'Hi Abha what's the news?'

Ujjwal was there with his friends, again.

'I made it Ujjwal. Today I am going to complete the formalities.'

'That is great. Hey, Abha are you from Bengal? Only Bengali girls have such beautiful eyes.'

'No I am from Uttar Pradesh.'

How come Abha had not cut off his rather stupid way of flirting? Simran wondered. In the bus, Ujjwal and Abha chatted non-stop. At the Stephen's bus stop when Ujjwal got off, he said to Abha, 'I'll come and see you in SRCC the day the University opens.'

The day Delhi University opened was cloudy. The first pre-monsoon showers had lashed Delhi the day before. Abha and Simran had agonized quite a while on what to wear, deciding on jeans and top as the best bet. Together they got off the bus and stood outside the portals of SRCC. The dark red brick building with the watchtower seemed imposing. The thought of belonging to the institution for the next three years was exciting. There was also a sense of trepidation in both their hearts as they walked quietly towards the college building. The boys loitering around the corridors were a new, strange and thrilling sight. The lack of uniform and the sense of freedom was exhilarating.

The two of them turned into the corridor towards the administrative office when a group of senior boys surrounded them. Probably the diffidence and uncertainty of being freshers was writ large on their faces. One of the boys ordered, 'You see the lawns. Well ladies you are going to play a tennis match there. Start.'

It took a while for both of them to realize that ragging had begun. Their jeans rolled up and with make-believe racquets, Abha and Simran started playing an imaginary game of tennis in the lawns made muddy by the rains. Mud-splashed and dirty, they were laughing as they got to know that group of seniors. Very soon, another group of seniors took over. At every step that day, they found themselves doing something uproariously funny and strange. The fun and frolic of the first day of college life was exiciting and liberating.

It was a day of discovery. They explored the huge classrooms with wooden benches, the long corridors with pillars and the auditorium in the college. The best part was that there was no bell ringing, and there were many gates in the college. It was unlike school, where the solitary gate used to be under strict vigil all the time.

A group of third year students took them to the canteen. Up the stairs, in a small building in the corner of the college campus, was the canteen. Full of rickety chairs, cheap sunmica tables and lots of noise. The leader of this group of seniors was Sunny Singh, a dynamic sardar. He ordered tea and samosas for all of them. Sunny spoke about the college activities, festival and other details of college life.

'If you girls have any problems don't hesitate to ask me.'

'Come on Sunny, *tera propaganda shuru mat kar* (Don't start your propaganda). Girls, he plans to contest the college elections this year, so remember him. Okay.'

The canteen was filling up. It was nearly 2 pm. Abha was full after three samosas and two cups of incredibly sweet tea. The group broke up when Sunny spotted another group of freshers. Abha and Simran came down the stairs.

'It is nearly time for the 2 pm U-special. We should try to catch it Abha. Did you get the timetable for your classes?'

'Yes. Can we not hang out for some more time?'

'Why? I am quite tired with all this stuff now. I want to go home and have a nice bath.'

Simran noticed Abha was looking at the crowds, as if searching for someone. It suddenly struck her.

'You are waiting for Ujjwal? Shit, Abha what's gone wrong with you? He must be busy with his own thing. You can't be serious.'

'Let us go and catch the U-special.'

University specials were a great thing. Rahul, in second year, had told Abha and Simran all about them during the course of the day. They were Delhi Transport Corporation's yellow-green buses, earmarked for students, running at a specified time on specific routes. They stopped at fewer destinations, but covered a large part of the city. The U-special was a good place to make friends from other colleges, and get ragged if you were a fresher. Simran and Abha walked to Patel Chest Institute. Hordes of students were standing there. They found the bus going towards Dhaula Kuan and jumped in. The ride was uneventful because on the first day not many people could make out who was new and who was not.

'Mummy was saying the other day that Papa might get posted out of Delhi—Simran, then I will have to find a hostel. Our college has only one for boys.'

'Once we are in the University system I am sure something will work out. Do you like the idea of going to hostel?'

'I really can't say. I will miss Mum a lot, that I know for sure. Maybe hostel will be nice. But anyway, it is not certain yet, so we will cross that bridge when we come to it.'

'See you tomorrow morning Abha. Be careful, you seem to be developing one big thing for this guy Ujjwal. Yaar, he isn't even the kind you like. He is not even good looking!'

'Shut up. I just enjoy talking to him. That's it. Okay?'

At home, in the evening, Papa was on the phone. As usual.

'Well my daughter has joined Shri Ram College of Commerce.'

Aarti Devi was amused at the pride dripping from her husband's voice as he told a colleague about Abha's admission.

'How was your day Abha?'

'Mummy, we had a real good time. I must say ragging can actually be fun. It is a nice way to get to know the seniors. I guess classes will begin from tomorrow.'

'Abha, be serious in college. Attend classes and don't waste your time with friends. College is where you learn to be responsible for yourself.' Her father interjected authoritatively.

Aarti Devi always wondered why her husband and daughter had a continually sparring relationship. They never talked, rather they challenged each other most of the time. Maybe it had become the style of conversing in their household. Over years of attrition, the house had become a ceasefire zone. Calm, but always simmering beneath the surface. Couples often fall into strange patterns. For Aarti Devi and her husband it was one of constant dissatisfaction with each other, where neither cared about reaching out to the other. Like countless other couples, they simply bore their crosses. Safe behind the shields of children and society, they carried on.

The phone was ringing again. Simran was on the line. Aarti Devi could not understand. The two girls had spent the whole day together and now they were on the phone again. Bina did not have friends like this. That her two daughters were different in temperament and their approach to life, was obvious to her.

'Mummy I need money to buy some clothes for college. Now there is no uniform, you know. Over this weekend Simran and I want to go to CP and buy some clothes.'

Although her father was sitting in the same room, Abha addressed this demand to her—as she had always done. Sometimes relationships get tangled for no apparent reason. However, her husband never noticed these things. He saw things around him through a certain prism where as long as there was no distortion nothing bothered him. It was a very uni-dimensional masculine perspective—Aarti Devi had realized long ago.

'Don't buy see-through clothes or any skirts, understand?'

Sound advice of a father, but said again in a tone that brought out Abha's hackles. Daughters are supposed to be like Bina—gentle and docile. But Abha, the defiance in her eyes, in her posture, something about her seemed to challenge the person in front of her.

Abha was now the focal point of Aarti Devi's dreams. She wanted her to have all that she never had—freedom, opportunity and the companionship she had always longed for. It was the eternal story of women. They want their daughters to have a life different from their own—better, freer and filled with more choice. That is why women's lives do change with generations. If it were not for this desire burning in the hearts of their mothers, it would never be.

In Simran's home, it was just another day when she returned from her first day at college. Her mother was in the kitchen, Shikha was ironing the clothes, while Seema was lounging on the bed. Her father was not home from office, and Ravi Bhaiyya was on the phone. No one asked her about her first day at college. She bathed and started helping her mother in the kitchen.

Ravi Bhaiyya came into the kitchen and announced, 'Amma I am going on a tour for four days. Simran, pack my suitcase. *Arre tera college kaisa raha (Hey, How was your college)?*'

'It was nice, Bhaiyya. Amma I need to buy some clothes for college. *Ab uniform nahin hai na (Now we don't have a uniform).*'

'Here Simran take five hundred rupees and enjoy.' Ravi Bhaiyya took out the money and gave it to her. A thrilled Simran ran to call Abha.

That the world was male dominated was quite clear in college. There were only six girls in Abha's class of over thirty. In fact, girls were a minority in the college. Initially, the six of them sat on two front rows together. In class, Abha discovered Rekha. Pretty and confident, with the sense of ruling the world that Punjabis often carry with them, Rekha was always well informed about all the events and happenings in college.

'They are auditioning for the declamation contest to be held in the forthcoming college festival. Coming with me?'

'I have never debated or done something like this before. I am interested in dramatics you know.'

'Let us find out what is up. You can do the drama thing.'

The festival fever was catching up in the college. Committees and groups were buzzing all over. In no time Rekha and Abha were in the thick of planning and organizing the festival. All over college and the University campus posters announcing 'Crossroads' were put up. As the festival date drew closer, college was transformed. The dark red building was illuminated, decorated with festoons and banners. Abha jumped headlong into the activities, bunking classes and going home late every day. Simran stayed away from all the hectic work.

'Crossroads' was beginning the next day. Rekha came to Abha's drama society room and invited her for a lunch in the boys' hostel mess.

'Its allowed during festival time Abha. Girls can go for a meal. This guy on our committee has invited us. Let's go.'

The mess was full of boys lunging hungrily at the food. There were three other girls on another table. Maybe because girls were present there was a sense of order that day.

'SRCC hostel has the best food in the whole campus.' Their host was telling them.

'But how many times in a week do you get non-veg food here?'

'It's more than any other DU hostel, and it is not how many times, but how the food is, that matters, Rekha. You are a day scholar, you will never understand till you live in a hostel how important mess food is for existence!'

'Whatever, tell us what this whole bonfire thing is on the last day.'

'The college invites a band and they play, there is a bonfire, lots of beer and lots of other stuff. It is the best part of the festival. It simply rocks.'

After lunch as Abha and Rekha walked towards the U-special bus stop, Rekha asked, 'Abha will you be staying for the bonfire?'

'Where will we go, Rekha, once its over even if we do decide to attend the bonfire? I really don't know if, in the first place, my parents will allow.'

'You don't have to say you are staying for the bonfire. Say the festival is on and you will be late. We can stay at my friend's place in Kamla Nagar. She will also be coming. She is in third year in Miranda House.'

Rekha lived in Model Town with her parents and younger brother in a rented first floor apartment. She got off the U-special and walked towards home. In her mind she was planning a strategy to get her father's consent for her overnight stay in the campus on bonfire night.

Their landlord, an old migrant Sikh from Pakistan, sat in a small patch of green outside and soaked in the winter sun.

'*Sat sri akal ji*,' Rekha shouted, greeting him in Punjabi as she sped up the stairs. Her story was ready.

When the door opened Rekha found the sitting room crowded. Hardayal Tayaji was there with his family. Now she would never get permission. Rekha was disappointed. Ever since her father had left the army and settled down in a private sector job, Hardayal Tayaji had been calling them to visit Hoshiarpur, their hometown.

Rekha joined the group sprawling in the sitting room. There was a lot of talk, pakoras and tea going around the room. With sunset, whisky also would make an appearance.

'We are planning to go to Amritsar to the Golden Temple with Hardayal Bhaisahab and his family. Then we will go to Hoshiarpur for two three days,' Papaji, Rekha's father, informed her.

Rekha winced inwardly. She won't be able to get out of this. Why did Hardayal Tayaji choose this time to visit? What would she tell Abha and the others? They were all banking on her.

Rekha was fond of Hardayal Tayaji. She remembered with great happiness the holidays she had spent in Hoshiarpur when she was younger. That was then. Now she loved Delhi, her life at college and in Model Town. It had been some years since they had gone to Hoshiarpur. Since Papaji left the army and settled down in Delhi, they had never been there.

'Biji, I have tests going on. I cannot go.' As soon as her younger brother said this, Rekha saw light at the end of the tunnel.

'Papaji, Bubble and I will stay back. I am also busy in college. We will go in the holidays.'

Papaji and Biji conferred and then agreed to the proposal. Rekha was elated. She could now attend the bonfire without any hassles. She wanted to jump with joy, but sat there with a helpless expression, as if she had made a great sacrifice for her brother.

Simran and Abha met often during the day in college, but being in different courses their timings clashed at times. Due to the festival they had barely met. Snatching some time from her hectic schedule, Abha had gone with Simran to the canteen for a much needed cup of tea. They gulped down some oily bread, omelette and tea.

Simran was dead against Rekha's plan of attending the bonfire, as she was not comfortable with the whole thing. She resented Rekha's pushy approach to things. There was something awfully Punjabi about her and Simran could not understand why Abha was friendly with her. Simran tried to persuade Abha out of the bonfire.

'Abha your mum will never allow you to attend such a thing if you tell her the truth.' The sauce with the omelette was deadly as usual. Even the sweet tea did not drown out its tang. Abha kept quiet and continued to sip her tea.

All of a sudden Ujjwal walked into the canteen, surrounded as usual by a group of friends. He had many former schoolmates in SRCC, and was seen more often in SRCC than in his own hallowed college. After settling down at a table at some distance, and placing the order, he sauntered up to the table where Simran and Abha were sitting.

'So you girls joining in the bonfire day after tomorrow?' Although he addressed both of them, the question seemed meant for Abha only.

'Maybe. Why don't you sit?' Abha replied. But Ujjwal had already spotted some other friends.

'Okay, then see you there.'

Simran knew she had lost the battle. They paid up and walked towards the bus stop. All the way back, in the bus, it was the other way around. Abha was trying to talk Simran into joining in the plan. 'Simran, if Mummy knows we are together it will be better. Come on it will be an experience. We don't have to be there for the whole time.'

Abha was always persuasive, Simran knew, however, now there was the added allure of doing something thrilling and out of the ordinary. It did not take long for Simran's defences to crumble. During the bus journey back home the stories were rehearsed and matched, and later in the evening consent of the parents obtained.

Night fell early on the bonfire day, it being winter, and rather cold. Rekha had gathered a group of classmates and some seniors around the bonfire. The ground behind the auditorium was set up with a stage and large speakers. Music was streaming from the speakers and the mood was festive. There was something thrilling about it. No parents, no elders, just a sea of youngsters ready to party through the night. It was nothing like Simran or Abha had ever experienced before. The music blared and small sparks from the bonfire flew all around their group. Sunny Singh, the newly elected president, had assumed leadership of their group. It was obvious that he had taken to Rekha. Simran watched as he tried to find a place to sit close to her. Soon they were chatting away in Punjabi. The music was growing louder. The beer bottles opened, and soon Campa Cola was doing rounds in glasses.

The glass came to Simran and she caught the whiff clearly. It was reeking of rum. The same smell came when Ravi Bhaiyya's friends came home.

'Abha, it is mixed with rum don't take it,' she whispered into her ear above the music. But Abha took it and sipped tentatively.

'Hey it's not bad Simran. Do you think I will get drunk if I have it?'

'You will and so *do not*. This was not what we had agreed on.'

Reluctantly, Abha kept the glass down. Then her eyes began to scan the ground around. In the dim flickering light of the bonfire, the ground was shrouded in mystery. It was impossible to clearly identify any one in the other groups.

'You looking out for him? Ujjwal?'

'No, Simran I am just looking around. Is that a crime?'

But Simran knew Abha was searching for him. All around the bonfire, groups sat huddled. Many couples sat wrapped in one shawl. The band was loud, too loud at times. Neither Simran nor Abha knew much about rock or jazz music. For them Hindi film music was the big high. Simran looked at some of the couples sitting around; it was a place to be enjoyed with a boyfriend. She was feeling rather cold. As the hours passed and the stars moved in the sky, the chill was increasing. Abha had stopped looking around the ground quite some time ago. She conversed animatedly with one of the boys from her class. He looked quite drunk. Simran wondered if Abha had surreptitiously washed down a rum-cola. The empty glass in front of Abha was rolling on the grass. Abha had downed the damn thing. To Simran's trained eye, she was not looking drunk, simply dazed. Rekha was virtually reclining on Sunny's shoulder. Simran was sure she had downed a few of the rum-cola glasses. It was nearly two in the morning when their group decided to call it a day. In the flickering light, to the tune of a loud band, many couples were born. Like it happened every year.

Sunny Singh was the college president. He was also a suitor for Rekha's attention. He tried hard to balance the two demanding engagements. They zipped around on his bike. He dropped Rekha everyday some distance from her house. They went for a morning show once in Batra cinema nearby, and exchanged rather passionate kisses in the dark hall. When Sunny tried to put his hand down her top, Rekha pushed his hand away. He, nevertheless, pressed her breasts rather hard from outside. That was the last time she went out with him. Rekha was not looking for anything serious just yet; Sunny was also not her type of guy. He faded from her life. But he had given her an interesting insight about SRCC.

'Abha the guys here are boring. You know why? They all have these goddamn family businesses to fall back on. No one has any ambition beyond going and sitting at the shop or whatever it is there. Totally avoidable yaar.'

Rekha and Abha were sitting, swinging their legs by the stairs near the auditorium. It was a nice place to sit, secluded and yet they could observe what was going around the college. Just a few months, and it seemed that they had been here forever.

Abha was smiling. Rekha wondered if she had taken to the guy with whom she had talked non-stop on the bonfire night. 'What about Shiv? That's his name right? Is he also in the same category as the boring SRCC guys?'

'Oh yes and you know what Rekha, he has really started pestering me. With cards and all. He just came on so strong, I got put off.'

Sunny Singh came towards them and said a cheery 'hello'. They both looked back and smiled. He hung around them for a while, but Rekha's cold shoulder was amply clear and he understood that there was nothing to try anymore.

'Where is Simran? Abha you don't think she is impractical? I always get the sense that she lives in la la land.'

'She was not well today so she bunked.' Even as she asked the question, Rekha's mind had moved off. She never dwelt on things for too long, specially when they did not matter to her. Her life's prism was simply 'herself'. She could see the new entrant in Abha's life, Shiv, coming hurriedly towards them.

'Hello Abha. Coming for coffee to the canteen?'

'No Shiv, I am going home,' and Abha walked off.

'Don't waste your time yaar.' Rekha patted Shiv's arm and walked after Abha.

The spectators were shouting and screaming. St. Stephen's and SRCC were having the last basketball match of the year. It seemed madness to shout like that, but when the college team is playing on home turf everyone turned up to cheer.

'Hi girls, Abha, do you think your team will win?'

Somewhere from behind where Simran and Abha were sitting, Ujjwal had popped up. Actually, he had started to annoy Simran. She instinctively felt that Abha had developed a soft corner for him. He would make sporadic appearances and then disappear. He would say 'I will come by tomorrow' and then not be seen for days. Simran knew Abha waited for him, though she had never admitted it to Simran yet. Then he would appear suddenly and re-start the conversation from where it had ended the last time. There was something in Abha's face when she looked at him. Simran wondered if Ujjwal was blind.

'Of course, SRCC will win Ujjwal. You just wait and watch. And how did your tutorial go?'

'Fine. You are looking nice as usual, Abha. You know, Indian clothes look much better on you. By the way, Mum was asking about you. She wanted to know if you are going for the rehearsal tomorrow, you seem to have missed a few?'

Simran could never make out if he was flirting with Abha, as he said things with a deadpan face. Also Abha and his mother were doing a radio play together. They had met at the radio station, and only during the course of rehearsals had Abha realized that she was Ujjwal's mother. Abha had gone to his house a few times for a cup of tea on his mother's invitation. Abha now knew the entire family.

'I am going. I missed it two days running. Soon enough the play will be recorded. You didn't call me the other day. You said you would.'

'Something came up. Well, I will call you tomorrow. What happened to your hostel thing? You made any progress?'

The two of them were chatting again. Endlessly. Going through all that had happened in their lives, while the match went on amid much screeching and shouting.

'Hi Ujjwal. You here again? Always hanging around our college? What's up?' Rekha always said what to her was most apparent.

'SRCC has prettier girls. Just look at yourself,' Ujjwal's reply irritated Simran no end. What Abha saw in him she could never fathom.

'Hey, I am not interested. So lay off. Okay?' Rekha sauntered off. She had sensed that Abha was interested in this guy. But nothing had happened there as yet. He was glib and charming to talk to, but one could never take what he said seriously. There was this constant banter in his manner.

Many couples had emerged in the first year of college. Going around was the most 'in' thing. It was fashionable to 'go around'. It normally entailed walking around the campus hand in hand, going for movies, followed by some frenetic groping in the dim movie hall. Rekha got a taste of the whole thing with Sunny in the last few months. There was also some serious sex going on, as it always does, in every day and age, but it was still few and far between. None of the people they knew had jumped into bed with someone. Not yet.

Where did these two fit in—Simran wondered as Ujjwal and Abha chatted. One year nearly over in college, and she knew that they had never held hands, never gone to a movie or really dated. Abha had evinced no real interest in any other person, although she had tried to distract herself. There were some like Shiv, who pursued her quite relentlessly. In the few times Abha and Ujjwal had met, they had talked to the exclusion of all others. Well maybe what Abha said was true—they were just friends. Then why did she look at him the way she did? The match was nearing its end and Simran was alone with her thoughts. Rekha had walked off towards the library, and Abha was busy with Ujjwal.

St. Stephen's won the match and with the all-encompassing statement that 'Stephen's is the best place in the world and I will see you tomorrow,' Ujjwal left.

'Hey, now the exams are around the corner Simran. I better work hard if I have to make it to the hostel.' Within a matter of minutes, Abha was back to prosaic and mundane things. Abha's father had been transferred to Bombay and she was looking around for hostel accomodation desperately. The University Postgraduate Women's Hostel allotted some seats to girls studying in mixed colleges that had no hostel for girls. The allotment was on merit and that meant that she had to do well in the forthcoming exams. They walked towards the college gate with the realization that first year would be coming to an end soon.

'I am glad you got admission in the hostel Abha. It really sorts out things for us. Now we can move as soon as you settle there. This is a hostel for postgraduate girls. They would be much older than you. Take care and don't get into any bad habits. You are at an impressionable age. I expect you to be sensible and clear-headed.'

Aarti Devi wondered if it was the prospect of Abha leaving, which made her husband sound vulnerable as he spoke. Abha gave her father a hug. Aarti Devi was feeling rather depressed. She had herself stayed in one of the Lucknow University hostels while doing her BA, but then her sister had been in the same city. In addition, her mother had many children. In her case, once Abha left the nest, there was going to be no one at home. Her children were out of the house.

When second year began, Abha's parents and Simran went to drop Abha at the hostel.

'What a small cramped room,' thought Simran, as she helped Abha arrange her things. On the top floor, the small room seemed to have a swathe of vapours hanging around it in the monsoon heat. Downstairs, in a gloomy common area, was a coin-driven phone and a rack of pigeonholes for letters.

'One phone and so many people? How will we ever speak to each other?' Simran was nearly in tears.

'Come on, we will meet in college everyday.' Abha tried to be brave. As she hugged her parents, she started to cry. The pain of leaving home had hit Abha hard. It didn't hurt less simply because she was nineteen. Standing at the hostel gates she waved to them, alone and forlorn. The hostel gate then swallowed her up.

Rekha and Abha were having lunch in the St. Stephen's cafeteria. Rekha was looking out for the new friend she had made in the U-special. In third year at Stephen's, he was everything she wanted in a guy. Smart, intelligent and focused. It did not matter that he was a Tamilian; Rekha simply fell for him.

Each day Rekha waited for him to board the U-special at his stop, two stops after her own. She tried to take the same special back as him. On the fifth day, after consistent following, Rekha had walked up to him in the bus and said, 'I see you get off at the Stephen's stop. You studying there? I need to check out a book in your library.' After that they chatted everyday. Rekha had decided it was time to visit him in his turf. Abha would accompany her to St. Stephen's, she knew. Ujjwal was there.

They had timed it such that they arrived around lunch break. The place was crowded with day scholars. The 'nimbu pani' and mincemeat cutlets of the cafeteria were legendary, being actually served on china plates with forks!

'Abha, no wonder these guys are somehow out of touch with reality. Imagine a college canteen that is like a restaurant.'

As they ate, the latest man on Rekha's horizon walked in with a girl. Rekha was slightly rattled. She had not thought that he could have someone in his life. Nevertheless she walked across to their table and started chatting. By the time she came back, she had extracted a promise from him to come over to SRCC for a cup of tea in their canteen.

'Let's go back Abha. We have a class at 1.45 pm.' Rekha had accomplished her mission, although she knew Abha was disappointed as they had not met Ujjwal. As they walked towards the back gate of the college, Ujjwal appeared from behind the chapel in the college premises.

'Hi. What are you girls doing here?'

'Came to see you.' Rekha, as usual, blurted out the truth. Her candour was a blessing or a curse, depending on the situation, but often people did not recognize it as such.

'As if I don't know this friend of yours. She has time for everyone but me. Okay, bye. Abha, speak to you later today.' And Ujjwal was off towards his college library.

They walked through the small road that lead to the Arts Faculty campus and then crossed the road to SRCC. Rekha was busy tying up the forthcoming visit of her new find in her mind. She did not see the perplexed look on Abha's face.

It was more than two months since Abha's parents had left for Bombay and she often went over to Simran's place. Fed up of hostel food, she would drop in for the weekend. A childhood spent together was a great binding force. Abha still did not feel as comfortable at Rekha's house, though she had gone there two weeks ago. In Simran's room, which had not changed much over the years, they lay on the bed as they did in school and stared at the ceiling.

The fan was whirring slowly, it being autumn. In the house somewhere, the TV news was blaring and Simran's younger sisters were shouting at each other. Abha could feel the familiar smells and sounds of home.

'Simran, what do you think Ujjwal feels for me?'

For the first time in more than a year, Abha had spoken about it. At last it was out in the open. Simran had been waiting for this.

'You have asked him?'

'Not directly, but sometimes I have tried to probe him and then you know he just takes off. Like he always does. Saying things he doesn't mean.'

'Why don't you ask him directly?'

'I can't, Simran. It's too important for me. I just cannot.'

Abha had at last admitted it. It had taken her more than a year to speak about it. Simran could not understand. If it had been her, she thought, she would have begun talking about it to Abha from the start.

'Well, I will then.'

'No, not till I tell you to.'

'Abha there are so many guys, other than him. Don't you want to go around with someone? You know I really like Vijay in third year. He asked me out for a movie last week. I feel like going—just to see what it feels like to zip off on a guy's mobike for a movie.'

'Actually Simran, I find it amazing. How can one just go out with a guy for the sake of going out? He should interest me, right? Some of these guys in college—they really put me off. They think all a girl needs is a bunch of flowers, some sweet talk and a ride on their bike! Go with Vijay if you feel you can tolerate him for three hours. Look how quickly Sunny and Rekha broke up.'

'Rekha is different, Abha. I don't understand you. You let that creep Sridhar kiss you in school and now you say that you will go out with a guy only if he interests you.'

'I wanted to know how it felt that time, Simran, but needs and desires change. Now I feel that I would like to go out with someone only if I can relate to him. What Rekha said was right. Most of the guys in SRCC are boring. No one is interesting. And by the way Simran, Rekha is not that bad Okay?'

'Like Ujjwal is interesting, right?'

'Right, but he has no interest of that kind in me. I just don't figure him out. Anyway. Can you imagine we are in second year now? What have you thought about the future? I better start preparing for the civil services exams from now on.'

'Nothing as yet. Now I am sleepy. Goodnight.'

Outside, the autumn night had developed a stillness that had the hint of winter hidden in its fold. Simran turned over. She could never admit to the pig-headed Abha that she often dreamt of a life where she would be waiting for her husband to come back from office, dressed up, with a cup of tea ready. She dreamt often of a nice home, with children and a man she was meant to keep happy. That was the life Simran looked forward to. She did not know then it would never be so.

Simran watched Abha, as Abha watched Ujjwal sprawling next to a girl a little further away. They were sitting on the sun-bathed, groomed lawns of St. Stephen's listening to a music group crooning away as part of the college 'Winterfest'.

'Let's go Abha. This is so boring. I'm tired too after the wedding.' Over the weekend, they had attended a wedding of Simran's cousin. Abha did not respond. Rekha was there too, busy with her Tamilian. He visited her often, although they were not an item yet and moved around in a group. But Simran knew, Rekha would have her way if that was what she really wanted. Rekha and that soft-spoken boy did not seem to make sense, but then these things often did not.

'He is too busy, Abha. Flirting away as usual. Let's go.' Simran tried again. This time Abha got up without a word, waved to Rekha and they made their way out of the small back gate.

'Abha wait. Why are you girls going? The nice music is just about to begin.'

Ujjwal was panting from running to catch up with them. Why couldn't he let Abha be? Simran was exasperated.

'The *mehndi* on your hand is looking really nice. You have such slender and beautiful hands Abha.'

In more than a year, this was the first time Simran saw Ujjwal holding Abha's hand, even if it was on the pretext of *mehndi*. She could not stop herself.

'Why, Ujjwal, she brushed you off did she? The girl you were chasing on the lawns. Your friend Amrit says these days you are running after some girl from Miranda House. Is she the one?'

'Simran, I spend all my time chasing your friend here, where will I have time for anyone else?'

He said it in a light and nonchalant manner. It was impossible to decide whether to take him seriously or not. It never sounded offensive either. Simran looked towards Abha, but she was concentrating more on the road in front. Ujjwal was difficult to pin down or slot in any manner. Sometimes Simran felt like catching him by his collar and shaking him, but one could never be seriously angry with him. He had never crossed the line with Abha, but he never let her go either. Simran had seen it over the past two years.

'No Ujjwal, we are going now. Simran is staying with me in the hostel tonight.'

'Okay then, bye. See you around. If you don't have classes, why don't you come at around noon to college tomorrow? We can have lunch in the cafeteria.'

As they walked off down the road, Simran turned and saw that Ujjwal was still standing at the small gate.

'Abha, doesn't he drive you mad at times? Why don't you just clear the air between you? Don't tell me you are going to Stephen's again tomorrow?'

'We are going Simran, although I am quite sure he will never turn up and then later just say "something came up"!'

'Then why will you go?'

'Because ... Simran, just in case he does come!'

That night Abha and Simran snuggled into the small bed in Abha's room and started chatting.

'Do you miss home a lot, Abha?'

'Actually I had thought I would be really happy away from all the bickering that went on at home and the fights with Dad. But you know Simran, I miss home like mad. The whole concept of home. You go, open the fridge, eat what you want, when you want. Create a fuss for something you want. Everything. Hostel is, well, just that—a place that gives you a bed and food.'

Outside the window, the moon was shining on the clear winter night.

'People always say that hostel means much more freedom. At home, you have to explain all the time. Where you are going, with whom, why... ?'

'I used to think so too. But after a time you want someone to show some concern for you. Simran, here there is a night-time curfew, that is all. No one really cares about you. Anyway, we did have freedom at home too. I most often did what I wanted.'

There was a knock on the door, and they were dragged to a neighbouring room. Being a minority, the undergraduate girls had formed their own group in the sea of the postgraduate and PhD scholars. At every age, people look for company of their own age group. Dreams, desires and excitements change so quickly that age becomes a critical factor, especially when one is young. The postgraduate girls seemed old to the younger group of nineteen-year-olds.

Sitting around a small table the group of girls were sharing a cigarette. To Simran's surprise Abha took a drag before passing the cigarette ahead.

'You started smoking again?'

'No Simran, but I do enjoy a drag once in a while.' The smoky room was full of gossip and chatter. It did not seem as if it was midnight, there was so much energy floating in that small room.

After sometime, someone started chasing coke. Simran was utterly shocked. Abha had told her that this happened quite a lot in the hostel, but she had never seen it. Not everyone joined in. Only two of the girls present were busy chasing coke.

'You tried it Abha?' Simran asked in a hoarse whisper.

'No. Not drugs Simran. Its not something you should ever try, I believe that. But as I told you, it is not uncommon, especially now that it is festival time in the University.'

'You know these girls?'

'Of course. They are like you and me, just have different choices. So much goes on here in the hostel Simran. You can either be swept away or find your feet getting firmer and your resolve stronger. Each time I see this going on I remember what Papa had told me when I was coming to hostel.'

For the first time in all the years they had known each other Simran heard affection in Abha's voice as she spoke about her father. It felt rather nice.

After nearly two hours of chatting and gossiping, they came back to Abha's room. Abha slept almost immediately. The night raced though the sky but Simran lay wide awake. Where would they be in the next few years? It was nearly the end of second year of college and the uncertainty of life after college was looming large. The apprehension was much more than when school had ended. To Simran it seemed as if the whole wide world was waiting to swallow her up at the end of college. It was scary. Abha was chasing her civil service dream and Ujjwal … . The irony of Abha's entanglement with Ujjwal was not lost on Simran. Abha, the so-called ruthless one, had lost her heart to someone even more casual and ruthless. And she? She was waiting eagerly to get married as soon as her father found her a suitable boy.

Even the most placid years have their ups and downs. The college office summoned Abha just before the exams and dropped the bombshell. Abha did not have the requisite attendance so she would not be allowed to sit for the exams. A letter to that effect was being dispatched to her parents.

'How did this happen Abha?' Simran was worried. They were huddled around a table in the canteen trying to formulate a damage control strategy. Rekha was clear as usual—'This comes from all the running around you do to St. Stephen's and all the drama group and festival thing you took on yourself!'

'What about you? You are more in Stephen's than me Rekha. I barely go there. I don't like such statements.'

'Hey I trained him better Abha. He comes here when I have time.'

'Is there any point in all this?' Simran tried to broker peace between them.

'What do we do now?'

Abha and Simran looked hopefully towards Rekha. She was always more clued into all the college happenings.

'Okay let me talk to the college president and see.' Some new guy was college president, but Rekha kept her finger on the pulse of the college.

It was a week fraught with unimaginable tension. The idea that she might not be able to take the exams was unimaginable for Abha. She made innumerable trips to the college office and had long confabulations with the college union. There were quite a few in the same boat as Abha, but that could not make matters better for her.

Simran could clearly visualize the reaction of Abha's father if such a letter reached him.

'I worry more about my mum Simran. She will be shattered if I lose a year. My case is not so bad. I am on the borderline. I think I missed a lot of classes in the festival organization without realizing it.' And she burst into tears. Simran put her arms around her and tried to console her. At that point Simran decided that someone in Abha's family needed to be taken into confidence.

Bina di was the only one Abha could think of. She called her from a post office. Bina di was quiet for a while and then said 'Try and sort it out, otherwise I will get Kishore to speak to someone in college.' The questions would come later.

Sisters are a blessing. They come packed in a wrapping of understanding and support.

Aarti Devi was happy as the house was full. Bina had delivered a son and Abha was home for the vacations. Together they were thoroughly enjoying the young one in their midst. Before the children came, the house was deathly quiet. With her husband's rise up the organizational ladder, the size of the houses had grown too. Now in Bombay they had a sprawling flat in Colaba right on the sea shore, but only the two of them lived there. Sometimes it seemed too quiet and eerie to her, especially when her husband was out of home on his innumerable inspections. Aarti Devi often wished that the government would allot houses in the opposite manner. When officers are young, have children and need a big house, they get small flats. When the children have left, they are given palaces to maintain. This imbalance did not make sense to her.

While her grandson slept, the three of them chatted over steaming teacups. Across the road, the Arabian Sea was hitting the shore at regular intervals.

'Abha, how are all your friends? Ujjwal, Simran, Rekha?'

'Fine Bina di. Ujjwal is planning to go to the US for further studies. Rekha is going to sit for the IIM exam and Simran—she remains as unfocused as ever.'

Aarti Devi was glad Abha had settled down to hostel life. There was also a certain quiet in her now. The raging fire had settled into a steady flame. Abha and her father had fewer arguments. They spent hours discussing a winning strategy for the civil services exam. Often he would tell her in the familiar challenging tone, 'It's tough you know Abha. It needs real effort to make it into the civil services.'

Maybe he had observed that she took up his challenges and tried to meet them. But Aarti Devi knew her husband had no time or inclination for such mind games. He was simply a father trying to warn and guide his temperamental daughter.

'Bina di, how much leave will you take for the baby?'

'Well three months is allowed officially, thereafter I will see. My mother-in-law has offered to take care of him, but I would need to find a good maid before I get back to work.'

'Do you enjoy your work?'

'Abha, it is such a difficult question to answer. We all have great notions about our own importance while we sit in our small rooms and push files. The government is one huge gargantuan machine that moves at its own time and pace.'

'Bina di why do you sound so cynical? I think we can make a difference as individuals.'

'You are not in the system as yet Abha, and you have the idealism that belongs to the young. Give it some time once you are in, and we will share notes. Often, I feel that once we are ensconced in the gilded cage of a government job we lose all touch with ground reality. We are far removed from the public we are supposed to serve.'

Aarti Devi cradled her grandchild in her arms and heard the conversation. It gave her a deep sense of comfort and achievement. Instead of discussing recipes and in-laws her young daughters were discussing work. Life definitely had its own rewards. The phone was ringing. Bina leapt to take it so that its bell would not wake up her sleeping son.

'Abha, call for you. It's Ujjwal,' Bina di handed the receiver to her.

'Hi Abha, how are you doing?'

'Fine, and what's up with you?'

'Well I was missing you. Delhi is colourless without you around. When are you coming back?'

'Really? I am back on the day the University opens again.'

'So how does it feel to be a "Mausi"? How are Bina di and the kid?'

'It's a wonderful feeling. I never knew a newborn is actually so small. I feel he will just slip through my hands!'

'That's interesting. This is a STD call from my Dad's office so I will call off now. Come soon. Am missing you. Will call you when you're back.'

'Where will you call me Ujjwal? The hostel has one call booth which you know is eternally busy.'

'Then you call me. Bye.'

Bina instinctively felt Abha had a soft corner for this boy, but Abha always had a 'no entry' sign on such issues. Although they were very close, they never discussed such topics. However, they did discuss the attendance issue when their mother was out of earshot.

Rekha had worked hard in getting the matter sorted out, using all her influence with the student union. The union had negotiated with the college administration, leading to a decision wherein borderline cases had to provide an undertaking that they would have an extra five per cent attendance in the next year. Abha had taken her exams. This had been her first brush with the maze of rules and regulations. It was clear that rules had scope for varied interpretations, but it did not mean that they were any less harrowing.

The vacations passed quickly, the newborn kept them completely engaged and soon Abha was back in a train bound for Delhi.

When she met Abha on the first day of the third year of college Simran knew that she was happy.

'Oh Simran, Bina di's son is so cute. It was a wonder to hold him. Ujjwal too called me quite a few times during the vacation at home. It really made my holidays. Am quite stupid, right? Anyway,

I have to call him today. I'll call from the college PCO, the hostel one means a long wait in the line.'

As they stood in the small line near the college PCO, Simran mentally crossed her fingers. Ujjwal's unpredictability was a havoc to deal with.

'Hi, Ujjwal, its Abha, I got back yesterday.'

'Hi. You don't have to say it, I know it's you. Welcome back. Settled in? Actually, I am running out of the house right now. Have to go somewhere. Catch you later. Bye.'

Simran uncrossed her fingers. It had not helped anyway. In her opinion, the biggest problem with Abha and Ujjwal was that they never squarely discussed this tenuous thing between them. It was a rather intense interaction, and there were expectations, but no means of expressing them. It was definitely not a relationship in the mould of the 'going around' category. Abha, hidden behind her 'I don't care' façade, burdened by her own image, could never peep out from behind her massive ego and simply ask. It was hopeless.

Nearly six months of third year were over. The only major event in Simran's life in the last few months had been Ravi Bhaiyya's marriage two months ago. It had been exhausting, but great fun. Simran had watched her Bhabhi's radiant face. Through all the ceremonies Simran had imagined what her own wedding would be like. The thought gave her immense joy. Ravi Bhaiyya had left for Madurai, where he was working, with his new bride in tow. The house had become quiet since he had left. Simran was lying in her bed reading a book when Amma came and sat next to her. Simran took Amma's hand in her own. Her hand was rough and calloused with years of hard work. Simran kissed it softly. 'Your papa was saying that he will now start looking around for a boy for you.'

Simran felt a thrill go down her spine. She kept quiet. Nothing was expected of her.

'*Phir Shikha and Seema rah jayengi* (Then Shikha and Seema will remain). Their turn will come after a few years.'

Amma slouched on the bed, and Simran put her head in her mother's lap. Without any formal education, her mother had managed to live in Delhi, support her father and bring up four well educated children. There was something remarkable about it.

Night fell outside, while mother and daughter bonded in silence, each eyeing the future with anxiety and hope.

The third year seemed to pass in a flash, leaving all of them breathless. They no more discussed cute guys or girls while sprawling in the college canteen. The buzz was all about what to do next. Most of the SRCC boys had family businesses to fall back on. Many had already joined them, much as Rekha had predicted. The bikes had given way to cars in the college parking. There were some who were looking abroad. GMAT, GRE and TOEFL were the operative words for them. Still others were cramming away for the forthcoming IIM entrance exams. There were also the CA hopefuls, and a few like Abha aiming for the civil service.

Abha and Rekha lounged in the college canteen trying to have a glimpse of their nebulous future in their steaming teacups. Rekha had decided to sit for the IIM entrance exams. She wanted to be as good as her Tamilian boyfriend who had gone to IIM Calcutta that year.

'Abha, why don't you think out of the box and try for management or something. Opting for the civil services, is rather passé now.

'I have never thought of anything else Rekha. It is a dream I have been chasing since childhood. I can't and don't want to give it up. Also, it is not that out-of-date. Look around, all over DU and JNU, people are working for years towards just this goal.'

'Maybe. So what are you going to do after college?'

'I'm going to enroll for a course in Law so that I can take Law as a subject in the civil services exam, and get a professional degree too. And you Rekha? Are you only following your boyfriend or is this what you want to do?'

In a long time Rekha actually took time to think before replying. She remembered her childhood at various army stations. It had involved constant shuttling from one city to another, and frequent change of schools accompanied with a search for new friends each time. Then, at last, her father had taken up a job in the private sector and they had moved permanently to Delhi. Their lives had looked up then. Become more comfortable and enjoyable.

'Abha, I know I want to climb the corporate ladder. I like the good life and I want it such that I can provide it to myself. Not be dependent on anyone to have the kind of life I want.'

It was not a surprise that Abha and Rekha had crystallized their ambitions well before the third year ended. What was surprising was that Simran had overcome her hesitations and started going around with Rohit, a classmate and hosteller. While waiting for college to end and get married, she was for once truly busy and focused. Whenever they sat together, Simran was full of all the glory of college romance.

'Hi. How are things?' Simran came and pulled up a chair and joined them. As happened often, when Simran arrived, Rekha always remembered she had work in the library and left the two of them alone.

'Abha, you have really wasted your three years in college hanging around for Mr. Undecided. It is such fun to have a steady boy friend around.'

She called for some tea and samosas. Simran was evidently happy. There was a spring in her step and she looked much brighter.

'Hmm. Have you thought about what you are going to do after college?'

'Not again. You have become such a bore. Yesterday we went for a movie and then he smuggled me into the hostel.'

'It's not allowed you know. Girls going into the boys' hostel. You can get into trouble. Be careful.'

'How come you never ask me what goes on in there? Aren't you curious?'

'Simran if you lived in a hostel like me you would never ask this. We say guys "kiss and tell". You should see the girls. They spend hours describing their boyfriends—how long they take to get it up, how long it becomes and how long they can keep it up. Beyond a point, it is actually nauseating. I believe it is really an exclusive and personal thing, not to be discussed like this.'

'Sometimes you surprise me Abha. In some ways you are so frank and in others so goddamn shy. Don't worry, I am still a virgin.'

'Not that I doubted it. If there were a timeline, I would put you last amongst the three of us in this!'

'So go and beat Rekha to it. She would be the front-runner right? We still have three months in college. Go around just for fun yaar.'

'Right now, other things are more important Simran. The race is on for getting onto the right track. Becoming something.'

Rekha was studying. It was nearly 2 am. The entrance exam for the IIMs was merely a week away. The pressure sometimes made her feel as if she would burst.

'You are still working? Go to sleep now. Study in the morning.' Papaji rubbed sleepy eyes at the door of her room as he said it.

'Papaji, it is the last week. I have got to give it all I have got.'

'Do you have a plan B Rekha? It is important in life.' Papaji came and sat on the bed near her study table.

Rekha shut her tired eyes and leaned her head on the chair. Plan B? She had not thought about it. She would make it to the IIMs if she worked hard and wanted it enough. She believed so.

'Papaji, I'll think about a plan B if I don't make it. Right now it will only dilute my efforts.'

In the light of the table lamp, her dashing father looked old. Rekha wondered how he would react if he knew she had a Tamilian boyfriend. She banished the thought. It belonged to another time in the future.

Time flew and suddenly the third year exams were over and they were all saying goodbye to each other.

Three years of fun, frolic and growing up were behind. Staring in the face was the real world, which demanded that each of them catch on to the thread of their future.

Simran was depressed. Rohit had taken admission in a University in his hometown, Bhopal. It was the end of their time together. She had known all along that this was how it would end.

College romances often meet this fate. They simply become memories. Life beckons beyond the portals of college. The dreams and time spent together in college remain just that—a dream. The boys need to find their feet. For the girls—if not working, then waiting for marriage becomes the next best thing.

Rekha had successfully entered the portals of IIM Calcutta. The three of them decided to celebrate Rekha's success. They met at Janpath, had coffee and sandwiches at DePaul's. Milling all over were youngsters and they suddenly felt grown-up. They were feeling quite sentimental and for a change, Rekha and Simran also got along. Abha knew she would miss Rekha. Simran and she were going to remain in Delhi.

Rekha left the next day by air for Calcutta. Simran had decided to enroll for an MA and wait around until her father found her a suitable man. She still had some time to kill before marriage claimed her.

For the vacations, Abha went to Bombay to be with her parents. She would return when the Law Faculty opened. Simran went to the station to see her off. Standing near the compartment with Abha was Ujjwal.

'So Abha, I am off in June to the US. I got admission for a Masters. Hope by the time I come back, you would have achieved your dream of joining the civil service.'

'Are you planning to come back Ujjwal?'

Could he not hear the hope and anticipation trembling in that question? Simran felt a rush of pure anger.

'I plan to, but let's see how things shape up. We'll be in touch.'

Hope not. Simran nearly said it. It was a blessing in disguise that he was going so far away. Hopefully Abha would be free of the strange thing that tied her to him.

The train was about to pull out. Ujjwal reached out and lightly caressed Abha's cheek in farewell. There was such longing in the gesture that Simran felt a lump in her throat. Didn't Abha sense it? She decided to speak to Ujjwal the moment they were alone.

He stood for a long time, waving to Abha's receding figure. Then he turned and said, 'So Simran, the tough part begins now, right? What are you planning? A cute girl like you should find a nice guy and get married soon. Don't waste your time anymore. You are meant to make a guy happy.'

The moment was lost forever. It was, as if, with the train, the curtain had dropped on his vulnerability and he was hidden behind his bantering self.

Abha was back in hostel, loaded with books and a detailed plan for the exam. Sociology was to be her second option for the main exams other than Law. Simran lay on the bed in Abha's hostel room and watched her childhood friend work like a maniac. She imagined Abha researching the techniques of preparing for the exams all through her vacations. Her civil service dream drove her relentlessly. Perhaps if she had been equally persistent about Ujjwal then things would have worked out between them.

'Ujjwal called you before leaving?'

'Yes.'

'And …'

'What and? He called me three-four times. The last time was the day he was leaving. He gave me the address and asked me to write.'

'Nothing else?'

'Well he did say just before putting down the phone. "I'll be back. Wait for me." That's it.'

'What do you mean that's it. What more could he have said?'

'Things are different now Simran. We are both chasing different dreams in different places. It's just too hazy.'

The more Abha ran after certainty the more it seemed to elude her. She did not have the ability to live on promises and dreams alone, always needing something more concrete to hold onto. If this meant being practical, Simran disagreed with it thoroughly.

'You know your problem? You can't say to the guy that you love him unconditionally. You always have these strange expectations lurking in your head.'

'Love? Who the hell knows what love is Simran. Right now, there is so much I want to do. My mother's expectations always greet me before I meet her.'

Outside, dusk was descending. Simran got up and started leafing through the papers lying on the stool next to the bed. There was an unopened letter from Rekha lying there along with other papers.

'Hey Abha take a break and let's read Rekha's letter.' She opened the letter and started reading aloud. It was full of the course at IIM and of course her boyfriend. She had managed to get that Tamilian after all. Amongst themselves, they simply referred to him as TamBhram. Abha went back to her books and Simran gazed out of the window. Between them, the companionship born of growing up together swirled comfortably.

'Did you write to Ujjwal?'

'Yes twice, but now it's been three months he hasn't replied.'

'He must be busy Abha.'

'I guess so. Apart from an "I reached" kind of letter, he has not written to me. Anyway, I don't think about it. I am too busy.'

'Do you wait to hear from him?'

Abha put her book down. 'You want to hear it loud and clear. Yes I do. Everyday. It is actually painful and it hurts like hell. When I enter the damn hostel, I go first to the pigeonhole allotted to me to check for letters. Happy?'

'Sorry.'

Simran lay back on the bed. It seemed so far away, but only last year she had been thinking as to where they would all be in a few years time. They had all scattered apart. Rekha was busy in Calcutta, Ujjwal was in the US, Rohit—she did not even know where he was. Abha and she? They were still together, but only physically. Abha had her civil service dream to work towards, but Simran had nothing yet. Her father was looking around, but nothing had worked out. How life changes, she thought, as the autumn breeze set the leaves fluttering in the courtyard.

Then life changed dramatically. On 31 October 1984, Indira Gandhi was assassinated and Delhi caught fire. Death, desolation and fear stalked the streets. Simran frantically tried to get in touch with Abha, but the hostel phone was perpetually busy. North Delhi and areas around the University were one of the worst hit areas. It was impossible to step out. Delhi became a ghost city as smoke curled up on the city skyline in a menacing manner. Inside the hostel premises throughout the devastating days, Abha was able to see from the hostel terrace the circle of flames that illuminated the skyline around. All the girls huddling on the terrace watched speechless, each feeling in their heart that this violence was going to change many things forever.

During that mad fortnight, one night there was a rumour that the water tank that served the University had been poisoned. Food in the hostel mess had already become bare subsistence level—roti and *aloo sabzi*—now, water had become suspect too. It took nearly a fortnight for the nightmare to subside, but it was clear that it would haunt the city for a long time.

The day it became possible, Simran went to the University to visit Abha. 'You cannot imagine Simran, the kind of fear one felt. It was all around, but not too close and yet the cold clammy fear gripped the heart. I couldn't sleep for the first few days at all. Then when the army started patrolling the University streets in their trucks, I suddenly realized what the terror of Partition must have been like.'

'But its better now. Things are slowly limping back to normal.'

'We think so Simran. I had joined a peace walk organized by the Students' Union to the neighbouring areas. Simran, houses were burnt, shops looted—there was devastation all around.'

'Abha I really hope that this recedes into the background. Can you imagine life in Delhi without the sardars? It is unimaginable.'

'True Simran. Let's hope that we can go to Bangla Sahib Gurudwara and have some *karah parshad* soon. You know Simran, what I learnt—anything can happen at any time.'

Rekha had sent Abha a long letter. The happenings in Delhi had shaken her. Hardayal Tayaji, her father's elder brother was a Sikh, while her own father was not. They visited the local gurudwara and temple with equal verve. It was a mixed family like many others in Punjab. Papaji had called her and asked her to stay in Calcutta and not rush to Delhi. Rekha had valiantly signed off the letter with 'Abha this will also pass. These things do. There is too much that is similar and meshed together.'

In class, Abha noticed that her good friend Gurdeep was now wearing a *kesri* dupatta everyday. The growing alienation of the Sikh students around them had became apparent. Many of the Sikh boys returned to University with their hair chopped and beards shaven. There was anger and anguish and a desire to escape from the madness that had gripped Delhi that autumn month.

Gurdeep stopped wearing her *kesri* dupatta everyday, although Punjab still simmered. Abha cleared the preliminary exam; she skipped her vacation to prepare for the mains exam. More than a year had passed and she had not even realized. Simran had stopped asking her about Ujjwal. After one birthday card, he had not written to Abha. Then the air was cleared finally.

One day in the University lawns, while Abha and Simran were crossing the road towards the Law Faculty, they met Ujjwal's friend Amrit. After some pleasantries Abha asked, 'So how is Ujjwal? Any news of him?'

'You still hung up on him Abha? Don't waste your time. I heard he is shacking up with a blonde out there.'

Simran could not decide what hurt Abha more in that instant. The realization that Ujjwal's friends knew she had a feeling for him, or the fact that Amrit had said it in her face so patronizingly or the news in itself.

'Don't take him seriously, Abha. Amrit always had this habit of talking loose.'

Abha remained silent all the way as they walked towards the Law Faculty building.

'I'm glad we met him today, Simran. It is time to move on.'

Ujjwal was never mentioned between them again. He got lost in the hectic preparation for Abha's exams, in the flow of life, in the distance between continents and in the pursuit of other dreams.

When Abha's exams were over, Rekha announced that she was going to be in Delhi for the winter break. After a long time the three of them would spend some time together. Now Simran and Rekha got along. Their mutual antagonism had been left behind in college. It was a nice, relaxed and lazy winter, spent watching movies, roaming Janpath and eating *chaat* at Bengali Market. The typical lull before the storm.

The day after the results of the civil services mains exam were declared, and Abha did not clear them, Simran's father died in a road accident. Knocked off his scooter by a speeding vehicle, Simran's father had lain on Wellington Crescent, bleeding. While he was dying on the road, Simran was watching *Chitrahaar* on TV with her mother and two sisters. How meaningless everything became when someone died. The numb pain never seemed to disappear. Even three months after his death, Simran had a burning anger within to catch the person who had knocked her father down and changed the course of their life. Ram Manohar Lohia Hospital had been only two hundred meters down the road, but her father had bled to death on the road as life raced by. The police cannot do much in 'hit and run' cases. The local inspector had been co-operative, but with no leads, he could not offer any solution.

Once the inevitability set in, it was time to move on, pick up the threads of life and figure out how the four of them were to live. Her mother and the three sisters. Ravi Bhaiyya, the good big brother had rushed from Madurai, done all the last rites and gone back. He had a job, a wife and two children of his own. He could not offer anything further by way of physical or economic support. Simran's father had built a small house in Ghaziabad, and they moved from the cozy confines of the centrally located government accommodation.

Life accosted Simran and demanded its pound of flesh. After Ravi Bhaiyya returned to Madurai, her mother and sisters looked to her for direction. She was now the eldest child in the house. She knew that her father's pension would not see them through. Not with the two younger sisters still studying.

Confused and hurt by things she did not understand Simran sought refuge in Abha's hostel room all the time. Cloistered in the room, she often hoped that when she stepped out reality would be different from what it was. 'Simran, I am sitting for the civil services exam again. You also take them with me. We will prepare together. You are intelligent, you only need to focus and you will make it.'

'Abha I never wanted to work. I hate the idea of being tied to a job and all the hassle of that life. I wanted a husband to provide for me and I would have made him really happy.'

'Life doesn't always give us what we want, Simran. You have to shoulder responsibility now. You have no option. Marriage will also happen, but you need to be able to support your family right now. These are forms for some of the Bank Officers' exams that are coming up. Fill them up.'

Simran filled up the forms with dread. Her life was slipping from the ordered, neat path she had always drawn for it. Aren't these the times that sons are desired for? Was it not for this time that Ravi Bhaiyya had been given priority in everything in their house? To take up the reins when their father passed away. Why was Ravi Bhaiyya not responsible for them? Why was it falling on her shoulders? There was no one to answer the questions that raged in Simran's mind. They brewed underneath and simmered for years creating spaces and silences in the family that could never be bridged.

Despite all the uncertainty, Simran cleared one of the exams and became a trainee officer in the Bank of India. When she gave the news to her mother, the light that came in Amma's tired eyes made it worthwhile. Life seemed to be slowly limping back to normal. After absorbing the shock of failure the first time, Abha also immersed herself in reappearing for the year-long exam. She had again cleared the preliminary and was trying to give her best to the main exams. This time, her mother had come to stay with her in the railway guest house to provide her moral support.

Aarti Devi watched Abha studying long days and nights. The guesthouse room was strewn with books and papers all over. When Abha studied late into the night, Aarti Devi would keep a flask of hot tea and sandwiches nearby. It was satisfying to be with her daughter while she worked hard to achieve her dream. Aarti Devi had despaired when Abha had failed in her first attempt. Her husband had started out with an 'I told you so' lecture, but along the way, he had encouraged Abha to take the exam again.

He had also started looking around for a suitable boy for Abha. On Aarti Devi's insistence, this matter had been postponed till the main exams were completed. Aarti Devi had never been religious, never felt the presence of any august God in her life. While Abha studied, she prayed fervently, to any power residing in the skies above, for her daughter's success.

Rekha and her TamBhram had been engaged two months ago. Much to Rekha's surprise her parents had accepted a South Indian as a son-in-law without much fuss. Their only desire was that she should have a ceremony in the gurudwara, and that had been accepted. They had decided to marry only after they joined their respective jobs at the end of their course at IIM.

Simran had to go Jaipur on a training programme while Abha was taking the main exams. Every weekend, she came home to be with her mother and sister. There was no one at home to understand her desire to get married. After her father's death, there was no one to look for a man for her. Ravi Bhaiyya, in Madurai, was too far away. There had to be some way out for Simran. Her life had to change. Simran was posted to a branch in Delhi by the time Abha's final results came out. 'Simran I made it. I qualified. I am so thrilled.' Abha had yelled down the phone. Simran dashed to be with her.

Abha's face was lit with joy. Aarti Devi had been the happiest. Her daughter had lived up to her dream.

'So what service are you joining?'

'I don't think I will get my first option as I am in the first hundred… .'

The phone was ringing. Her father was on the line from Mumbai.

'Papa I am so happy. Now you can be proud of me … . No, I haven't given railways as my second option. It is the police. Papa I have always dreamt of joining the police. Of course, we can change the options within ten days of the result. Bye.'

'Police, Abha?' Simran was shocked. It seemed a dreary and awful job to her. She wanted to add something, but decided to let Abha enjoy her big day unhindered.

The next day, Abha's father had flown down to Delhi from Mumbai and the great war had begun.

'Abha, you will not take up the police. It is not a job fit for women. Even for men, you have to be of a certain temperament to be fit in the police service. You are always interacting with the scum of society. No fixed hours, no holidays, you are on duty on all festivals. Just no way.'

'But Papa, I just love the idea. I love the uniform, and the authority that goes with the job.'

The arguments had continued relentlessly into the next few days. Aarti Devi had decided to remain neutral in this battle. She sensed what her husband said was true.

At last, Abha had relented. The opposition was too much from every quarter. Even Bina di and Kishore ji had joined cause with her father. Abha had agreed on the condition that she would not join the railways, 'Papa, there I will always be known as your daughter. I don't want to be in your shadow.'

'In service these things help Abha.'

'No means NO.'

It was her father's turn to back down, and on the last day left for changing choice of service Abha opted for the audit service, much to Abha's sense of loss and her family's relief.

The day Abha gave in her changed option she dropped in to Simran's office for a cup of tea.

'Why is it like this Simran? Why couldn't I have been allowed to make a choice I wanted?'

'Sometimes it's better to listen to the elders in these matters. And you only said to me Abha, life doesn't always give you what you want.'

'Anyway. It is a decision taken. Now I am only looking forward to what lies ahead. I leave for the training in Mussoorie at the end of August.'

Abha's ability to start looking ahead was a boon, thought Simran. It was essential for life.

Within the next fortnight the big news that came to Simran was that Abha was getting engaged. The wedding would be held in December after the three months' training in Mussoorie got over. Simran had actually felt a pang. If her father had been alive, things would have been different for her. But then Simran would not have met him. The love of her life, she thought. Should she tell Abha about him? It was unthinkable that she was keeping such a thing from Abha, but it seemed better to wait.

Simran called up Abha from her office.

'Abha, you are going in for an arranged marriage? Makes no sense to me. What about all your great things about the guy interesting you and all?'

'Simran, its different now. I have to get married at some point of time. My own success rate at finding someone is clearly low. I have to admit. So might as well agree to the person Papa has found. Seems all right. We met and chatted a bit.'

Everyone except Simran was getting married. In January Rekha and her TamBhram would be married in Madras. One ceremony was planned in the traditional South Indian style and another in the gurudwara. Blessings of all Gods were needed for a successful union.

As Simran took the bus home in the evening she wondered about their lives. So this is how they had ended up. With set careers and practical and down-to-earth marriages. Life—the big leveller. In her own case, there was some time still.

Over the weekend, Abha and Simran went shopping to Janpath. Abha, as usual, was full of the life that awaited her in Mussoorie. Simran wondered how Abha could be more excited about her job than her impending marriage. Simran had still not mustered the courage to tell Abha about him—the love of her life. She wondered how Abha would react. She would tell her about him once things between them had crystallized a bit more.

How come neither of them saw him until he was right in front of them? 'Hi Abha, how are you doing?' In his burnt red tee shirt, Ujjwal was actually looking nice, Simran thought with a shock.

Between the three of them, he was the one who overcame the surprise first. Abha seemed to have lost her tongue. It was close to three years, since the day all three of them were on the New Delhi station together. 'Ujjwal, when did you come back? Are you back for good or just visiting?' Simran tried to fill the strange silence with a host of questions.

'I came in four months ago. I had said I will come back and I did. Congrats Abha for your success in the civil services exam. And also congrats for your engagement.'

How did this man, he had become a man as they had all become women, still have the knack to start a conversation from where it was left off nearly three years ago? Simran wondered.

Then Abha found her tongue. 'Thanks Ujjwal. How about you? What are you doing now? How are your parents?' They chatted in the midst of bustling Janpath like the old college friends they were. They exchanged numbers and addresses and then moved on towards their respective destinations.

'It was unnerving to meet him all of a sudden. Wasn't it Abha?'

'It was actually nice. He has grown up and matured. I'm glad that he is doing well.'

It was better to leave it at that. So many things in life had to be left behind simply to move on. It is a different matter that often they never left, however much one tried.

Aarti Devi and her husband moved to Delhi much to her delight. In the few months preceding Abha's wedding they would be together. The tension between father and daughter had abated a lot over the years, leading to a grudging affection. Since her children had left home, Aarti Devi had tried to carve out a space for herself. She had turned to writing, finding herself drawn to writing for children. Simple stories of life, full of innocence and love. Was it an escape for her or a fantasy? She never stopped to find out. Her favourite characters were fairies, with coloured wings and light bodies, holding promise of a world that was sweet and tranquil.

While many women of her generation were turning to religion and gurus, Aarti Devi was manufacturing fairies. In her view, the pursuits were similar. Whether a guru or a fairy—a belief that something or someone offers a respite, a haven, was essential for existence. Abha would shortly leave for her training and three months later would be married. For Aarti Devi, it was the fruition of a long journey she had embarked on in the lonely days in the railway colony of Delhi. She—the mother of two daughters and not of a son—had daughters as well placed as their father. No other girl in their extended family had actively taken up a career. She was extremely proud of her children and was aware of her own contribution to their success.

The doorbell rang and Simran walked in. Aarti Devi had seen Simran change since she had started working. There was a confidence in her step and a focused look on her face. The vague sweetness of girls simply waiting to marry had vanished. The result was much more charming.

'*Namaste* Aunty. Where is Abha? I took half a day off to be with her. Now she will come only on the weekends, right?'

'It really depends on the rules at the Academy. How is your mother Simran?'

Just then, Abha walked in from the market and the two disappeared in Abha's room for last minute packing. The phone was ringing endlessly in the house.

'Abha, call for you Beta. He says he is Ujjwal. Is he the same one you knew in college?'

'Yes Mummy.'

Aarti Devi was surprised. In all these years, there had been no news of him. Abha never mentioned him. She had known that he had gone away to study in the US. She had also known that there appeared a softness on her daughter's face when she spoke to him. It happened to all girls that age. Aarti Devi purposely did not look at Abha as she spoke on the phone that day.

'What did he say Abha?' Simran was curious.

'He just called to wish me luck for the job.'

'Has he been calling you since we met that day?'

'No this is the first time. Don't worry Simran. All that is behind now. We were always friends more than anything else. It was just that I liked him slightly more. Nothing wrong with that, I am sure.'

'Your fiancé called you?'

'Yes, this morning.'

They got busy with the last minute packing. During the course of the week, Abha left on a new journey, towards a new life.

Simran eagerly waited for Abha's weekend visits. Her training seemed much more interesting than the rather drab work in the bank. Cabinet ministers, well known social activists and prominent personalities would address them at regular intervals. There was an endless stock of stories from Abha each time she visited Delhi. After the gruelling one year civil service exam, this was the fun time. A bunch of young people, with a secure lifelong career awaiting them, trying to understand how to administer a country.

Abha had dropped in to Simran's office on Saturday as it was half day for her. Abha was telling her that a week ago, Sam Pitroda had spent a morning with them. His talk on the way technology could change the workplace had fired Abha's imagination.

Computers—they heard about them all the time now. Simran had even seen a machine installed in the branch manager's office, but it was yet to come out of its protective cover.

'Simran, can you imagine they officially teach us something called OLQ—officer like qualities. It is simply hilarious. The other day, one of our friends wore a skirt to the classes and she was turned back. She was told that it was against OLQ for ladies to be dressed in such casual wear in working hours!'

'It sounds like fun.'

'It is. You know I tried horse riding for two days, but it hurts the rib cage like mad.'

'You like any of the guys?'

'I am engaged, remember? But seriously some of them are cute. You should see the hectic pairing and mating that goes on there, Simran. Everyone is looking for a life partner, especially the girls. Now what about you, tell me what's happening in your life?'

They were leaving Simran's office. Simran had decided that on this trip she would tell Abha about him. It was about time. As the two of them climbed down the steps of the office building, Simran saw him.

'Hi. I thought I might catch you here on a Saturday afternoon once Simran's bank closes. How is it going Abha, training to run the country?'

Why was he there? Simran somehow felt nervous. Ujjwal's knack of arriving unexpectedly all the time had not changed one bit. In shirt and tie, he was the young private sector executive to perfection. Was it Simran's imagination or was there a sense of appeal in the way he stood on the steps before them.

'It is really interesting Ujjwal. How is your work getting along?'

The conversation seemed to flow as easily as if they met Ujjwal everyday on the steps of the bank waiting for them. Abha and he were leaning on a car and chatting. As usual, Simran became the onlooker, the outsider. Some things never change.

'Tell me Abha do you have any second thoughts about your marriage?'

'What is that supposed to mean?' Abha's voice had a deadly sharpness to it.

'Nothing. I just thought that I must ask you. If you do, let me know. See you around. Bye.' And he had walked off to cross the road.

Abha watched his receding back and her eyes were seething.

'What was that Abha? Was he trying to propose?'

'Was he? I never heard it. If a man wants to propose, he has to say it loud and clear, in so many words. Right? Oh, just forget it.'

'Come on Abha, he didn't come here for nothing. He was trying to say something.'

'So what? We are not in college anymore Simran. We are grown-ups. We can say what we really want to say without beating around the bush. And should I tell you the truth Simran? This hide and seek with Ujjwal tired me out a long time ago. This constant emotional seesaw. Does he? Doesn't he? What did he mean, did it mean this or that. No Simran that is not what I want anymore.'

What can mere mortals do against the plans of destiny? Simran had developed a strong faith in the guiding hand of the stars. Look at the way her life had changed. So they left it at that.

Abha's marriage was a glittering affair. She looked the proverbial beautiful bride. She had always looked gorgeous in traditional Indian clothes. Simran could not recollect when she had last seen Abha in Western wear ... perhaps in the first year of college. They had walked a long road together—from childhood, teenage, college to womanhood and marriage. Often, in the long years of friendship, Simran had wondered if she was actually an integral part of Abha's life, the way Abha was a part of hers? Abha always had other friends, other dreams, other longings. There were days when Simran had felt that if she walked up to her, Abha would just brush her off. It was not meant to be rude, but at that moment, Simran was not part of Abha's scheme of things.

Over the years, Simran had learnt to accept and understand. Abha cared, but she was driven to give her undivided attention to whatever claimed it at that moment. Whether other people or other dreams, her attention never diluted. That was what was special about her. That was why like Simran, Rekha felt close to Abha and so did all the others who thought of Abha as a friend. In a group—Abha was the quiet one, the observer, but at a one to one level, she connected wonderfully.

Bina watched as her younger sister got married. She looked radiant and stunning. Kishore had rightly named Abha the firecracker in the family. There was tremendous energy in her—in her eyes, in her whole personality. Bina had always felt Abha was an intensely private person, making if often impossible to understand her mind. As sisters they shared everything, but not the matters of the heart. In their case Abha's heart, because Bina did not have a complicated heart, in the first place. Even at that moment, Bina could not gauge the excitement in her sister's heart. She could only guess.

Rekha stood hand in hand with her fiancé and wondered how Abha was feeling. She was looking gorgeous as brides are meant to be. They had stuck together since college. For Rekha, Abha was her friend. Simran was Abha's friend. Like a bridge, Abha kept the three of them together. Rekha watched the *jaimal* exchange, and clutched his hand tighter. There was something sentimental about such moments. Marriage seemed so final.

Aarti Devi was nervous. Her temperamental younger daughter was undertaking a different journey. In her heart lurked all the fears that a mother has on her daughter's wedding day. The fear of the unknown, a hope for happiness juxtaposed with sadness at the prospect of a child leaving. It all added up to a tremulous stir in her heart that kept threatening to pour out from her eyes. Abha was looking soft, beautiful and gentle. Aarti Devi knew of Abha's anger, impatience and strong will, but she knew of her other side too. She knew her daughter was blessed with sensitivity, which when combined with a sharp intellect could lead to a lot of pain. As the marriage ceremony progressed, she said a silent prayer to the fairies above to spare her daughter any pain.

Simran watched as the *pheras* were taken. The moments when the couple tied by a knot, circled the fire, signifying a lifetime bond, were so sacred. She felt a lump rise in her throat. She wondered if ever this day would come in her life. Abha was getting married and Simran was yet to tell her about Hussein.

The same Thursday in May

Bina watches the small gathering in the room. Papa is looking relaxed. The heat outside has captured the room also. The AC and the whirring fan cannot combat its vicious onslaught. The clock ticks away as they all wait. What conversation can one hold while waiting in an office room for a marriage ceremony? By now, Bina has read more than once the brown board behind the empty chair that displays in golden letters the names of previous incumbents of the position. The gathering has drunk water, tea, nibbled on biscuits and discussed the weather. They now sit in silence, waiting for Mr. Mathur, the Additional District Magistrate and marriage officer, to return from a meeting and solemnize the marriage.

In a deep purple silk sari she purchased on a recent official tour to Chennai, Abha is looking very pretty, much younger than her thirty-eight years. Her fiancé is also looking nice with a tilak on his forehead. The tilak is the only visible symbol of the ceremony they are about to solemnize. His relatives are shifting uncomfortably on the leather sofas in the room. Like Bina and Papa, his relatives have also brought two garlands. The flowers in all the garlands have begun to wilt in the heat. Bina wonders what each person in the room is thinking.

Her thoughts are with Abha. She really wants her sister to find happiness and joy—the kind she has shared all these years with Kishore. Bina wonders how she would have dealt with life, if faced with the same kind of trials as Abha. Bina admires Abha's courage, tenacity and ability to move on. It is difficult to talk to Abha about unpleasant things. She is intensely private about her grief and troubles. Despite their closeness, they never discuss many issues. Is it essential? Does intimacy mean sharing everything or is it about understanding and relating to what is unsaid too? Bina's mind goes to Mummy, lying in her hospital bed. Mummy has grave doubts about what is happening. Her main concern is Parul. Papa on the other hand is happy that his daughter is getting remarried. Their parents are now old and simply pray and wish fervently for this marriage to work.

Bina looks once again at the two of them. They have been through a long journey to reach here, each with baggage of their own. The way forward could be full of strife or it could be a smooth journey. She wishes, for her sister's sake, that it will be the latter.

'Abha, should we enquire again when Mr. Mathur is likely to come?'

'Bina di, his secretary has already said that she doesn't know. He was called to the Prime Minster's Office suddenly for a meeting.'

They have been waiting for nearly two hours. Waiting for a marriage to be solemnized in an office, is difficult and rather strange. No one in the room has a clue as to how the ceremony will be performed. All of them are first timers in such an event.

Parul walks into the empty apartment. Reena Didi starts fussing around her. She dumps her bag in her room and walks into 'their' room. Hers and Ma's. That is how she describes the two rooms in her mind. One is hers, and the other belongs to her and Ma. The room is neat and empty. Reena Didi has tidied up the house after they went. There is nothing in the room to tell her that her mother has gone to get married.

Parul feels her tears well up from inside. Yet again. Gaurav Bhaiyya calls her to have lunch. But she does not want to eat or talk to anyone. She runs into her room and locks it from inside.

Delhi, Again

'What do you mean 'what happened?' Simran, I did not expect you to ask me this.'

'I mean what happened that lead to this Abha?'

'Everyone asks the same thing in this awfully concerned yet inquisitive tone. It grinds and grates on my insides.'

'Abha, be reasonable. People just want to know why it happened and how it came about. That is all. You shouldn't resent it.'

Abha winced inside. 'What happened?' Was the statement that 'it did not work' not enough to explain what happened. Was it possible to explain to others the slow and steady decay of dreams and aspirations? Why did people ask 'what happened' as if she could say 'one fine day the marriage collapsed because … .'

It was never so simple.

'Simran, a bad marriage is like an interval in one's life. Before that the movie is going on—full of life and colour. Then the interval comes. In the interval the movie pauses, you hang around the hall looking for something to occupy you till the movie begins again.'

'You now have a daughter also, Abha.'

'Yes that is the biggest blessing. Imagine not even having her at the end of it all.'

'That is not what I meant. You must reconsider your decision Abha. If not for yourself, at least for your daughter's sake.'

Abha sipped the tea placed on the desk. Simran's office tea was miserable. She had heard these statements hundreds of times ever since she had taken a transfer back to Delhi from Baroda, and decided to file for a divorce.

The stench of a bad marriage can suffocate—it stifles, it stagnates and until a decision is taken to either bear it or leave it, the interval is never over. It was extremely difficult to explain the feeling.

'Simran, people marry for the sake of their parents, their families, they stay in hopeless marriages for the sake of children, but divorce—it is the most selfish and personal decision a person can make. It is one decision in life which a person takes primarily for oneself, purely. What is important is to take responsibility for this decision. I am ready to do that. I can sustain Parul and myself in every way. Why then is it so difficult for people to accept this?'

Abha wondered whether this conversation that began with 'what happened' would ever leave her life. Even Rekha had asked her that over the phone from Bombay, but quickly followed it up with a 'hope you know what you are doing'. Parul, all of two years, was the only unquestioning person in her life. The ultimate joy.

'Let's leave this discussion for another day. Tell me did your brother finally agree to Hussein?'

Simran was in love with a Muslim. It had been difficult to accept and rather disconcerting. Hindu and Muslim marriages remained few and far between. The only exception seemed to be the world of Bollywood where many of the reigning Muslim male actors were married to Hindu girls. However, in ordinary, everyday lives—it was a situation fraught with uncertainty and opposition.

Simran had met him while she had been on her training in Jaipur. He worked for an insurance company. Simran had been drawn towards him irresistibly. The void created by dreams of a marriage that seemed nowhere near the corner was filled by the feeling of an intense attraction for him. The incurable romantic, she had not stopped to think or rationalize. She just fell for him all the way, sliding down the ladder of love.

It was only a year after Abha's marriage that Simran had told her about Hussein. It had worried Abha—somehow the relationship did not seem to have a future. But Abha had been caught up with the arrival of her daughter, her job, new city, new husband, new challenges. Along the way, Simran had been posted to Agra and Hussein had also moved there. In Agra they had sort of lived with each other, maintaining separate residences and meeting only on the sly. Then Hussein had moved to Chandigarh. At that juncture, Simran had broached the possibility of marriage. He had told her, 'Get your side to agree first, and then I will talk to my family.'

Simran, the believer in true and unconditional love had taken the bull by the horns and spoken to her mother. After some initial hesitation, because Seema was still unmarried, her mother had relented. Her only condition being that Ravi, the absent man of the family, should concur.

Then the storm that had brewed under for so long had burst. Ravi had descended from wherever he was working and given an emphatic 'no' to her marrying a Muslim.

Simran could not understand how Ravi got the right to say 'no'. He was never there for the family, never thought it fit to find a suitable boy for Simran. It had suited him that she was there to take care of their mother and sisters, while he lived with his own family.

Arguments and bitterness had raged in Simran's home. All the things that had simmered beneath suddenly ignited and exploded. Simran had tried to get Hussein and Ravi to meet, but Hussein was adamant that only once they agreed to the proposal would he meet anyone from her family. Caught in the quagmire of religion and between two unrelenting men Simran had spent the last year trying to find a way to marry.

Ever since Abha had returned to Delhi, the only two topics Simran and she discussed were Simran's saga and her own. Was Simran's mother using Ravi as a shield? Abha often wondered. There never were simple answers to simple questions

After some time, Abha left Simran's office and made her way back to her parent's home. Papa had retired and now lived in his own house in East Delhi. Abha and Parul were with them now. Parul would be waiting for her. Parul was her only distraction. A light of innocence and love.

When a marriage collapses, like the wedding, it becomes a family affair. Mummy and Papa had called in Bade Mama and Kumud Mausi for innumerable conferences. Hours had been spent simply discussing the issue. All the elders in the family had their own views, the common thread being that with a child between them Abha should try again.

Try again and again and again. Couldn't they realize that no one marries with the idea that he or she will divorce one day? Could no one comprehend the throes of uncertainty, fear, pain, and desolation that she had to go through before deciding to walk out? Could all these people, who were her well-wishers, not see the truth—she had taken the decision only after trying again and again.

Often Abha wanted to shout back, but she had understood that much like her, her family too would have to go through the entire gamut of conflicting emotions before they could come around to accepting the finality of her decision. At times, the sense of failure she saw in her mother's eyes made her feel guilty. Abha often wanted to tell her—'Mummy, this is not anyone's failure, least of all yours. If anyone failed, it was I. But, actually, I don't think so too. Divorce is really an accident. It can happen to anyone.'

'Let us wait for sometime before doing anything. Maybe after a few months Abha will change her mind and decide to go back.' Kumud Mausi's suggestion had let the matter be for about three months. Then Abha had discussed filing a petition with a lawyer friend. That action had spurred another round of conferences.

'Abha, I think you should not hurry, maybe after a few years you will feel differently. In fact, I feel you should go and live with him. He has not asked for a divorce, he wants you back. Everything sorts itself out over a period of time.'

A few years? Was life meant to be spent waiting for things to set themselves right on their own? Don't we owe ourselves the responsibility of taking life in our own hands? Bade Mama's suggestion had blown the lid off Abha's patience with the elders.

'Mama, if you are so keen, go and live with him. I will never do that.' Her statement had ensured the end of any sympathy the extended family was to show her thereafter. They sympathized with Papa and Mummy. But Abha? She was not how girls in marital trouble were meant to be. She never cried, never expressed her grief or desolation. Abha never elaborated on the details of why her marriage broke down. She never asked for compassion and sympathy. She refused to be a martyr and no one forgave her for that.

Her life seemed to be stuck in an impasse. She took decisions everyday at work, gave directions and participated in national policy-making, but her own life was beyond her control. She hated going into the house everyday at the end of work. The pall of gloom that had descended on the house made her feel very guilty.

Abha parked the car and Parul ran out with her arms outstretched 'Ma, Ma come back from ofich!' The warmth of the hug, and the sheer joy Parul emanated rubbed itself on her. Abha picked her up and hugged her, and for a moment, all her troubles seemed to disappear.

Bina di and Kishore ji had come over from Lucknow. They all sat together over dinner and talked of different things. Once Parul had gone to bed, the never-ending dialogue about Abha's marriage began.

'Abha what happened?'

'Bina di it did not work out. I don't want to get into details. That is for the court proceedings. Why isn't it enough that I don't want to continue in this marriage? I am not a fool. Credit me with some sense on such major things please. I want to be out for good.'

'Are you sure?'

'After years, in my life, I am sure about something.'

Sisters are wonderful creatures. Bina di, the considerate and gentle woman, always willing to adjust and compromise never once advised her sister 'Think it over again. Go back and try.'

'If you file for a divorce what about Parul?' When Abha heard Mummy's question she knew things would fall in place. If Mummy came around and took her side, she could overcome anything. Like Parul, Abha was the little daughter seeking refuge in her mother.

'Mummy, of course I will ask for her custody. I have been discussing this. If the woman is working and willing to keep her child, it is rare these days that the child will go to the father. And especially when it is a girl.'

Bina di convinced Papa that the time had come to follow up on Abha's decision and act. That clinched it. The interval was over. Abha filed for divorce, along with claim for Parul's custody, and life began to move again.

Lutyen's Delhi is laid out with broad avenues and big roundabouts to celebrate spring. The roundabouts become a kaleidoscope of colours with blooming flowers. The green trees seem to glisten and shine. As she drove the car, the fresh spring air made Abha happy. She loved the spot where Tilak Road opened onto the vast opulence of India Gate. To reach her office, she drove up the majestic Raj Path. Delhi was like a regal queen residing up Raisina Hill, with North and South Block as two ornate sentinels. It was simply breathtaking; she loved this time of the year in Delhi.

Abha reached the North Block parking and then walked up to her room on the second floor. She had managed a room to herself in the notoriously crowded North Block. Tucked in one of the remote recesses of the second floor, its solitary window opened out onto one of the broad courtyards in the middle. It was her haven. Away from all the thoughts that chased her when she was at home or alone. In her office room, she was in a different mould. Once the door shut, and Abha sat at her desk, everything else seemed to matter less.

There was something unnerving about being in the twilight world of a separated or divorced person in the Indian setting. While sitting in a lunch group Abha could not become a part of all the domestic talk that went around.

'Yesterday we went there and met … .'

'My husband's brother is around … .'

Suddenly as a single person, there was no status in the much-married world. People were not rude, they did not exclude on purpose, but there was no escape from being the odd one out. The first causality of new-found singledom was the lack of acceptance in 'married' circles, especially for the woman.

In office when anyone met Abha for the first time, after a few questions she was always asked, 'What is your husband doing?' Abha always wondered why they never asked male officers 'What is your wife doing?'

'I am in the middle of a divorce' was her stock reply. The responses varied dramatically. Some of the people looked shocked and then muttered a 'Sorry', as if it was their fault. While others said 'What happened?' Still others queried 'You have children?' While still others maintained a silence. She had become adept at handling all responses. Despite the minor irritants, office and work provided a source of relief and comfort. Long years ago, Abha had imbibed the mantra that as long as you do well what you are supposed to be doing, other things fall in place. She was competent and sincere at work, so what if her marriage had not turned out well. That was another part of life.

The phone on her desk had begun to ring. Another day at work beckoned. When Abha had started out a few years ago, she had dreams of doing great things, changing the way the system worked. Down the line, she had learnt slowly and surely that in a bureaucracy there was acceptability as long as one steered through the maze in a state of grand mediocrity. The survival strategy was to do the assigned job well and remain impervious to what happened around. The bureaucracy had taught her well how to live in compartments. And in a way, Abha was grateful. Her life was in small compartments, each co-existing within her with ease. There was Parul, the divorce proceedings, things at home, managing work and the outside world and tucked in one corner there was her own self. Deep down, the lowest on the rung—her vulnerability, her sense of loss along with her faith that life is beautiful. Despite all the adversity in her life, this belief never left her—that life is beautiful and has a lot to offer by way of beauty, warmth and knowledge. This was her hidden mantra; the one thought that propelled her on.

The intercom on her table was buzzing.

'Abha come for lunch today to my room. Many batchmates are coming over.'

'Thanks, Raghav. Will be there at 1.30 pm.'

'Batchmate' was a precious concept in the civil service. Joining the service in the same year, when they were idealistic and young, they had been trained together for a long time. Thereafter, spread out across the country they formed a reliable network of support. In practice, batchmates were like siblings in the service. They fought, competed and at times hated each other, yet they were together for nearly thirty years in the same system. The bond remained something special.

Abha would go for batch lunches like the one in Raghav's room sometimes. It was an opportunity to catch up and get to know what was happening around.

The buzz at lunch that day was about computer training. They had been hearing about it for a long time. Computers would be entering the work-place in a big way soon, all officers would receive training and soon they would enter the paperless world! It sounded exciting, but in government, they knew that until something happened actually, there was little point in planning.

Abha watched with interest as the lunch boxes opened. All her male colleagues, with wives at home, had perfectly laid out lunches, there was *sabzi* in one container, nicely packed roti in another, some salad and even *achar*, while the working women's lunch boxes had the look of a hurried hand. Rotis stuffed in with some *sabzi*—haphazardly.

'What working women need is a wife at home!'—the thought made Abha smile. She looked around the group that was busy eating. Could she call anyone of them her friend? There was no one. In the job, she had made good acquaintances, but her friends were all outside the system and dated to a time much before.

'Abha, I am celebrating my son's birthday on Sunday. Please bring Parul at 7 pm and stay for dinner'—Raghav's invitation was a revelation. Abha realized that although she had lost her acceptability as a wife, she had it as a mother. She was not invited to couple events, but she was welcome for a child's birthday. Relationships shaped how people interacted with you—this realization struck her all over again.

The solitary fan in the cubicle was whirring away, trying to bring in some of the fresh outside air. In Patiala House, the lawyers' chambers are small, windowless cubbyholes cluttered with paperwork. The dusty documents on the shelves represent lives spent trying to secure justice. Abha would spend long hours there, poring over the paperwork that mounts unendingly in a court case. She was sure no one ever read the reams of paper. However, each line was important because when it would become the key issue was never certain.

When she had started looking for a lawyer, Abha discovered that lawyers worked in stages. They would first suggest reconciliation.

Next, since she was a woman they would highlight the problems of a divorced woman in the Indian context. If still she refused to reconsider they targeted the child. It was only when the entire process had been gone through that they would approach the business at hand.

'I think you should let the child go to her father. Why should you take the lifelong responsibility of a daughter? She will be an impediment to your subsequent marriage.'

When the lawyer they had approached had said this for the second time, Abha had got up and left the briefing.

'Mummy I will change the lawyer. When my lawyer doesn't agree with my point of view, how will he ever put it across in the court?'

'You should think about what he is saying,' Ram uncle, Papa's friend, who had helped them in the search for a reliable lawyer, said quietly.

Had she given birth to a child to give her away? Subsequent marriage? If she were to marry again, it had to be someone who realized that Parul was a part of her life, part of her identity, her existence. Abha had wanted to scream out.

But she did not. Convincing others about what you want and why you want it was important only to a point. Abha had firmly decided that the way she looked at life would henceforth be through her own prism and not anybody else's.

She had landed in Patiala House with a new lawyer. A repeat of the whole process of 'Do you really want it? Do you know what it means?' had been gone through. The new lawyer had never suggested that she should give up her child. So she had stuck with him. The battle had commenced. A divorce proceeding is akin to a fight for life and there was no escape from the fine lines, the reams of paper, the accusations and the counter accusations. It was a dreary and dirty fight, worth it only because at the end of the tunnel there was hope of her life becoming her own again.

While Abha read the latest papers to be filed, her lawyer said, 'At the next hearing we have to provide visitation. You will have to bring Parul to the court.'

'I know.'

This was the most painful part. The innocent infant was taken at intervals to the revolting and drab environs of the courts at Tees Hazari. To shed the unwanted baggage of life there are many crosses to be borne, and Parul too could not escape them. It was amazing, thought Abha, that once you know what you want—clearly and unambiguously—the price you have to pay for it becomes immaterial. The journey towards the decision is much more painful than anything that comes after that.

It must be the same thing that drove Simran. Simran never fought the truth. Within a few months of meeting Hussein, she had known that he was the man for her. Subsequently, she faced everything that came in the way with courage.

Abha had met Hussein once when he had passed by Delhi. He was a man of few words, taciturn and rather dour in his demeanor. How a chatterbox like Simran could be with a person so difficult to speak with, Abha never understood. But when Abha had seen the look on Simran's face as she looked at Hussein she knew—in these things there is no formula. They just happen.

Amma was sitting in the sun outside, in the small open space near the gate. Age had caught up with her knees. She found it difficult to walk, but continued to remain active as far as possible. Simran was sitting on the steps near the door. Quietly they watched the world go by on a lazy winter Sunday afternoon.

'Amma, this time when Ravi comes to Delhi, whether he says yes or not, I am going to invite Hussein home. You can meet each other then. *Kab tak Ravi ke decision ka wait karoon* (Till when should I wait for Ravi's decision)?'

'Call him Ravi Bhaiyya. He is your elder brother. *Tujhe jaldi hai itni to court marriage kar le* (Get married in court if you are in such a hurry).'

Simran's home had become a battleground because of Hussein. There was no one to support her.

'Amma, I would do it, but Hussein says it is important for families to agree.'

Amma kept quiet. The phone inside was ringing and Simran went inside to attend. It turned out to be a wrong number. Simran came outside and saw that some people from the local temple were chatting with Amma.

'Simran go and bring fifty rupees from inside.'

'*Arre* Amma, for the Ram Mandir only fifty rupees, give at least hundred.' The man standing near the gate said.

Simran was irritated. The rising crescendo for a Ram Mandir in Ayodhya had reached her doorstep. She went in and hurriedly brought the money and gave it to the group. Grumbling they left and knocked at the next house.

'So who will you side with Simran—the mandir or the masjid? *Hosh mein aa ja* (Wake up).'

Simran was quiet. Whether there was a temple or a mosque in Ayodhya did not matter in her immediate life. Her life depended on Ravi Bhaiyya's assent. She bristled inside, but knew she had no choice but to wait.

Abha was also waiting. She was waiting for an end. The drive home from North Block to East Delhi was the time when all the thoughts that remained at bay during the working hours came rushing forth.

It was lonely to be single again. The evenings were the most difficult. How much TV could she watch? Talking with her parents was difficult because the conversation always came around to the divorce and all its attendant problems.

Parul provided Abha's life with colour, relief and unconditional love. Abha often wondered why people always expound on how much they loved their children; children return the love in immeasurable quantities. Two-year-old and full of her small victories and defeats, Parul spoke to her unceasingly through those lonely evenings. She slept with her small form wrapped around her mother. Seeking and providing security and love.

That evening when Abha had reached home, Parul was screaming in the house 'Papa phone'. She called Abha's father 'Papa', and her mother 'Nani'. It had been a natural progression since all the children she played with had a Papa and a Mummy. When one is young, it is simple to live through falsehoods. Only as we grow older do we hanker for the truth, and more often than not, the truth hurts. Abha hugged Parul and went inside.

In the night, after Parul was asleep, Abha went to her parents' room. She needed to speak to them.

'Mummy, today the housing form was circulated. I have applied for a government accommodation.'

'No way Abha, you are not going to stay away from us. It is not correct and who will look after Parul?'

Papa had not lost his authoritative manner. Maybe Abha had imbibed her fighting spirit from him. In her late twenties, it was possible to see her father as an individual, not simply a father. He was driven, ambitious and loved his work. Mummy and he had been two distinct individuals, with different needs and aspirations. It could never have worked well. In this strange crisis that his younger daughter had put him, he supported her, after some initial hesitation, like the Rock of Gibraltar. Relationships changed over time—within the same household, friends become foes and the other way around. Nothing remained the same.

'Papa, it will take sometime for the allotment to be made. I can always decline, so can we discuss it when the time comes.'

'I think that is right. Abha, I think it is time we also started looking for a full time maid, I get quite tired running after Parul. She is growing up.'

Her mother's statement seemed to be her hidden manner of saying that she agreed with Abha's decision.

The intercom on Abha's office desk was buzzing. In North Block's corridors, the intercom could disrupt well-made plans at regular intervals. It usually signified summons for an unscheduled meeting.

'Abha can you please come to my room when you have time.'

It was the new Joint Secretary on the first floor again. He was neither her direct supervisor nor the division head. However, since his arrival in the last two weeks he tried to call her to his room on some pretext or the other. There were many like him in the bureaucracy, while there were many others who were wonderful. Abha had dealt with many of them, and was learning new ways of dealing with them constantly. Abha ignored his call and continued to do her work. Towards evening he buzzed her again on the intercom.

'Abha you did not come. How about my taking you out for dinner one of these days? You must be quite lonely.'

Abha felt her anger mounting within her at his persistence. These things irritated her more than anything else.

'No thanks sir. I am doing fine.' She firmly put the phone down on him.

Just then, the external line rang.

'Hi. How is it going lady? What's new?'

Rekha. Just what she had needed to give vent to her irritation and anger. Rekha was now working for the Bank of America in Bombay, while her TamBhram was busy selling tyres.

'What yaar. Sick and tired of these lecherous types in the office. Rekha, why don't they get it? As a single woman, I can surely decide whom I want to be with. It really exasperates me!'

'Cool it. Just forget it. What single woman Abha, it happens all the time even to me. You just learn to deal with it. So why doesn't this single woman choose someone?'

'The time for that will also come Rekha. Not now. I have too many things on my hands. So when are you coming to Delhi next and how is the husband?'

'Out on travel, as usual. He is back this evening.'

'Why don't you two have a kid?'

'For that you need to do it right? Well, I really don't remember the last time it happened. Anyway, how come Abha, it is always me who keeps calling. Why don't you ever call?'

'Because you are in BOA and me in poor GOI. At my level in government, we do not have STD in the office, okay? Now got to do something. Bye.'

Rekha put the phone down and looked out of the window. Her office was on the top floor of a building at Nariman Point. Down below the city of Bombay raced past. Even through the tinted glasses, the energy of the city was palpable.

Rekha looked at her engagement list for the day. There was no party invitation for the evening. That meant the two of them would be home. What would they do? Often these days, when they had no social engagement, her husband and she spent the evening in separate rooms, not exchanging a word. They simply did not have much to say to each other. It bored her to death.

At parties, on the other hand, they were transformed. They became the cool couple, well placed, happening and devoted to each other. The myth and the reality!

Rekha caught her reflection in the mirror on the opposite wall. She looked rather nice in her new hair cut. It was a nice feeling.

She picked up the phone on her desk and called 'Hi Monica, what are you guys doing tonight? Why don't the four of us meet for dinner at the Taj? 8 pm. Okay. Great, see you there.'

Then she got back to work. Now the evening would be well spent.

In the middle of a messy divorce proceeding, nothing else occupies the mind. Abha had often felt that she was living from one court date to the other. The days in between would be full of reading petitions, and finalizing replies. All other things, including work, had become fillers, the divorce cast an overbearing shadow on her mind.

Sometimes good news came along. Simran and Abha sat hunched over a tumbler of coffee in a Udipi restaurant near Simran's office.

'Ravi *finally* agreed. He has given his green signal to the marriage. The only condition is that we should marry under the Special Marriage Act.'

'Meaning what?'

'Well that means no religious marriage on either side. We marry under civil law.'

'Hussein and you have discussed this?'

'Not yet. You come to the modalities of the marriage when everyone agrees, isn't it?'

'I called Hussein and told him. On Ravi's next trip they will meet.'

The thrill of possibilities, hopes and dreams—that is what kept life going. Abha watched as Simran's face lit up with the movement forward in her life.

'Sometimes I wish I could peer into this cup of coffee and see what is going to happen in the future. I still feel very unsure.'

'Come on Simran. It is working out now.'

'You know Abha, I have been visiting so many astrologers and pundits—they have all told me that by next year I will be married to the man of my choice.'

'Simran, when you lose faith in yourself—in your own capability to shape your life—that is when all this becomes important. Don't get carried away with these things.'

Abha's own parents had started believing in astrology since her problems began. They consulted astrologers and pundits with hope and ancipation. For Abha it was the same as going to a psychiatrist. When in trouble, people sought different avenues for a glimmer of hope that things would change.

And they did change. Dramatically.

Soon after that cheerful cup of coffee, when Simran's dream had seemed closer. In far away Ayodhya, the Babri Masjid got demolished. The incident reverberated all over the country.

Simran sat with the phone in her hand. It had gone silent, after the person on the other end had put it down, tersely informing her, 'He continues to be on leave.'

It has been over two months since that fateful day when the events in Ayodhya had unfolded. Simran was at home on 6th December when the news had started coming. As Simran saw the pictures in the newspapers the next day, for the first time she had felt a shiver of apprehension going down her spine.

As soon as she reached her office the next day, Simran had called Hussein's office in Chandigarh.

'He has gone on leave for a fortnight to his hometown.' Hussein had gone to Azamgarh? Simran needed to speak to him desperately, but decided against calling on the Azamgarh number. She had never called there. What would she say if someone asked her who she was? She decided to wait.

After a fortnight Simran had called Hussein's office again and got the same terse reply. In the interval, Bombay had burned, people had died and hatred had become the prevailing tenor. Simran could not understand what had happened. Hussein and she had been together for a few years, and religion had never come between them. It had remained on the periphery.

With every passing day, the knot in Simran's stomach was getting tighter. Hussein had made no attempt to contact her. The blank space between them was getting etched sharper with every passing day. Simran had told Amma, who had only given her the 'I told you so' look, but had mercifully not said anything. Abha was caught up in her own battles, and could only offer 'Hang on, he has a job. He is not going to disappear. He will be back.'

A few days later, Simran called Hussein's office again. She hated herself for her desperation, but she needed to speak to him.

'Hussein here.' The voice at the other end announced. Simran was struck dumb. He had come back. She felt a burst of relief and then a slow sense of anger started knocking within.

'When did you come back? Why did you stay away so long? You never contacted me? I was so worried.' The words tumbled out as Simran came close to tears.

'Well Simran things have changed. All around us. I was planning to call you today. First things first. Forget the marriage thing. It is not possible between you and me anymore.'

'You married someone else?' Simran barely whispered on the line.

'No. But between us it cannot work. Not anymore.'

Just like the disputed structure, Simran's world came crashing down all of a sudden.

'What's up? Why hasn't Simran joined us?'

Rekha and Abha had met for lunch, as Rekha was in town. Rekha was well groomed; she carried an air of authority accentuated with the security that money provides. They were sitting in an expensive restaurant courtesy Rekha's expense account.

'She is yet to get over the blow. What is impossible is that she still insists on meeting him. He also meets her, but has told her in no uncertain terms that he cannot marry her.'

'Will not may be more like it. At least the guy is honest.'

'True, Rekha. You know she even told him that she was prepared to convert to marry him, but he declined.'

When Simran had told her that, Abha had been angry. There is a limit to what one can do to make things work. Despite everything Simran was prepared to do, it had not worked.

'I don't understand why she still sees him. She needs to break away to really start over in her life, Rekha.'

'Must be the sex. Good sex can be a great binding force, you know. If you don't know you better make it your business to know.'

'Rekha, when did you become an expert on sex?'

The secret had come tumbling out. Rekha had met him in a conference in Bangalore. By design or accident, she could not recollect, they had landed up in bed and Rekha's journey of discovery had begun.

'I never knew Abha what pure joy it can be. You just feel great. And to think I have been married for nearly six years, and went around good and proper for two years before that. Still I never knew what it really was. If and when we got down to doing it, it was like a chore that had to be preformed. But with him, it is different. I find I manipulate such that we meet and there is nothing that I look forward to more than the groovy sex.'

'How will this work out on your marriage Rekha, and what about him? What is your lover's marital status?'

'As of now I find I feel much kinder about my dear husband, since I started seeing "my lover" as you call him. About later, who knows where this is going. At this point I really don't care. It is the best thing that happened to me in years. Oh and he is one of those confirmed singleton types.'

Why had they tangled up their lives so much? Abha wondered. Was it not possible to have simple straightforward lives? Nothing shocked or amazed her anymore. She had ceased to be judgmental, and accepted things as they came across. Abha looked across the table at Rekha and felt a surge of affection for her. In the long years that had gone by, they had come closer even though they met only occasionally. She looked around in the restaurant—maybe all the people sitting there had some secret, some crazy fantasy lurking around. Life—the great mystery!

As they were leaving, Rekha told her, 'Remember the guy from St. Stephen's who used to hang around our college a lot, Ujjwal. Well I met him in Bangalore too; he is based in Bombay. He was asking about you. He asked me to give you his number. Thank God, I remembered. Take it down.'

Ujjwal. After all the years, she heard of him on the steps of a restaurant in CP! Ujjwal—a rather grainy image of him came to her mind when he had stood on the steps of Simran's bank the last time they had met. It seemed like another lifetime. Time had such a knack of rubbing a coat of dust on everything. Abha wrote down his number and wondered if she would ever contact him. The years in between, with all their rough and tumble, seemed to be a great yawning gap.

All the three women were cuddled up and chatting away since Bina di was in Delhi for a meeting. Papa fiddled around the house, and sometimes entered the room where the three women of his life were bonding over steaming cups of tea. Such moments made up the flavour called home. Encircled in happiness and warmth, Abha loved the atmosphere in the house. At least for a while, reality was kept at bay.

'Bina di can you imagine Parul is due for school beginning of next year. She will be three plus. The admission process in Delhi is a nightmare. I had to put her in a play school to train her for the damn nursery interviews.'

As if on cue, Parul sailed in and recited a poem for her Mausi. It sounded cute and innocent, but it was unimaginable why school authorities expected that toddlers would open up before total strangers. Interviews for three plus children was indeed an absurd idea. Abha worked with her each day, but often Parul forgot what she was taught the very next day.

'Bina di, the play school principal told me that schools don't take kindly to the fact that parents are separated or going in for a divorce.'

In fact, the principal had even suggested to Abha that she should either take someone along and introduce him as the father or say that the father was out of station. To Abha this was anathema; the life of a child cannot begin based on such a big lie.

'I don't think you should do any such thing Abha. I am sure there are many children in Parul's situation in cities like Delhi.'

'Even if they are not, I do not intend doing any such thing. I just found the whole idea preposterous.'

'Any hope of the divorce thing finishing soon?'

'There is some hope emerging of a divorce by mutual consent, let us hope for the best.'

'I am sure he too wants to get on with his life now,'—Papa who had walked in, interjected and provided the male perspective.

Time had such a way of sorting out perspectives. Papa, who had been horrified at the whole idea of divorce, was already thinking about 'what next'. The quintessential father of a girl, his mind had already moved to the next logical step. The key to his personality was a never-say-die approach. Life was meant to be forward looking. Abha had unknowingly imbibed this spirit from her father.

Abha watched as her parents and sister pampered her little daughter. In that moment, as in countless others, she knew she was blessed. She had the love and support of those who really counted.

The courts had closed for the winter break. Usually in the court vacation, Abha would concentrate on the pending paperwork in her case. However, as the possibility of a mutual consent divorce had opened up, she would be free in this break. So when an official tour to Bombay came up, she grabbed it.

The Rajdhani Express lurched out of New Delhi station while Abha waved to Parul and Papa. She came back to her berth and watched New Delhi fade away outside the darkened windows of the train. Two days of a different kind of life awaited her. In the midst of all the mess in her life she acutely felt the need for space at times. Space from her work, her child, her office, her home, almost everything. She could not explain it to others, this need to be with herself. In the crowded by-lanes of her mind, she often forgot the road that led to herself. The train hurtled towards Bombay, and Abha thought about the city she in some way loved. Maybe it was the nice times spent while Papa was posted there. Or it was her love for the sea. When the sea breeze hit her face, she always felt an exhilaration that was incomparable. She often dreamt of taking a posting to Bombay, but for the time being most of her dreams were on hold.

Travelling in the Rajdhani has a charm of its own. Ensconced behind the tinted glasses of the train, everything outside loses some of its harshness. The cool environs of the train, the food that comes on time to the berth, the lesser halts—make it a smooth and peaceful journey. Sleep claimed her while Abha tried to plan the next two days in her mind.

On the day she arrived she was busy in official meetings. In the evening, she strolled on Marine Drive, and let the sea breeze take her with it. A crowd milled around the NCPA and lights were slowly coming on along the sea. Abha had many batchmates in Bombay, but this trip was a time she had carved out for herself. She strolled near the sea and let Bombay's pace and ambience soothe her soul.

The next day, as she sat in the office, Abha remembered Ujjwal's number. It was lying somewhere in her bag. Ujjwal was in Bombay—only a phone call away. As she dialled the number, Abha wondered why she was calling him. She did not stop to think what she would say.

'Hi Ujjwal this is Abha … '

'I know, you don't have to say it. How are you? Where are you?'

'In Bombay. I am leaving by the Rajdhani today. Rekha …'

He cut her short. 'Why don't we meet up for lunch? Can you drop by at my office? It is at Nariman Point. 12.30 Okay?'

Abha took a cab to his office with a strange flutter in the pit of her stomach. Their lives had changed since their last meeting on the steps of Simran's bank years ago. They probably looked different too. Abha was curious to see how he had turned out and hoped that he was not too different. There was a sense of comfort in the idea that some things remained the same.

She was escorted to his room. He had a wonderful view of the sea. It was the first thing Abha noticed. He had filled out, in a nice mature sort of way. The chair one occupied for seven to eight hours a day definitely rubbed off. The innocence of college days, the light heartedness of youth seemed to have gone into hiding.

'Abha, so nice to meet you again. You are looking as charming as ever.'

Thank god, some things never change. Abha was relieved. Ujjwal's style and manner of greeting had remained the same. With that one sentence, she relaxed considerably.

'Let's hop across to a nice place for lunch round the corner. You don't mind walking, I hope.'

As they walked across the road, Abha saw their reflection in one of the numerous glass doors that lined the road. She was in a sari and he in a suit—not the kind of dress they had ever seen each other in before. In a manner they were strangers.

They sat across each other at the restaurant table. Abha braced herself for the next round of questions.

'So tell me Abha, how are you doing? How is life?'

'I am in the middle of a divorce Ujjwal. I have a daughter who is almost three and she is with me.'

He was quiet for a minute.

'Is that what you want?'

'Yes. I have filed for it and for the custody of my daughter. And you?'

'I got married two years ago. My parents are settled in Chandigarh now. How is your work coming along?' With these few questions, they crossed the years that lay between them with ease.

Often when people meet after years, soon enough, after catching up, they start looking around for something to say. Some common ground to cover. Life is but a chain of memories, and unless common memories are built on a continuous basis, relationships tend to disappear. Long intervals leave silent spaces difficult to navigate. But with Ujjwal it was not so. Abha did not realize when two hours had elapsed. She looked at her watch.

'If I don't run now I will miss my train.' He helped her catch a cab. She sat inside, and then he bent down and patted her head.

'I'll call you.'

As the taxi swept down the road, Abha felt a strange lump in her throat. A pull at her insides, which seemed to bemoan the loss of a precious promise.

Delhi engulfed her on her return. Abha had a court date in the very same week. Whenever Abha went to the Tees Hazari courts, a sense of dread filled her. The long dusty corridors with dreary rooms, where lone judges sought to dispense justice were incredibly depressing. Each time she had her court date, Abha would peer at the list hanging outside the courtroom to see her serial number for the day. The way the cases were numbered indicated the year in which they had been filed. It was clear that matrimonial cases remained pending for decades. Abha would feel a shudder go down her spine. Waiting for the matter to be called, the two parties who had promised to be together for a lifetime stood as opposite parties. It was a sad and tragic waste of time and energy—this whole business of ending a dead marriage.

On that day, there was some respite for Abha. The first petition for divorce by mutual consent was filed. After a mandatory waiting period of six months, she would be free. When uncertainty transforms into certainty, the relief brings with it a fatigue that goes into the very bones.

'You can safely assume now that you have got the divorce and the custody of your daughter. Anyway, men give up daughters more easily. If you had a son he would have fought tooth and nail'—her lawyer tried to put things in their natural perspective.

Abha drove back home from the court and thought of her bright-eyed and perky-nosed child. Was the child important only on the basis of its sex? Abha wondered. This strange discriminatory world did not exist in her mind. Her child mattered to her to the exclusion of everything else in the world.

With the divorce proceeding sorted out, the next item on Abha's agenda was the government accommodation she had been allotted at Pandara Road. She had accepted it without disclosing the news to her parents. That needed to be dealt with.

She gave the news to her parents over dinner, the same day.

'Why should you live alone there? I do not understand. What will people say?'—Papa had many misgivings about the impending move. A few years back such a situation would have broken into an argument, but Abha had matured. She understood at a certain level Papa's disquiet with the idea of her moving out.

Mummy had tilted the balance in her favour. Her mother, the traditional Indian woman was brave to the point of being unbelievable.

'Abha must set up her own home. Parul needs to feel that she has a house of her own. It is important for the child's growth and Abha must learn to live on her own.'

'She is not going to live alone forever. She must get married again, I have started looking around for her. Till she marries she will stay here.'

'No Papa. There are going to be no such conditions. I am not saying no to marriage, but not just yet. And I do want to have a home of my own. It is closer to office too.'

Slowly Papa came around. With age, the inevitable becomes easier to accept. It is youth that dreams and dares to think that life is invincible and immortal. With age, acceptance becomes the best form of defence.

Over the next weekend, with her parents and Parul in tow, Abha had gone to see the house. When she opened the lock to the bare two-roomed apartment, Abha felt a lump in her throat. After a long time, she had a home which she could call her own. Parul pranced around the small apartment and came back.

'Ma whose house is this? It is empty.'

'It is ours—yours and mine.'

After running around the apartment again. Parul came back to comment, 'How can it be a house—the kitchen has no gas!' The little girl understood that a house did not become a home until it had a hearth with a fire! 'But who is going to live here Ma?'

'You and me.'

'What about Papa and Nani? It has only two rooms. They need more space.'

'Papa and Nani will live in their house. We will live here with Reena Didi.'

'No, I will live where Papa and Nani live. Not here.'

Why was it that the child was not spared a wrench at every step? It made Abha feel guilty at times.

'Parul beti, we will come here often. Also, your Ma and you will come to our house every weekend when Ma has a holiday.' Mummy tried to placate her.

'Promise Ma?' Parul looked hopefully at her mother.

'Promise.'

It was simple to appease a child. The power of promises.

Slowly Abha furnished her apartment. Some things came from Papa's house, others she bought. Much like her life, she avoided crowding it with too many things. Soon enough, the all women household of Abha, Parul and the maid Reena started functioning.

Simran was their first guest. Much mellowed and subdued. After lunch they sat in the small covered balcony of the apartment and Simran informed Abha, 'I have been transferred to Hyderabad. I am going to pack up and go after two weeks.'

'Why are you going so far? Why don't you seek a nearer place? I am sure it will be considered.'

'I want to go away from Hussein, Abha.'

'That is fine, but you don't have to punish yourself for that. Your mum is here, you don't know anybody in Hyderabad. I also think it is about time we take out an advertisement for you in the matrimonial columns.'

'I am actually going so that he can get married to someone else if he wants. This way he too does not move in his life.'

How could Simran still think of it from his point of view? Abha wondered. Were people actually so different in their approach? This was something she could never have done. Simran, her childhood friend, sort of drifted along in life, never sure of what she wanted. Then she found one thing she really wanted and she was ready to gamble away her life for it?

'Let me take an ad out for you Simran.'

'Let us wait till Hussein gets married.'

After two weeks, Abha had gone to New Delhi railway station to see off Simran on the Andhra Express. She looked forlorn and dejected. They hugged and Abha felt near tears.

'I will really miss you Simran. I cannot imagine Delhi without you. There will be such a vacuum in my life.'

'Me too. You at least have Parul.'

The train was off and Abha stood at the platform waving to Simran. What did they have? The three of them as they entered their thirties. She had Parul, Rekha a marriage and a lover and, Simran a steadfast dream and longing for a man who refused to hold her hand. Not much, when life has so much to give. Yet each of them stood at this crossroad by choice—that was the biggest gift.

Parul secured admission in a good school. Her play school principal had been wrong; Delhi schools were open and understanding about single parents. Life had suddenly started moving at a frenetic pace. Abha sat in her office with a piece of paper that proclaimed her freedom. A piece of paper with a few lines and a seal, the outcome of a long struggle. There was a sense of anti-climax as Abha held the divorce decree in her hand. It seemed just that—a piece of paper.

The external phone near her desk rang.

'Hi. Abha how are you?'

Ujjwal. He had called her a few times since her return from Bombay. He never asked any questions, simply absorbed the details of her life. It was refreshing to talk to someone who was not judgmental all the time. They spoke of other things, because life was full of so many other things.

'Ujjwal it's over. The whole thing is over.'

'It worked out the way you wanted?'

'Yes. The whole thing.'

'Good. I am coming to Delhi for a meeting. Will call you when I am there. Hope we can meet up.'

When she put the phone down, Abha had felt an urgent need to share the news with Simran. But Simran was far away, hiding from pain and reality. In the office, there was no one that Abha could tell. It would just trickle around over time. Such information had a way of doing so. Whenever Rekha called next Abha would tell her.

What next? Suddenly Abha felt a strange emptiness inside. As long as the battle was on she was incredibly busy, now a sense of void confronted her. It was similar to the kind she used to experience years ago after a long spell of exams. The work waiting on her desk provided an ideal escape.

In the weeks that followed Papa swung into action. He set out to find a suitable spouse all over again for his daughter. It led to an interesting discovery. There was a huge subsequent marriage cohort. Friends and acquaintances started giving references of divorced or widowed men. There were plenty of people who sought to give marriage a second try.

Papa would present proposals for Abha all the time. At times, the other party would magnanimously put across word that they would not mind if her daughter stayed with her. No one tried to consider separately a man and his child. The man always came with his baggage, but she being a woman had to negotiate for her child.

Abha wanted a break from all this for some time. She had often asked herself—did she want to marry again? The answer would always be an unequivocal 'yes', but it was also 'not yet'.

Abha was once again in the Rajdhani Express as it hurtled away towards Bombay, for official work. She tried to read, but the steady movement of the train induced extreme drowsiness. Simran had written to her some time ago. Her loneliness and frustration came through the letter clearly, but how to help someone who did not want to help herself? Rekha remained busy with her not so new lover. This time she had moved up the latitudes, her lover was from Andhra, but she had this knack of finding someone below the Vindhyas each time! Ujjwal had passed by Delhi quite a few times, but they had not been able to catch up with each other. Abha wondered if she would meet him in Bombay.

The last time she had been on this train, her mind was under stress. This time the pressure had been lifted, and Abha could observe life with more equanimity. Almost as if from a distance.

She was learning to live alone in Delhi with her child. It was not easy. Unwanted men from office would sometimes call up at her house, or arrive at the door unannounced. She had learnt to be rude, callous and ruthless. It had worked; the attacks, as she liked to call them, had decreased. The everyday needs of life, bills to be paid, the ration card, the gas connection—she had learnt to deal with all of them. Mummy and Papa were there to help her out too. Slowly the urge to dress up and look good had also resurfaced. It was as if gradually, she was rediscovering herself. Abha relished the feeling.

The next day after finishing her work, Abha met Ujjwal for lunch near his office.

'Has internet connection come to North Block as yet? Email is going to revolutionize the way we communicate Abha. '

'Not at our level as yet. I have heard that some very senior officers have it. I am likely to have a computer installed soon, but I wonder if it will really change the way government works. I attended a training programme sometime ago in basic computer operations, found it quite interesting.'

'You are looking much more relaxed from the last time we met.'

Abha smiled. Why was it easy to talk to some people while it was so difficult with others? From where did masks and guards pop up all the time? As a woman, why were her defenses always on high alert? People cannot be who they are most of the time, always hiding behind some manufactured image or the other, Abha thought, as she watched the sea across the road from the restaurant window.

'Abha, where are you headed post lunch?' Ujjwal had broken her reverie.

'Back to the guest house. I have a meeting in the forenoon tomorrow and then I catch the Rajdhani back to Delhi.'

'Then I will drop you there.'

They walked back to his office, and he took out his car and they drove through the crowded Marine Drive.

'I love Bombay Ujjwal. I plan to take a posting here sometime.'

'I prefer Delhi, for me it is the only city I can call home.'

Delhi, the image of the city that had been her home since childhood suddenly swam before Abha's eyes. Its beautiful green avenues, the flower filled roundabouts and the underdeveloped trans-Yamuna area. The city had seen her grow from a young girl into a woman. Suddenly Abha realized that she loved the city with a passion.

'You are right Ujjwal. Whenever I return to Delhi, and the train passes over Tilak Bridge, as soon as I spot a yellow and green DTC bus, I feel so happy. I feel I have come home. Maybe Bombay is just a dream or a thought of escape.'

'Why did you reject me Abha?'

In a flash, he had crossed all the years and distance between them with that question. Abha wondered if she had heard him right, but the silence in the car waited for her answer. She could have chosen to brush it aside. There are moments in life when suddenly realization dawns that certain questions would never leave unless faced squarely.

'I did not. The question of rejection doesn't arise. You never asked. Did you?'

'I did. I came to meet you even though you were engaged, and asked you if you had second thoughts about your marriage.'

'Is that a proposal?'

'How else do you go and ask a girl who is engaged to another man? Tell me.'

'You just expected that one day after years you will appear, talk to me in that roundabout manner of yours and I will understand?'

'It was just over two years. And my manner all along was any thing but roundabout. I told you straight before leaving that "I will be back. Wait for me." What more was needed? And you know I have always been a person who cannot talk where it matters.'

When he had said it like that for the first time, Abha looked at things from his perspective. Was that her failing? That she had never looked at this from any other perspective than her own. But is it possible when one is young? Then the only thing that counts is what you think, how you feel. It takes some growing up to find space for another in one's psyche.

They reached the guesthouse, and Abha invited him in. This one conversation had to run its course. They could not run away from it—either of them.

'But you never wrote to me from the States, apart from three general letters. I know, because I still have them.'

'I was always a bad letter writer and I always thought we understood each other. Your being in India was a major factor in my decision to come back.'

'What "understood" each other? Did we ever talk about "us"? It was always a guessing game for me. It really exhausted me.'

How come these feelings had resurfaced with such intensity? As if, they had lain in wait, to be recalled some day. Never forgotten, just not thought about.

'We were in college Abha. I couldn't promise you anything then. I was also young. And you never told me anything positive either, just brushed off what I said. Made me feel so inadequate.'

How had she given him this feeling? Ujjwal of all the people.

'We actually did not communicate with each other Ujjwal. Not what was needed or mattered, despite all the talking we did.'

'Are you trying to tell me after all these years that if we had spoken to each other our lives may have been totally different?'

Why does it often take so long to understand simple things in life? Each of us have to learn our own lessons.

And then, more than a decade after they had met near a water cooler in Delhi University, in the lengthening shadows of Bombay they kissed. Abha was not surprised; she fleetingly wondered why it had taken him so long. The seeds for this moment had been sown long ago. When a lifetime ago, he had held her hand, caressed her cheek and then not so long ago patted her head. It was like fulfilment of a promise, making love to someone she had known and loved for so long. There was pure and sublime joy at the fruition of a long wait. They could not have passed by life without that shared moment. It reinforced the trust they had reposed in each other all the long years—the culmination of a long journey.

It was 2 pm on a hot muggy Friday afternoon in Delhi. Abha had been unable to go home for lunch, as a meeting had stretched endlessly. Before approaching the spicy and oily *chhola bhatura* placed before her for lunch, courtesy her peon's search, she dialled home.

'Hi Parul. How was school today?'

'Ma, not coming for lunch today? I am waiting.'

'Don't wait Beta. It is not possible today, but I will come early.'

'No, no, come.'

'I can't, okay? You have your lunch and then rest or play with Reena Didi. Bye.'

Children of single parents develop a streak of independence and stubbornness that probably is their line of defence. Abha tried to go home for lunch everyday. A luxury in the chaotic city, possible only because her official accommodation was situated within a seven-minute drive. The days she could not go home for lunch, Parul would resent it very much. She had got used to having her mother home for lunch. Otherwise, Parul had no problems with the long hours Abha needed to keep at times in her office.

Parul and Abha would spend quality time together before bedtime. Resting their heads on the same pillow, Parul would tell her about happenings in school, and Abha often found herself telling Parul things that happened at office. They would be way beyond the understanding of a four year old. Perhaps without realizing, single parents treat their children like companions.

On Fridays, Abha would leave office early. It was a ritual that on each Friday they would lock their house and drive to Papa's home in East Delhi, and return Sunday night. However, that day she hurried home as Simran had come to stay.

Simran had come from Hyderabad for a few days as her mother was unwell. It automatically fell on her to travel all the way to look after her mother. Being unmarried and working it was expected that she would take on all such responsibilities, although officially, the brother remained the man of the house. Some things change very slowly.

'How is Hyderabad doing Simran?'

'Fine. The work is the same. Just the south is more orderly than the north. In fact, Abha, when the train crosses the plains of North India, things become cleaner, more disciplined. It is like two different cultures. Day to day things are simpler there.'

'Made some friends?'

'In office yes. Otherwise no.'

'What news of Hussein?'—There was no way this question could remain unstated for long. Although he was not in her life, he remained the pivot around which everything turned. Abha found it incomprehensible, but she had understood that with friends many things needed to be simply accepted

'He is fine. He has now got posted to Lucknow.'

'And you? Have you thought of anything for yourself? Want me to run a matrimonial advertisement for you? I could give my address.'

'Not yet.'

What was Simran waiting for? Abha often wondered. Was it possible to wait indefinitely without any glimmer of hope? Maybe if Hussein got married, Simran would be free. How hopes and desires changed. Sometime ago Abha had hoped that they would marry. Now she was hoping he would marry someone else! This was what life's journey was all about at the end of the day. Some hope or desire had to be chased, even if it was diametrically opposite to the one that preceded it.

'What about you Abha? What are you thinking about your life now?' It was easy to ask questions, but extremely difficult to deal with the ever-changing answers. Abha mulled over this question herself every now and then.

'As of now, nothing Simran. I am actually enjoying the present even keel of my life. I am enjoying my child and the space that I have. Papa keeps popping prospects at me, but I am not keen right now.'

The fan was whirring away on the ceiling. Outside it was a muggy monsoon evening. Drenched after a monsoon shower, Delhi could be ugly and beautiful at the same time. The roads clog up, everything becomes muddy and squelchy, but the trees glisten as if after a good bath. Freshness envelops the atmosphere, before the heat gets suffocating and it becomes humid again. In the city, every season could be savoured in all its glory and squalour.

'Simran Aunty. See the drawing I made in school. This is my family—Ma, me and Reena Didi. I did not make Papa and Nani because our teacher told us to make a painting of those who stay in the family.'

Parul proudly displayed her latest accomplishment. Simran admired it and then Parul wandered off.

'Abha she doesn't ask you as yet about her father?'

'No. Sometimes I feel there is within her some innate understanding, but she has not yet come out and asked me.'

'What will you tell her?'

'The truth. When she asks me I will tell her.'

'Will she understand?'

Understanding. It was a difficult thing to find in life. One searches for it always—that one person, one relationship that could provide understanding as a basis for life.

'Kids accept things first Simran, then they try and understand them. Makes the process much easier. I think we adults should also follow them in this. My only endeavour is to build a relationship of trust with Parul; wherein she knows and accepts that if there are any questions in her life, her mother will answer her truthfully. Even if at times the truth hurts.'

That is why good friends are so essential in life. Abha had thought about these issues many a time as she lay in bed while sleep eluded her. It was only with Simran that she had articulated her thoughts and put them in a clear perspective.

'You met Ujjwal in Bombay last time. How is he?'

'He is fine. Calls up occasionally and generally keeps in touch.'

Abha had not told Simran everything. What was there to tell that could be easily understood. After that evening in Bombay, Abha had wondered where their relationship would go. Ujjwal and she had known each other far too long to have an affair. Some relationships are too precious and valuable to be sacrificed at the altar of an affair. They need to develop their own dynamics or they disappear in the mists of time.

Like innumerable circulars that crossed her desk, the one Abha held in her hand was for a two-year training programme in Japan. She had started filling up the foreign training circulars that passed her table. It was simply a whim—to go abroad and spend some time there. In the corridors of North Block, as in other government offices, foreign trips were the most sought after 'goods'. People planned careers around postings that gave the maximum trips abroad. Once the thrill of travel had worn off, the dollars one earned on the trips kept people going. In the hallowed precincts of Government of India, foreign trips were fought for, manipulated and chased.

Abha filled it up as usual, with no hope of success. The amount of chasing and effort it required was not something she could do, but trying was in her hands, and that she did with great enthusiasm. Her boss encouraged her in this effort. Abha had a boss who had a working wife. The attitude of men with working wives was infinitely healthier and easier, it was just sad that they were still a minority. However, there was hope; a majority of the younger generation of girls were opting for a career.

The phone near her desk rang.

'Hi Abha. How are you? What's new?'

It had become Rekha's standard form of greeting. 'What's new?' As if life had something new to offer all the time. In her tone, there would be an expectation that seemed to say if nothing new was happening then something was amiss.

'Nothing. As usual. What about you? Where are you?'

Rekha's calls came with a regular periodicity these days. Abha sensed that something was brewing in her life, but had not asked. It was as if after the gap of a month or so Rekha needed to call Abha—just to touch her youth through her again. Maybe.

'I'm moving to Hong Kong. Next month. We filed for a mutual consent divorce.'

Somehow, it had not surprised Abha. It had been just long in coming.

'Everything settled?'

'Of course. We did not have a kid to wrangle about. We decided to divide our things. You know Abha since the flat was from my company lease, I gave him the choice to move out his things and left the keys with him. He took virtually everything. Everything that was mine, as well as the things we had invested in jointly. Shocked me. But I let it be; at least he was letting me go.'

'Oh Rekha, if there is any thing that makes one indifferent to possessions and material things it is a divorce proceeding. You just get over possessions once you have been through a divorce.'

Rekha's marriage had broken up not when her husband had learnt about her affair. It broke when he had told her that it was all right with him, as long as she kept it discreet.

'Imagine Abha, how could I live with a man like him? He did not protest, did not fight. Just let it be. It was insufferable. I couldn't take it.' Abha remained quiet.

Why do we always want things to take the expected route, even as we ourselves take the unconventional one? And why does it shatter us so much when things do not. Her husband's capitulation crushed Rekha's last illusion of love and affection between them. The total vacuum that existed between them had found eloquent expression. For him probably, it had been a gesture of accommodation and maybe even love, for her the futility of the relationship. They were simply different points of view.

'And what about Mr. Perfect Lover? Where is he in all this?'

'Nowhere right now. I got this offer to move to Hong Kong and I am doing so. We will see what happens later.'

As Abha drove home that evening, she thought, were they all running away from the truths of their lives? Simran hiding in Hyderabad, Rekha moving to Hong Kong and Abha herself was filling up all forms that came her way nurturing her hope to go abroad.

The screeching of parrots as they roosted on the trees by the side of the road drowned the sound of vehicles. New Delhi's tree laden avenues announced the change of seasons in their own fashion. Summer would glisten in the fire of the bright yellow Amaltas and fiery Gulmohar, with the purple Jacaranda giving a soothing touch. The beautiful Tesu heralded the advent of spring. In autumn, leaves would cluster upon the ground as they cascaded down in a steady stream from the trees. For Abha autumn brought a deep nostalgia, a sense of sadness. As she drove home, the slight nip in the air was sharp. It was clear that winter was waiting around the corner.

The cacophony of the evening rush hour was floating through the open window. Rekha lay in bed in the silent apartment. It still amazed her, the manner in which her home had been cleaned out. Her clothes still hung in the cupboard. Thank God for small mercies!

All the years, and it was over like this. Rekha felt a great sense of relief. There was also a tinge of sadness, but it lay at the bottom of the heap. She was now looking forward to Hong Kong. A new city, new job, new experiences—it was what she needed at this point of time in her life.

Papaji and Biji had been very upset. They had kept asking her 'What happened?' Then Rekha had understood Abha's irritation with the question better. Her parents had accepted whatever Rekha told them. They would cope, they had to.

Rekha had in a way moved into another orbit, out of their grasp. She was happy to leave India. The world beckoned and Rekha waited with her wings in readiness for flight.

It was providence that Abha was at her parents' home the night Papa fell ill. She put him in the car and drove in fifteen minutes to the Railway Hospital in Connaught Place. In the ICU, they told her that he had had a heart attack. While the doctors tended to him, Abha went to the lone PCO in the dark hospital corridors and called Mummy. The phone lines had begun to ring from Delhi to Lucknow and beyond while Papa struggled.

As instructed by her mother, Abha tried to remain within her father's sight. She watched her father through the glass pane. He was conscious, and looked old and defenceless as he lay there with his head tilted down to keep the blood flowing to his brain. The doctors tended to him, while he struggled alone with his pain. Were moments such as these that entailed what is called 'growing up'? Abha sat through her lonely vigil waiting for the morning. She felt the years accumulating on her shoulders.

Winters in Delhi could be heaven or hell, depending on whether there is a haven from which to enjoy it or one is on the streets wrapped in newspapers. The long nights give way to foggy, damp and dreary mornings. Spending the cold winter night outside the ICU was a cruel reminder of how harsh winter could be.

By mid-morning Mummy, Bina di and Kishore ji had arrived. Only Parul remained ensconced at home—oblivious to what was happening.

'We do not have a heart specialist here. You need to shift him to some other place—AIIMS preferably'—the doctor told them. All through the night the doctor had asked Abha for someone from the house. By that, he had meant the 'man' of the house. Only towards morning had he realized that the daughters of this family were the 'men' of the house.

The All India Institute of Medical Sciences remains the 'promised' destination for anyone seriously ill in Delhi, and elsewhere in India, creating tremendous pressure on beds. Papa struggled to keep his life going, Mummy sat helplessly and waited for some miracle to save her husband. Her daughters got into the act of trying to ensure a bed for their father in the AIIMS cardiac centre. After innumerable calls and requests later that evening, Abha and Kishore ji had managed the miracle. Papa was shifted to AIIMS, and the entire family shifted to Abha's small house, which was much closer to AIIMS.

The long vigil had begun. In India's premier hospital, a family member was needed twenty-four hours outside the ICU. The nurses would come out, call out the bed number and hand a prescription to the waiting person. Then, a mad dash to one of the chemists who operate around the hospital for medicines. However, for this waiting member there were no chairs, no waiting hall. They would have to sprawl at night in the corridors outside the ICU and during the day just sit around, most often on the floor.

Abha and Bina di had divided the vigil between them. Abha sat during the day as Parul was small and needed her in the night, while Bina di took responsibility of the harsher night duty. Kishore ji managed their home in Lucknow. Mummy managed the food for the patient and the care—givers. It was like an enterprise—looking after a patient admitted in AIIMS.

Before Abha and Bina exchanged their shifts, they sat on the steps of the hospital and shared their fears and fatigue. A new bonding emerged. The shared responsibility of siblings with old and infirm parents. When a parent falls grievously ill it is a watershed in life. Abha remembered Simran's father's death when they were younger. The sense of loss had been acute, but then life had seemed to stretch out eternally. At this later stage, a parent's illness seemed to bring one's own mortality into focus. The mantle of life had come and enveloped their shoulders.

'Bina di sometimes I feel maybe Papa got this heart attack because of all the stress he had to go through on my account.'

'There is no point in wallowing in this meaningless rut of guilt Abha. It could have happened even otherwise.'

Some doubts however tend to linger on for a lifetime.

While Papa was recuperating from the angioplasty at AIIMS, Abha received the news. The two year Japan programme had accepted her, and she was to leave by end of March.

Why did the most cherished things come her way at the wrong time? Abha wondered. With Papa's illness she could not possibly leave for two years. There was Parul to be considered. Abha shared the news with Bina di, while they sat on the steps of the hospital in the fading sunlight.

By the end of February, Papa returned home. The spring flowers had begun to bloom in the roundabouts of New Delhi, and a cloud had been lifted from their home. Parul was the happiest to have her 'Papa' back home. Before her departure for Lucknow Bina di told

Abha, 'I have discussed your Japan course with Mummy. She feels you must go. I do too.'

'What about Papa? He needs medical care and check-ups. Mummy cannot manage alone.'

'Kishore and I are there to do all that. We will come here as and when required. You do not worry about all this.'

Were all sisters like this or was Bina di simply special? Bina di could have taken a very different stand, but then she was Bina di—always capable of looking at things from the other person's point of view. Bade Mama had put the first and deadlest spoke in the wheel. He had come to see Papa and said, 'How can you send a girl off like this abroad? Especially now, after a divorce and all. It will become very difficult to settle her on her return. And what about the child?'

Questions and more questions. Somehow, with women, issues were never uni-dimensional, they would not be discussed on their merit alone. All the baggage that comes with being a woman would become an intrinsic part of the debate.

Mummy had countered the pressures with a simple counter question—'Would you have raised the same objections if she was a boy?' However, once brought out in the open, such issues had a way of hanging around, and making their presence felt off and on.

Papa kept a stoic silence while this debate swirled in his household. He would go for his daily walk, take his medicines and rest on time.

For Abha, time was running out. She had to formally accept the offer, and then all the official paperwork would follow. She was undecided too. The change it would bring to her life was phenomenal. Going for a short-term training was different. Two years meant setting up home in Japan, to live as a student again at thirty-two. And then there was Parul. Yokohama National University had informed that it would not provide family accommodation, and she would have to fend for herself on that account. They did not know anyone in Japan; it was an unknown place. Maybe that is why she had got the course, not many people would have applied for a two-year programme in Japan. Abha tried to assess if she had the courage to take it on.

Apart from Bina di, Ujjwal had encouraged her. Over the telephone he had advised her from Bombay,. 'You must go Abha. It is a break you need. Also, studying abroad opens up your mind so much. It is an opportunity you should not give up.'

'What about Parul?'

'Once you are there you will work things out. Most of the developed countries have good arrangements. Go and then things will fall into place.'

There was a lot to consider. Life was in a pattern—comfortable and known. Change was scary and an innate resistance seemed to have taken hold of her.

Two weeks before the deadline, Abha was having evening tea with her parents. Parul was playing with her friends outside. The warmth and cosiness of home enveloped her. It threatened to be lost with her impending move.

'Abha, I spoke to one of my colleagues. He knows a senior Japanese working in Sony here. I have fixed up an appointment with him. Go and see him. I spoke to him on the phone. Mr. Murase said that Yokohama National University is a very good University in Japan.' Papa had broken his silence. He had been ferreting out information for her despite his ill health. This was her father. He always looked ahead in a practical manner. She had grown to respect and love him in all the years that had gone by.

'Papa you think I should go?'

'Yes.'

That one word made up Abha's mind The next decision was regarding Parul. Once again, others took decisions about her life, while she remained a mere receptacle of the aftermath. Parul would stay with Papa and Mummy until Abha found accommodation and school for her in Japan. Then Parul would join her mother. It fell on Abha's shoulders, obviously, to inform Parul. That night as they lay on their bed in Papa's home Abha said, 'Parul you know Ma is going to Japan for a two-year course.'

'Why?'

How should she answer that innocent question?

'Because her office is sending her.'

'I will tell your boss not to send you.'

If only life were so simple. How could she tell her child that the choice was deliberate? 'Parul, Ma is going first and then when I find a house and school I will call you to live with me. Till then you will stay with Nani and Papa.'

The dark room remained silent as the little four-year-old digested this piece of singular information. Abha waited for a response, but when she looked, Parul had already fallen asleep.

Did she hear me? Abha wondered. There were barely two days left for her departure. There was hectic packing going on. Bina di had come over to help pack for a two-year trip with a twenty kilogram limit on the luggage. There were so many things to sort out.

The next night, as soon as they had gone to bed, Parul asked, 'Ma, promise that you will call me?' She had heard her mother after all, and probably thought about the new development in her life for the whole day. Abha felt close to tears.

'Yes Beta. Promise. As soon as possible. I am not leaving you and going away for ever.'

'Are you leaving your job?'

How did such young children have these sensitivities? Abha realized that Parul understood the importance of her job in their life.

'No. My office is sending me there. I am not leaving my job. When I return I will go back to office.'

'Tell me Ma, in your absence if I need something will I ask Nani?' Was Parul trying to understand in her own way the arrangements for her life in her mother's absence? Abha was amazed. We tend to underestimate our children most of the time. They have a fine understanding of reality and its fragilities.

'Yes Beta. I have opened a bank account with her. Anything you need, Nani will give you. Okay? Stay sensibly and don't trouble Papa and Nani too much. Listen to them.'

'Hmm. Ma when will you call me?'

'Soon. My first job will be to find a house and school for you.' Parul had then clung to her tightly, like she would never let her go.

The day Abha was to leave passed away in a jiffy. Mummy came to her while Abha was sorting out her handbag alone in the room. 'What do I tell Parul if she asks about her father in your absence?'

There were so many issues to tackle. Our decisions often placed strange and unknown dilemmas before those we love. Abha felt a stab of guilt.

'Mummy, tell her that her mother will answer all her questions. I will handle this issue myself.'

Parul came scampering in and Abha felt her heart in her mouth. How was she actually going to do it? Leaving her little girl and embarking on an unknown journey.

'Ma. I will go with you to the airport. I have never seen an airplane from close.'

Children cope by focusing on the immediate. Why can't we learn from them, instead of always thinking that we could teach them?

'Yes Beta, now change quickly. Bina Mausi is coming with us. Papa and Nani will stay at home.'

When the car rolled out Papa broke down. He had not cried like this even when Abha had got married. As Mummy held his hand and steadied him, Abha watched their receding figures from the back pane of the car. Did her parents resent her for leaving her responsibility on them or was it only unconditional love they felt for their daughter? The way she felt for Parul. Why do we understand and appreciate our own parents only when we become parents ourselves? Their car turned and the long road ahead beckoned.

Parul clambered onto her lap. Was it her small heart that thudded so loud or her own? A pause hovered inside the car. Bina di tried to keep some desultory conversation going, but Abha did not hear any of it. Delhi was floating outside, and Abha was bidding a silent farewell.

They had all embarked on their respective journeys. Simran had cried when Abha had called to say bye. Rekha had zipped off to Hong Kong, single and relieved. Abha was moving towards a country about which she knew virtually nothing. Towards a place called Yokohama, that she had discovered on the map, to be just below Tokyo. Towards knowledge and a student life all over again. In the car, her most precious relationship sat on her lap and covered her face with small sweet wet kisses.

'Ma, remember your promise. Call me there soon.'

That was the only sound that reverberated in her heart when the plane took off and the lights of Delhi became mere specks on the horizon.

Anxiety on Thursday

The mobile is ringing. Aarti Devi picks it up in a hurry.

'We just finished the ceremony Aarti. It took so long because the Additional District Magistrate had gone for a meeting. They have gone to his house. I am going to Abha's house now.'

Aarti Devi feels a sense of great relief. The ceremony had gone smoothly. Her younger daughter is married—again. She suddenly feels an irrepressible urge to meet Parul—not Abha, but Parul. She calls her husband.

'You bring Parul here. She will keep me company while Bina and you rest. It is very hot today.'

The most vulnerable member of the family is always the focus of attention. While Abha was going through her divorce, Aarti Devi focused all her energies on her. She did not visit her elder daughter even once in those years. She felt her younger one needed her more. After the divorce had come through and Abha had started to get back on her feet, her attention shifted to Parul.

Now she judged everything from its possible impact on Parul. The prism of her life is her ten-year-old granddaughter.

Was Parul so mature in some of her reactions because she was a girl or because she lived a different kind of life? Whatever the reason, her granddaughter was sensitive, intelligent and loved her mother. Ever since Abha's remarriage became an imminent reality Aarti Devi has felt torn in two. Try as she might to look at it from her daughter's perspective, it is only Parul's that dominates. When Abha had announced her marriage plan, the first question Aarti Devi put to her was—'What about Parul?'

The testing time has arrived now. Abha is married. Aarti Devi knows her husband is relieved and happy. With his infuriating uni-dimensional male perspective, he lives by the mantra that one by one things fall in place. In his opinion, Parul's interests will be safeguarded, and in the end, she will do fine. If only Aarti Devi could have the same confidence and certainty.

Parul is the light of Aarti Devi's heart. In fact, they are friends in a way she never was to any of her own daughters.

Yokohama, Discovery

Inside the small cubicle, with the handle of the dry shower in her hand, Abha felt close to tears. She had run out of coins and had still not managed to rinse her hair. Everything in this place seemed to run on coins. In the cooking area, the gas ran on coins. So did the laundry machine and the vending machines all over the campus. Suddenly life had to be measured by the time a coin could mark.

It had been a week since Abha had landed in Yokohama, a major port city about twenty-eight kilometres south of Tokyo. In Japan she had realized that she was illiterate—all signs, newspapers, magazines, TV programmes and public announcements—everything was in Japanese. English signage and usage was minimal all around. Since her arrival, she had not spoken a word of Hindi to anyone, except during a brief call she had made home, and ended up crying shamelessly as coins kept time.

Abha heard the bathroom door open and called out. Someone pushed a hundred-yen coin under the door, Abha inserted it in the slot near the shower handle and water started running again.

Outside the shower room a young Japanese girl waited. They could not talk, but the predicament in the shower was probably well known. Abha went back to her room in the dormitory and came back with hundred yen and handed it over to the young Japanese girl.

It was already time to go to class. Abha hurried towards the faculty building. During the last few days, other course participants had streamed in. She had met a few—two Chinese, one Malaysian, two Africans and one Mongolian. Some of them had trouble speaking in English. They were all considerably older than the young Japanese students crawling all over the campus. Yokohama National University's campus was not breathtaking, but it was of manageable size and green, with open spaces between faculty buildings. Abha had explored it during the first few lonely evenings as she adjusted to new sights, faces and sounds.

Life was slowly falling into a strange pattern at the University. In the morning, Abha would grab a few coins from the bowl she had made on her table and rush to the shower room down the corridor. Thereafter, coming back to the room, take more coins and conjure up a breakfast of milk, egg and bread in the common kitchen and then rush for classes; fish out more coins in the cafeteria for lunch—cold fish, cold rice and hot Mizu soup with a dash of soya sauce. The rest of the day was spent exploring the area around the campus. In the evenings, the common kitchen area was the hub. The young Japanese and the other women in her course inserted coins in the gas range and tried to get to know each other as strange and unknown aromas wafted all around.

Since her arrival, Abha's primary quest was to find a place where she could live with Parul as the University dormitory was for single use. She had been to the foreign student's wing and spoken to just about everyone who could understand English. The search was proving to be difficult, not because family housing was not available off campus, but because Abha discovered that on a student scholarship in Japan, housing outside the University campus was simply unaffordable. Yokohama was no different. Ever since she had landed in the city, her life seemed to hinge on coins, and escalating expenses. The staid security of a decade-long bureaucratic life back home in Delhi seemed a faraway dream. Here, each day, she woke up to a new struggle.

The human mind is like an elastic canvas. It gradually starts to assimilate and accommodate whatever is there before it. In a matter of a few weeks, Abha felt that she had been in Yokohama for a long time. Far removed from all that was dear and familiar, Abha was dogged by a strange loneliness and emptiness, but she was getting used to this life.

'Ma did you find the house?'

As Abha sat in class, Parul's sweet voice on the phone echoed in her ears crossing hundreds of miles. Children have such infinite patience; they are willing to wait because they believe in a parent's promise. Abha felt the prick of tears and tried to fight them. Outside, it was a spring day in the month of May. The Japanese cedar trees swayed gently to the cool breeze blowing on the pleasant sunny day.

Delhi must be a furnace right now, she thought. Suddenly the vision of Delhi drenched in summertime heat, blooming with mango buds, enveloped her. She could smell the heat in the classroom itself. Abha had never thought that outside India she would miss such things about home. There was much to miss—the sounds, sights, smells—the very feel of the place.

'Have you found a place yet?' Mary asked her. A coursemate from Namibia, Mary too was a single mother, with a twelve-year-old boy. They had found common ground.

'Not yet, but I am hopeful. I have been looking at some places. They are quite far from University, but at least they are affordable. Now I have to decide on the school.'

'Are you sure you want to bring your child here? She is small and you will be alone here with no help from family. I would advise against it. It is only a matter of two years. I explained that to Tony and he understood. So he stayed back, and now lives these days with my mother.'

How could Abha explain the significance of the promise she had made to her four-year-old before coming to Japan? Abha did not want to fail her child now, or for that matter, ever.

Between them, the power of promises was a binding force.

Abha could never have imagined the morning rush at Yokohama station. As people jostled her at the platform, she cringed at the thought of travelling in this rush once a week for an internship in Tokyo. The crowd was overwhelming, Abha felt she would suffocate. As the Tokaido sen pulled up at the station, everything changed within a split second. All the boarders waited for the passengers to get off, and only then got on in queues. The order was impeccable.

What a contrast to the chaos Abha had witnessed so often at the local railway stations in Bombay! The men in the train were a contrast too. Japanese men buried their nose in the newspapers when they could manage to read, or stared out of the window lost in the music that streamed into their ears through their walkmans.

Where Yokohama ended and Tokyo began was difficult to fathom. They seemed to merge into each other in the train window. Of course, the elusive Mount Fuji would often flash past playing hide and seek, as it were, between tall buildings.

Fuji san—the venerated elder of the Japanese. Abha had learnt at University that a building's highlight was the view of Mount Fuji it offered. From the train, as she watched the sun's rays fall on Fuji san on her first journey to Tokyo, Abha was awed without knowing how Fuji san was going to connect to her life.

The train stopped at Shinjuku station. Abha got off and took the escalator that indicated an arrow towards an exit. From one escalator to another, she floated upwards. Small wonder that Tokyo is such a fabled city. There were shimmering shopping malls, exotic eating-places, stalls and lots of people. The maze seemed never-ending. The exit seemed nowhere near as she swept past the levels on various escalators. The station was a glittering, throbbing city in itself. At last she saw daylight and stepped out on a street in the city of Tokyo.

Was she going to bring Parul here? How would Parul manage? Who would look after her while she was in class or on her weekly internship? Accommodation and school admission plagued her thoughts. She had found an apartment, with a school in the neighbourhood. Before going to see the apartment, she needed to check about the school admission at the local ward office. While an eager and well-meaning Japanese official made a power point presentation and haltingly addressed them in English, Abha wondered if this struggle was what she had actually anticipated. She knew of office colleagues who had gone to English- speaking countries and had a wonderful time. Housing, schooling, food, Indian community, all had been smooth sailing. No one had stories of this sort to relate.

In the evening, as she walked past slickly dressed Japanese girls and the never-ending shopping arcades within the station at Shinjuku, she wondered what she was doing here. Miles away from all her loved ones.

Simran. Abha suddenly missed her with an intense longing that took her with surprise. Simran's homely face that had matured into a melancholic yet warm countenance over their years of friendship seemed to dance in front of her eyes. Yet again, Abha felt tears welling in her eyes.

Minato san and Abha were in the bus on their way towards the ward office, which had jurisdiction over the area where Abha had found an apartment. At each halt, the name of the stop was announced. People got into the bus from the front door and got off from the middle one in a disciplined manner. Abha was tense and very nervous, as if she were going for an exam where she did not speak the language of the examiners. She had understood that unless the ward office agreed, Parul would not get admission into a school, which then would mean a host of problems.

The two of them got off at their stop and walked to the ward office of Asahi-ku—a small neat building, with lots of information posted on the notice board outside the entrance and not too many people around, with the staff in their seats. Why can't our municipal or other public offices be like this? Why do most of our public buildings always look unkempt and dirty? Why does the staff there never smile? Abha couldn't help but compare all the time.

Minato san and Abha were sitting at a counter in front of a young Japanese woman. Minato and the woman talked animatedly. Having checked all of Abha's papers, the woman checked her computer, and then talked with Minato san again. Abha suddenly realized that she was holding her breath.

'She says, Abha san, your daughter must be here before they can accept her for admission. How can they accept a child who is not in the country?'

Abha exhaled. She'd had a premonition all along—something would go amiss. When she heard the statement, it sounded logical even to her. Both Minato and the woman behind the counter looked extremely apologetic and sympathetic.

'Minato san, please explain to her. How can I get my daughter here without ensuring her school admission? Who will look after her if for some reason, the admission does not come through? She is only four and a half.'

Even as Abha said this, she herself was not convinced. The child should be present before admission is granted, the demand was logical.

Then the two women conferred again. How left out one feels when one cannot understand what people are saying, even though one knows what they are talking about. Abha scrutinized their faces, desperately trying to fathom whether the dialogue was going the right way. Suddenly Abha recalled Sarbati, the maid who had been around when they were growing up. Sarbati too would have the same hungry look on her face when Bina di and Abha talked in English about her. '*Chotto matte kudasai*,' said the woman at the counter and left.

'She has gone to confer with her boss. She cannot take a decision on something like this by herself.'

Abha sat still, her mind benumbed. This put everything in a different perspective. The renting of the apartment, getting Parul across—everything hinged on the school admission. The woman was back in ten minutes, and speaking to Minato san again. She looked extremely apologetic.

'Abha san they have decided to admit your daughter to school when she arrives. So you can get her across. She is sorry for the delay.'

Suddenly the room seemed to liven up and Abha had a strong urge to hug the woman across the counter. She too must have sensed Abha's relief because she gave Abha a bright and cheerful smile.

Abha's next stop for the day was the apartment. She had a detailed map from the University office, and the office had said that the landlord spoke English. The apartment was not near the train station—so it was cheaper, but it was connected to the University by a direct bus and close to the school. As she took the bus to her new destination, Abha felt lighter.

The apartment turned out to be in a double-storied building. Iwama san, the landlord, came downstairs and showed her into the small living area on the ground floor. It had a TV, some magazines, newspapers and many toys.

'Most people staying here are students and have families with children. Your daughter will have company in school. There is a Mexican couple whose son is of her age and he goes to the same school. I also allow my tenants to use the bicycles here—free of charge. That helps in buying groceries, taking the child to school, etc. Electricity and water bills are separate for each room. In the backyard there is a coin driven washing machine for common use … .'

Abha listened to him politely, impatient to see her new home.

'Come, now I will show you the place.'

He walked down the corridor and opened a door. Abha saw a room—probably three metres by four metres. It had a bed, a table a chair, cupboard, lamp, and a basin with an electric plate. That was it—her new home consisted of this living space with a small attached cubicle for a bathroom. A door in front of the bed opened into a small space—one could call it a balcony if one so desired.

Suddenly Abha felt she could not breathe. It was so small. There was no space. How would Parul and she live here? Her Pandara Road flat flashed across her mind. She had thought that was small, but compared to this room, it seemed a palace.

She stepped outside as Iwama san detailed the arrangements. Abha knew that she had to say 'yes'. She had been long enough in this country to know that she would not find a bigger place within the budget she had. In fact, this cubby hole was going to take up nearly half her scholarship. Thank God, school was free. But Parul would feel suffocated in this house.

On her way back in the bus towards the campus, Abha felt the euphoria of the morning ebbing away. She tried to visualize Parul and herself in that room for the next two years, and fought back a sense of panic. The bus stopped at Wadamachi and she got off. This would be her stop if she were to shift to the apartment. From this stop, the way to the campus was an uphill walk of about fifteen minutes.

That morning when Minato san and she had come down the hill towards the Wadamachi bus stop, the descent had not seemed so tough. Now as she climbed uphill and walked towards the dormitory, she felt exhausted. Nothing seemed workable—the room, the space, the walk up to University—nothing seemed to be right.

In the dormitory kitchen, Mary was waiting for her. They had dinner together whenever possible.

'I don't know what to do Mary? I am so confused. It seems a daunting proposition.'

'I have been telling you from the start. Explain to your daughter. Children understand, you know. Even Lin, the Chinese girl has left her five-year-old son with her husband.'

In fact, all the four men in the course had left their children and spouses behind too; it didn't seem to be an issue for them. No one commented on that or expected them to have their families over. Nor did they ever talk about their families joining them during the two-year course. Maybe there was a difference between how fathers and mothers relate to their children. Abha never bothered to figure it out. She knew how she felt and that was what mattered.

It was the day she called home. Most of her course mates had got telephones installed in their rooms. Abha had not because of her impending move. She walked to the public phone booth, framing in her mind the words she would tell Parul.

'It is difficult here Parul. The house is small. You will not like it … .'

'Parul I think you are happier there. It will be very uncomfortable here … .'

Nothing sounded good enough to placate a child about three thousand miles away. The phone at the other end was ringing and Abha had still not decided what to say.

'Ma. I was waiting near the phone. Today, you know our school closed down for summer. I told all my friends that I will not be there when school reopens because I shall go to my mother in Japan.'

Abha forgot all her planned sentences. The chirpy hopeful voice of her daughter could not be denied. She knew she had to get Parul over. She could not betray her daughter's trust.

'Parul, I fixed up the house and school admission today. Papa will buy your ticket and send you here by the end of the month.'

'Ma I love you. Speak to Papa.'

Abha's father gave all the details on the things they had packed for Parul. She could sense the uncertainty in his voice. His small granddaughter would be making a long journey.

As Abha walked back to the dormitory, she wondered if she would be able to tackle what she had taken on. It was going to be difficult to manage all alone with a small child in this different setting. An acute sense of dread and apprehension came over her. And with it, the ever-familiar feeling of being alone. A feeling she hated and constantly tried to push to the back of her mind.

Peter was giving the update for the day.

'Today we will get to know about our academic supervisors. You know it is a big deal. You have to write the thesis under the supervisor's guidance. I hope I get an easygoing guy, folks. I am going to take up a part-time job. I need to earn as much as possible in these two years so that my dream house back home in Angola can be built.'

Peter made them laugh the most. He was the one who brought the part-time job thing out into the open. Slowly Amrut, the Sri Lankan, and Ibrahim, the Malaysian, declared that they too were looking for part-time jobs to make some money. They were all high-ranking civil servants in their respective countries, but in the 'Land of the Rising Sun' they were students who could work part time on their visas.

More than the course content, discussions in the group focused on sharing information about the kinds of jobs available. At University, unlike in English-speaking countries, nothing was available because none of them knew Japanese!

As foretold by Peter, the afternoon saw them in a solemn meeting with the course professors. The supervisors for all the other nine participants had been announced. Abha was the only one left. Then Murai sensei stood up. He was the youngest among the faculty.

'I have the pleasure to guide Abha san.'

Abha was relieved. She preferred someone younger. The older professors seemed to resent her somewhat. She sensed it. She asked questions, demanded explanations and was always speaking in class. She was too new then to know or understand why an undercurrent of apprehension and resentment was always there. And she had no time to think of all this. There was too much to tie-up in the three weeks remaining for Parul's arrival.

After the meeting, Abha decided to visit Rashid and Vivek in the Science Faculty. Vivek was from West Bengal doing his PhD, Rashid was from Pakistan. There was also Amit from Madhya Pradesh doing a Master's in another Science lab. They bonded over language, food and a general sense of belonging to the same landmass. Abha often visited them when she felt low. It was a relief to sit in the lab and share her troubles with them. They would converse in Hindi and often share a meal together, cooked mostly by Amit. In a different land, so far away from home, all cultural and other differences seemed to disappear. Instead a feeling of kinship developed. Vivek was in the lab busy with some experiment.

'Abha ji, please come and sit down. I will just finish what is on hand and be with you.'

He was much younger than her, had been here for more than three years, spoke Japanese and had a Japanese girl friend.

'Vivek, I have decided to get Parul over at the end of the month. I have taken that place I told you about. It is so small.'

'All houses here are small. They just take some getting used to, you know. Things will work out. If you want, I will come with you to the airport the day she arrives.'

Suddenly Abha found herself crying. She felt ashamed, but could not help it. Vivek brought a glass of water for her, and waited for her to calm down. Then they talked of other things, just to help her overcome her gloom.

When they walked out of the lab, the sun had set and the dark trees were swaying in the breeze. By now Abha knew the names of some of the trees in the campus. The Icho noki and the Tsubaki were most common near the Science Faculty. It was quiet and serene at this time of the evening. Vivek and Abha walked silently towards the cafeteria. Over dinner in the cafeteria, it was decided that in order to keep costs down, piece by piece, Abha would transfer her luggage to the new place by bus. Vivek, Rashid and Amit, all would pitch in to help.

Abha was sitting in the computer lab with her mail inbox open. The latest entrant in her life in this techno-driven place was email. The University had provided them with an email account and unlimited access to the internet. Abha spent hours surfing the few Indian newspapers that were available on the net. She had pestered Bina di and Kishore ji to find someone who had an email account back home. In the mid-1990s, having email access in India was still a rarity, even in the larger metros. Kishore ji discovered a colleague who had an email address and was adept at using it. This established Abha's electronic connection with home, at last.

There was a mail from Ujjwal:

'I was blessed with a son. Can you suggest some names?

Ujjwal

PS: Hope you are going out with some men now.'

He always managed to make her smile, as in the days of college and despite all the years gone by.

As she typed all the interesting names for boys she could think of, Abha wondered whether he would understand her problems if she wrote to him about it. Then she decided to let it be.

There was also a message from Bina di about Parul's flight arrangements. Kishore ji and Bina di had found someone known coming to Tokyo on Air India and booked Parul on the same flight. So finally, Parul was coming to Japan. Abha felt a flutter in the pit of her stomach; the kind she used to have in school when exams were round the corner.

It was nearly ten in the morning, time for her first meeting with Murai sensei.

Abha walked into Murai sensei's room and was taken aback. There were books everywhere—on the floor, the racks, the chairs, the table—it was difficult to locate the man in the heap of books. Murai sensei got up from his chair and after bowing to each other in the traditional manner, on his suggestion she emptied a chair of its books by dumping them on the floor and sat down. Somehow, the room seemed overpowering.

'I know my room needs some organizing. I will do it in the holidays.'

That sentence broke the ice between them. Abha discovered he had books in English she could borrow.

'Have you thought about your thesis topic, Abha san?'

'Isn't it too early Sensei? I need some time to think.'

'Maybe, but it is better to be prepared so that you can start collecting information. It will be difficult to find material in English. You might have to get help from your country. I heard your daughter is coming to Japan. Do you think you will manage with her?'

And so it went on. Abha found that he was easy to speak to and unlike many Japanese she had encountered, he had a sense of humour and smiled often.

'Sensei, where did you learn English?'

The Japanese aspired for English language skills. There were numerous schools offering English-speaking courses. In trains and stations, often people struck up a conversation with Abha for the admitted reason of trying their English skills.

'On my own. By reading, listening and trying to speak. I learnt Spanish formally. I also play the flute.'

Murai sensei had interests other than the Economics he taught. The thought was somehow comforting. The meeting turned out to be good and Abha stepped out of the room full of books with an armful of English books to read. She was happy. Most of the books in the library were in Japanese, so English books, especially fiction, were hard to come by.

That night Abha decided to sleep in her new home. Parul was expected in a week and most of her things had come in as planned. In the glow of the small circular tube light that illuminated the tiny space that was her home, she stood before the mirror fixed on the cupboard.

She was past thirty-two. To herself, she looked much like when she was in her mid-twenties. She had put on some weight though. Her hair was still long, and flowing till her waist. She roamed this strange land in salwar kameez and her eyes remained the brightest part of her face. It had been quite some time since she had evaluated herself like this. She had never had the time in the last few years.

In bed, Abha lay awake for a long time. A new place is replete with new sounds, new smells and new whispers at night. As one grows older, the mind takes time to adjust to new surroundings.

When the bed creaked, the sound seemed to ring out in the silence of the night. The residential areas in Yokohama were silent even by day—no child playing outside, never a TV blaring, nor a dog barking. In the night, only the lights coming out of the windows of houses and passing cars made it the land of the living. She needed some time to absorb the silences of the land.

In a strange country, on a strange bed, in a strange room, it was easy to see herself from a distance. Here she was—a woman in her early thirties, a single parent with a marriage behind her. Things that hurt in Delhi had stopped mattering now. A change of place, the thrill of learning again, the discovery of new skills and competencies definitely lend a healing touch. In a way, it was a blessing that she had moved out of India. Once Parul adjusts, things will be fine, she thought to herself.

Abha never stopped being surprised by her sense of involvement with Parul, by this intense connection with her child. Whenever Abha tried to remember her life before Parul, it was a blur. She could no longer recall how it was when she was not a mother. No wonder people say that the birth of a child is a life-changing event. Difficult to understand till actually experienced.

As sleep came to claim her, Abha thought of Simran and Rekha. Simran and she had been exchanging long letters. Simran was still in Hyderabad, single and waiting for Hussein. That neither irritated nor surprised Abha. Many things in life were simply meant to be accepted—the only way to live with them. Rekha was in Hong Kong, a sporadic appearance on email now. Rekha's lover had also moved to Hong Kong and they were living there together. Yet somehow, Abha still thought of Rekha as alone.

All three of them alone in different parts of the globe.

They were hurtling towards Tokyo for the weekly internship lectures. Mary, Lin and she were now a group—three mothers who understood each other's problems.

Before Parul arrived, Abha wanted to register her presence in the Indian Embassy in Tokyo. It was one unequivocal advice given prior to her departure, 'Since you are going to be there for two years, you must connect with the Embassy.' In her diary, she had the name of someone she was advised to meet. After the class, she took the train to Kudanshita station. Once she came out of the depths of the station Abha looked around for a *koban* box, the ubiquitous police box. It was the best place to seek directions. Often when a cop could not speak English, he would walk Abha halfway to wherever she was going. Abha moved in the direction indicated.

On turning right from the road, she saw it. The tricolour fluttering in the wind. There was a strange pull at the heartstrings when she saw it in a different land. A clear sense of belonging and pride. It was a discovery. The incredible pull of one's country.

Once inside the building, Abha felt as though she were back in India. The reception walls were adorned with pictures of Indian tourist places, a big statue of Natraj stood in a corner and a general sense of languor prevailed.

'I have come to see Mr. Murthy, First Secretary. Currently, I am a student in Yokohama National University. Back home I am in the Ministry of Finance.'

After a very long time, Abha had mentioned her professional identity. Somehow it sounded strange, but as in India, it helped open doors here as well.

'He has gone for a meeting and will be back in about half an hour. Would you like to wait?'

'Yes, please.'

Abha sat down on the sofa in the reception area and picked up magazines lying on the table. In front, was a glass wall from where steps led up to the mysterious confines of the Embassy. Many Indians flitted around. It was difficult to imagine that outside the building, across the moat, stood the Imperial Palace of the Japanese Emperor. Inside and outside were two different worlds.

Another person came looking for Mr. Murthy and told the receptionist that he was going to the library and would return in half an hour. Abha quickly got up and followed him. The Embassy library was modest, but had many Indian newspapers and magazines. Abha devoured them hungrily. They made her nostalgic. She longed for home.

'Hello, I am Diwakar. I work for American Express here in Tokyo. And you?'

The man who had come in to see Mr. Murthy was addressing her.

'I study at Yokohama National University and am here for a two-year course.'

'That is long enough for you to know this place and start liking it. It is difficult in the beginning. Have you made friends in the Indian community here?'

'Not yet. I am too busy settling down. Trying to get my daughter over. She is nearly five. '

Abha waited for the eternal question that Indians never failed to ask, in India or abroad, 'What does your husband do?'

'You know children settle down much faster than adults. Their capacity to assimilate is greater. I have a son, nearly eight. He loves it here now. We have been here nearly three years.'

Waiting for Mr. Murthy, they talked. He was from Belgaum in Karnataka, a farmer's son who had made it big through personal initiative and curiosity. He also wrote poetry in Kannada.

'What is your telephone number? When we have a dinner at home next time, we must have you over.'

'I do not have a phone yet. But I do have email.'

'No phone in Tokyo! Quite amazing! How do you manage?'

He gave Abha his calling card; she gave him her email.

Mr. Murthy was a bureaucrat of the old mould. Very rule bound and extremely verbose—full of his postings, his experience and his proficiency in Japanese. Sitting on the other side of the table, Abha found him quite amusing and wondered if she too would behave like this some day. He must have been only three to four years her senior, but she felt he was decades older. She wondered how outsiders to the system like Diwakar handled such people. It was difficult to get a word in the conversation. Yet Murthy was considerate; keeping in view her student status, he offered that she could call home from the Embassy phone, after of course, enquiring about her 'absent' husband and 'present' child!

'Ma, I am now counting the days till I can be with you again. I miss you.'

'Miss you too. Give the phone to Nani.'

Abha felt the lump in her throat as her mother's soothing voice floated down the line. She hoped Murthy did not realize she was close to tears, though she had a strange feeling that Diwakar sitting next to her did, since he politely looked the other way. While she was on the phone, Diwakar had managed to get his work done. They left the Embassy together.

'I can drop you to Shinagawa station. From there you can get a direct train to Yokohama.'

Abha accepted his offer. She had never sat in a car in Japan. Just travelled the cities in trains or buses. Sometimes on the surface, at times underground. To see a city from a car window offered a different perspective—closer to the ground and people. From the car, she saw many trees and parks that she had never seen from the train. The pace of Tokyo appeared infinitely faster from a car.

'Are you a published poet?'

'Yes, I have published a collection of poems and am working on the next one.'

'Great. How do you reconcile the two—banking and poetry? They seem to be pretty divergent?'

'Each one of us is a poet. But only some of us get down to writing poetry. Even prose is poetry. And my work provides me a canvas that is different.'

A nice Hindi film song was playing in the car. The ride and the music made her remember the life she had left behind.

'That is Yoyogi Park. It has the most beautiful Sakura trees in season. That is Tokyo Tower.' Like a self appointed guide, Diwakar pointed out the sights of Tokyo.

The car stopped outside Shinagawa station.

'Best of luck for your daughter's arrival. If there is anything I can do, please do not hesitate to give me a call.'

In the train, Abha's thoughts came back to the issues at hand. What should she put in that room that will make it look like a home when Parul arrives? The school was primarily a play school-cum-crèche. Children played, recited poems in Japanese, ate and slept till the parents came to pick them up. How would Parul adjust there? At Yokohama station, Abha walked around aimlessly in the bright lights of the shopping arcades ruminating over the same thoughts again and again.

The answers would come only with Parul's arrival.

On Murai sensei's suggestion, Abha set out to pick up Parul with Kazuki, her 'tutor'. He was a Japanese student assigned to help Abha settle down. He would help bridge the linguistic divide on Parul's arrival at the airport.

They set off for Narita Airport by train. It was possible to plan a trip to the last minute while using public transport in the time-conscious nation. It was nearly a two-hour journey by train to the airport. Abha found it difficult to believe that it had been only about four months since she had landed here. It seemed a lifetime. She found she was now used to the ticket vending machines, the punching machines, the automatic doors of the trains—the total lack of human interface. The memories of what life had been back home were slowly fading. Yet the yearning for home would overtake her at the most unexpected moments. Just two days ago, it had rained. As she had walked to her new home, the smell of wet earth wafted to her nostrils. She could not remember the last time she had noticed the smell of the damp earth in Delhi. But here, in Japan, the smell, hitherto dormant in her consciousness, called out to her.

The half-an hour wait for the flight to arrive was unbearable. Abha paced up and down after giving up trying to keep going a desultory conversation with Kazuki. Despite the linguistic gap, they managed to communicate the bare necessities to each other. Then the flight was announced. And after a while, passengers started emerging from the arrival lounge.

When waiting for someone particular, the rest of the crowd becomes invisible to the eye. The mind's eye does not 'see' them. Then Abha saw her. A small forlorn figure, clutching a bag, following the airhostess, looking utterly terrified. Maybe Parul saw her before she was able to spot Parul, because the child just charged and flew into her mother's arms. Abha could feel her child's heart beating wildly against her own. As she held Parul, she realized just how much she had missed her little daughter—her feel, her smell, her being … .

In the train back to Yokohama, Parul curled up in Abha's lap, quietly clinging to her as the world outside whizzed past. She gazed curiously at the different-looking people around her. Kazuki simply stared at mother and daughter. He had a long way to go before becoming a parent.

At last, they stood at the doorstep of the new home. While Kazuki and Abha adjusted the new luggage in the small confines of the room, Parul sat on the bed shaking her tiny legs. She had not uttered a word since her arrival. Abha had tried to talk to her in the train, but she had fallen asleep after a while.

'Ma this is the new house?' She asked once Kazuki left.

'Yes.' Abha was expecting an outburst.

Parul got off the bed and slowly started looking into each and every corner of the room. She opened the cupboard, rummaged among the things kept on the table, went into the bathroom and inspected the kitchen table.

'Is it new Ma? Everything is shining!'

Japanese perfection did not fail to impress the little girl either. Abha breathed a sigh of relief; at least the first reaction had not been too bad. The realization of the confined space would probably dawn later.

Parul's first day in Yokohama was spent in adjusting her things in the room. With her toys, crayons and tiny clothes, soon the room took on the ambience of a home. After that, they walked hand in hand to a small shrine nearby that Abha had discovered during one of her long solitary walks. A wooden structure on a hillock, it remained mostly locked, draped in isolation and disuse. They stood in front of it and quietly invoked the powers above to see them through. How much Abha had missed the chatter, the incessant questions and the company of her daughter became clear with the arrival of Parul.

After having the rather sad dinner Abha had prepared, Abha started washing the dishes.

'Ma have you become a servant in Japan?' Parul's innocent question made Abha feel confident about her decision to bring Parul over for the first time. A different way of life would teach her many things. For the first time in months, Abha had no trouble sleeping. With the ever familiar breathing of Parul by her side, she slept in a matter of minutes.

Over the next few days, life fell into a pattern. Abha would drop Parul to school on the bicycle, park it there and take the bus to University. She would return in the late afternoon and pick up Parul, come home and cook. The pattern was punctuated by periodic rides on the bicycle to the nearby store for groceries.

The computer lab was now part of Abha's daily itinerary in the campus. First thing in the morning, she went to the lab as it was easier to find a free terminal at that hour. Half an hour of surfing and it would be time for the classes. That day there was an email from Ujjwal.

'I have given him one of the names you suggested—Ankur. How is Parul doing? Hope both of you are having a great time. Ujjwal.'

There was also an email from Rekha. She had resurfaced after a long gap.

'What's new? How is it going? Are you having some good sex at last? But Japanese men??? I wonder. Things are fine. Work good.'

Things change, yet remain the same. Rekha was living with someone, but only physically. He was not present in her consciousness. He was never mentioned in her communications. Maybe that is why despite his presence in her life, Abha always thought of Rekha as alone.

That evening as Abha and Parul sat down to have the disappointing meal Abha had rustled up in a hurry on her return, she waited for Parul to complain. Maybe things around Parul were new and different, so she did not complain about anything these days. Maybe. She asked, 'What do you do at school Parul? Your teacher tells me you do not eat the meal that is provided, nor do you sleep. You have also been crying.'

There was silence in the room. 'I don't like the food they give Ma. I can't sleep but I lie still at least. I miss you so I cry.'

Abha hugged her and wondered what the little girl was actually going through, with this dramatic change in her life.

'It will be better Parul, as time goes by.'

The giant ferris wheel was moving slowly. On one side lay the vast expanse of the dull grey Pacific with ships in the distance, and on the other, evening lights were coming on in Yokohama as the sun set. The highway in the distance appeared as if it were a moving necklace—a mesmerizing sight. Parul sat inside the cabin of the ferris wheel glued to the glass. Spread out below was Sakuragicho with its stupendous malls, wide walkways and beautiful waterfront on the shore of the Pacific. After getting off the wheel, Abha and Parul sat for a long time on the steps of the waterfront and heard the gentle waves lapping the steps. Lovers crowded around the steps that led to the ocean. Behind them the shopping malls glittered. It was serene and relaxing.

'Ma can't Nani-Papa come and visit us for some time. We can sleep on the floor and give them the bed.'

For the first time in the month that she had been there, Parul had given voice to something Abha had known all along—she missed her grandparents.

'Yes Beta. I have written to Papa and asked them to come. Let's hope they make it.'

Bright lights, new faces, new places become irrelevant with time. Slowly the way of life and the people who matter the most start tugging at the heartstrings.

Whenever Abha picked Parul up from the school, even as Abha settled her on the backseat, she would start an incessant chatter. Her monologue would continue till well past dinner. It seemed as if she were releasing something pent up during the day. Everyday.

'Parul why do you start talking so much the moment I pick you up from school?'

'*Arre* Ma. I can't speak a word to anyone there. They all speak Japanese. Even their songs are in Japanese. By the time you come I am just waiting to talk.'

Why had she not realized this? Abha recollected that whenever the Mexican boy came to play in their apartment, the two children played in absolute silence, just gesticulating for communication. She held Parul closer. Ship lights twinkled in the water at a distance.

'You should try and pick up some Japanese from your classmates.'

'Ma I can now count and even say *Watashi* Parul in Japanese. I am trying.'

Abha knew that Parul was making every effort to make the most of this tough situation in her own small and consistent way. Had it been an English-speaking country, things would have been very different.

They moved from the waterfront and went for a stroll in the mall. Japanese restaurant windows fascinated Parul. The food on offer would be displayed in an attractive manner through plastic replicas. For Parul it was a game, to test what she could recognize. But when it came to eating there was no choice. It had to be McDonalds, the child loved the burgers the first time Abha took her there.

After dinner they took the bus home. By the time they reached the apartment it was close to midnight. They walked hand in hand without a care in the world. The late hour and the lonely road were not intimidating. Abha appreciated this sense of security in Japan. There was no perception of threat of being mugged or harassed. Whatever the hour, on public transport, there was never any pulling and pushing, pinching, winks or lewd remarks. As they walked towards their apartment, Abha wondered when India would afford its women this real freedom—the absence of fear.

Time seemed to fly since Parul's arrival. The two-month summer break loomed around the corner.

While Abha was busy cooking, cleaning, keeping Parul entertained and attending classes, Peter and Amrut had found part-time jobs. They now worked nearly through the night in a factory making *futons*—Japanese mattresses. As a result, they were drowsy during most classes. Mary had also started taking English classes and earning some money. Abha seemed to be the only one in a spending mode. Each time she went to withdraw money from the bank Parul would ask her, 'Ma I hope there is some money in the bank still?' The change in her mother's financial status now that she was on a student scholarship was quite clear to her daughter.

Actually, things were not so bad. Just that Abha was not able to manage what most of her colleagues in the bureaucracy would have done in these circumstances—save money. Abha's expenses were high. The rent of the apartment, coupled with Parul's presence, made existence pretty hand to mouth. She waited with baited breath for the scholarship to come in at the end of the quarter so that when she saw her bank statement she would feel better. But there was nothing about her life that Abha wished to change at this point of time. She was managing with Parul all alone; Parul had also settled in and life was just perfect.

Perhaps that is why it did not last.

It happened two days before the University was to have a break for the summer. Parul and Abha had returned home from their weekly shopping. Parul's school was about to close down for sometime.

'Ma what will we do during the holidays?'

'We will roam around. Let me see if we can make a trip outside this area. We will watch movies and be together all the time.'

'My school in Delhi would have re-opened now. Shipra must be catching the Sumo everyday in the morning.' The wistful tone implied that Parul was missing her life in Delhi.

'Parul, I have got *Dilwale dulhaniya le jayenge* from Vivek Uncle. Do you want to watch it?'

'Okay Ma.' Both of them settled down on the bed to watch the movie on the second-hand TV and VCR Abha had purchased from an outgoing student. The charm of watching Bollywood movies abroad was two-fold. They entertained and managed to fill up a hole in the heart too. As Shah Rukh serenaded Kajol in the sylvan green expanse of Europe on screen, both of them forgot they were in Japan.

The next day was busy for Abha. She had a meeting with Murai sensei. By the time she reached Parul's school it was four-thirty in the evening. School shut at three-thirty, but some children stayed late till their parents were free to come and fetch them. When Abha arrived, Parul was swinging on the school gate. As soon as she saw Abha from a distance, she started waving frantically.

In the evening, Abha took Parul on a long bicycle ride around their apartment building. They discovered another shopping area to the north of the apartment and a nice playground further down. After dinner at the apartment Abha said, 'Parul once holidays begin, we can spend time in that colourful playground more often. It was good that we found it.'

'Ma can I go back to India?'

'No Beta it is too expensive. Maybe in winter we will try and make a trip, but not now.'

'Not for a trip. I want to go back to India, to my school, my friends and Nani–Papa.'

Abha who was washing the dishes, suddenly froze, then turned around and looked at Parul. Sitting on her favourite place on the bed, she was swinging her thin legs and looking out at the dark Japanese night. She couldn't mean that. She is just expressing something that I have felt many times myself, Abha thought.

'Parul tomorrow after school I will take you to the beautiful Yamashita Park near the sea. In season it has the most beautiful tulips. Then when holidays begin, we will have lots of fun.'

Parul seemed to have forgotten her statement. She switched on the TV and got busy watching a Japanese cartoon. She liked to watch them even if she did not understand a word.

The next day they were in the bus heading out to Yamashita Park when Parul said, 'Ma I want to go back.'

Something in Abha did not want to heed the earnestness in her daughter's voice.

'Parul even I want to go back, but you know I am here on office work. I have to finish this course before I can return. We will go back. Once in the middle and then at the end of two years for ever. Okay, now cheer up.'

'No Ma. I want to go back now. I want to go back to my school and to Nani–Papa. I don't like it here.'

It was finally out in the open. The fear and apprehension that Abha had thought were unfounded and behind her, were suddenly rearing their ugly faces. At that moment, she felt like giving Parul a tight slap. She felt inadequate, a miserable failure.

'Well then you had better start liking it. This is where we are going to live; you had better adjust to it. Okay? And I don't want to hear all this again. You think it is easy for me? You don't have this choice—of going back. I hope you understand that.'

Who was Abha really shouting at? Herself or for her sense of failure? Because the small child she was addressing her frustrations to was looking out of the bus window, tears rolling down her cheeks.

Despite the beauty and relaxing atmosphere of Yamashita Park, the trip was a failure and they returned home quietly. Abha did not know how to handle this. Nothing had prepared her for this. She had thought she would be unable to cope and manage Parul all alone in this strange country. But her child would not want to stay with her—for whatever reason. It hurt terribly.

The next few days seemed to pass in a daze. Each time Abha picked up Parul from school, she hoped her daughter would say something to change the situation. Abha waited for Parul to disown her statements. But it did not happen. Abha tried to argue the situation differently.

'Parul has it struck you that even if you were to go back home, Ma cannot return right now.'

'But Ma, you only said that we could visit in winter. So you come to India once in the middle and I will come and see you once more. Time will pass quickly, and then you will be back for good.'

When had the little girl thought out all these alternatives? Did children actually have such analytical powers or is it the simple rule that we all follow but never acknowledge—once we know what we want, everything else falls into place.

She sought out Mary's counsel; there was no one else she could think of.

'You must listen to her Abha. In a way, it is good. You kept your promise, so the child will not hold that against you. She has seen life here and made a choice. Hopefully she will be able to live with it.'

'Mary we are talking of a four-year-old going on five, not some adult that she will live with her choice. Once back in India, what if she wants to come back here? It cannot work like this.'

Abha's mind somehow refused to accept it. At times she felt betrayed by her own child. At others she dwelt on her own inadequacies, but could not pin-point anything. All the effort and trouble she had taken to set up a home with Parul in Japan seemed to have come to naught.

Holidays had begun and once again, Abha's life was in a spin. Parul's problems were over once she had mentioned her desire to her mother. She was back to her chatty chirpy self. Waiting for her mother to fulfil her wish. How simple it is to be a child. And how much as a parent one loves them. Abha watched as Parul played in the colourful playground.

The only person who could put this in perspective was her mother. The next day, Abha was on the phone trying to solve the muddle of her life. A child unburdening herself to her parent.

'Mummy, Parul says that she wants to go back for good. She doesn't like it here.'

'Fortunately we did not withdraw her name from the school here. Only took leave of absence.'

Why did Mummy have such a prosaic reply to something that hurt her so much? Abha wanted to shout all her frustration and pain down the phone line, but distance does have its advantages.

'But suppose she wants to come back after sometime? What then? I cannot keep doing this. Why don't you speak to her and tell her she must stay here.'

'Abha Beti I suggest you bring her here during your holidays. If she decides to go back, take her with you. Otherwise, leave her here. And don't worry, before you know, your course would be complete and it would be time for you to come back.'

Why had she not thought of that? Suddenly Abha's tension eased. Mothers are like that, they provide solutions and solace to the most vexing issues.

The winter trip was shifted to summer. Abha and Parul planned the visit home. Shopping and picking up interesting things for everyone at home and trying to locate the cheapest airfare took up most of their time. The happiness and utter joy at the thought of going home was unbelievable.

As Abha went to the computer lab for the last time, before leaving for home, she checked her mail.

'You are coming in now? I am going to be out of the country on a project during this period. Will not be able to meet you. That is sad. Anyway, let us see how it plays out. Ujjwal.'

What a pity! There was also a dinner invitation from Diwakar. Abha had nearly forgotten about him. Anyway, she would be at home in Delhi at that time!

It felt great to be back. After the glitter and shine of Japan, Delhi seemed a shabby dump, unimaginably dirty, with power cuts that lasted hours. The mosquitoes attacked Abha as if they had missed her. But this was home and she loved it. There was tremendous scope for improvement, but home remains the best place to be in! Delhi and its chaotic traffic, its teeming millions and its beautiful avenues—they all seemed to welcome Abha with open arms.

Parul had joined school and was revelling on her return. She spent the evenings with her friends, playing and shouting in the playground, running around, getting dirty and messy. As if the discipline of Japan was being cast off with a vengeance. Life seemed so complete and fulfilling back home. Watching the unfettered joy on Parul's face made Abha ponder.

'Papa I think I too should just drop out of the course. I can just give some medical reason and stay back here. No one will say anything. It happens all the time in Government.'

'If you feel like doing that, do that. But I would never advise it. You will be branded as a person who did not finish her assignment. It will be a black mark against you in your career. '

'I really don't care,' Abha said. But she did. Abha knew only too well. She was not going to be branded a failure in her professional life.

During the visit, Abha met Simran for lunch. Simran had moved to Delhi to look after her ageing mother. Her youngest sister, Seema, had also got married. Only Simran remained. No one seemed to be thinking of Simran's marriage anymore. Neither her elder brother Ravi, nor her mother—no one. Hussein remained a sporadic presence in her life. More like a peg on an empty wall.

Rekha was in Hong Kong. They were in touch on email. It was a long time since Abha and she had last met. Maybe next time when Abha came to Delhi they would plan a visit together.

The month at home passed all too quickly and it was time to test the waters as far as Parul was concerned. 'Parul, Ma has to go back. You know that. What about you? Do you want to go back with me or stay here? You must understand—I cannot come back before the two years are over, and once you decide to stay here, then that is final.'

She had to give these ultimatums to Parul. Sometimes life does not offer alternatives.

'Ma I will stay here. You promise me that you will come once in the middle and also get me over to Japan once again.'

Promises extracted and promises made. When separation and distance are inevitable, promises are the only hope. Abha was back at the airport once again. Leaving again for Japan. No anguish this time except that there was going to be no Parul to wait for in Japan. This time she was going to be alone in the true sense of the word.

'Ma, you will be alone there, but please don't cry.'

The small voice of her daughter reverberated in her ears till the lights of Delhi slowly shrunk, then disappeared from sight. Abha leaned her head against the backrest. This was not what she had planned. Leaving Parul with her parents was never her intention. But then nothing in her life had actually worked out as planned. Did it for anyone else? She often wondered.

'Come on let's go to the dormitory. I am hungry. What is it that you find interesting in a damn computer I don't understand. I find it tiring to sit before the screen even for the Econometrics class.'

Mary and Abha were sitting in the computer lab. Abha's eyes were glued to the screen while Mary looked desultorily all around. Back in Yokohama, Abha felt as though she had never been away. Everything here was now familiar and known too. Her mind seemed to move seamlessly from one known object to another.

There was an email from Diwakar.

'I am holding an exhibition of photographs taken by me in Japan at the address below. The inauguration is on Monday at 7 pm. Please find time to drop in. Diwakar.'

A banker, a poet and now a photographer. The man seemed to have diverse interests, Abha thought, as she sent a reply accepting the invitation.

'Mary, the Net is just fascinating. As if the whole world were at your fingertips. It enthralls me and I want to use this time to become a good user. By the way, where is Lin? I don't see her around in the dormitory kitchen.'

'She's found someone.'

'Meaning?'

'She's found a guy. She is busy with him.'

Life had obviously moved on in the month that Abha had been away. Away from her husband and child, Lin had found someone. If she had been a man, everyone would have winked and said, 'He is having a good time,' but for Lin there was an acute sense of disapproval in Mary's voice. The dilemmas of being a woman never ceased.

On Monday, as the train took her towards Tokyo for Diwakar's exhibition inauguration, Abha missed Parul. The apartment was empty without her. It had the feel of a home while Parul was there; now it was simply a one-room apartment. She also needed to talk to the University to see if she could shift back into the dormitory. It would save her some money.

At the station, Abha made a beeline for the washroom. She had learnt from observation the secret of the impeccable look of the Japanese girls. They freshened up at the station, removing creases of the journey.

At the venue, in the small hall, there were many people. Nearly fifty photographs were mounted on the walls with small captions underneath. Abha spotted Mr. Murthy and went over to him.

'Oh Abha san, this is my wife, Jyoti. She is from your state—UP.' Jyoti turned out to be a cheerful upbeat woman, quite unlike her somewhat drab and boring bureaucrat husband.

'You must come over someday for a meal. It is so good to meet someone who is not part of the Embassy crowd. I am working in a college in India. I am here on long leave to keep my husband company.'

The evening turned out to be a good introduction to the Indian community in Tokyo. Mr. Narayan who headed an organization of the Indian community seemed to be the key person of the group. The event was a whirl of saris, salwar kameezes, samosas, India bashing and Tokyo loving. Diwakar's wife and son Udayan were there as well.

The photographs were interesting. A whole kaleidoscope of Japan had been captured in them. More than landscapes, people in various moods were the focus. The last photograph was of Diwakar sitting on a sheet of snow in the *padmasan*, his eyes closed, with only snow all around him. The caption read, 'The gypsy tries to find roots.' Diwakar caught up with Abha in front of the photo.

'Did you like the photographs? Are you still on vacation? Then I have an offer. This exhibition is on for two more days. If you come here and sit through the day from around 11 to 5 pm, I can offer you a good lunch as compensation.'

Abha had nothing much to do, so she agreed. That evening she received innumerable dinner invitations from the Indian community present there. It seemed as if the primary occupation of Indians in Japan was to dine at each other's home. She also sensed that at each gathering she would meet a slice of the same crowd that was present at the exhibition.

The next day Abha came in the morning and sat in the small hall. A book in hand, she watched the small stream of people trickling in. They did not leave without writing in the visitor's book. Some wrote in Kanji, the pictorial language of the Japanese, while others wrote in English. At one sharp, Diwakar came from his office to take her out for the promised lunch to a small restaurant nearby.

'How did you take up photography?'

'It just happened. It is purely a hobby and all these photographs are from a normal camera, not a professional one.'

'They are good. How is work coming along?'

'Fine. You have settled in now?'

He had noticed Abha's stress the last time they had met at the Embassy. For the first time she took a good look at him. A rather plain looking darkish Indian face, from the south, with clear eyes and a pleasant smile.

'So you think you are a gypsy Diwakar?'

'Aren't we all? Some of us have it a bit more than the others and while some accept this, others deny it.'

'What do you think about the Japanese?'

'They can only be good imitators, never leaders. The need to conform is so great in this society that no one can really achieve his or her true potential. Everything has to be in a particular predefined manner; there is no scope for spontaneity. I feel if Japanese discipline could be clubbed with Indian spontaneity we can take over the world.'

It was an entirely new way of looking at the Japanese.

'You still haven't acquired a phone Abha? You must. It will help you remain connected.'

'Yes I am thinking about it. It will be simpler for my parents and Parul also to call me. Once I shift back to the dormitory, I will get one.'

Lunch on both the days was short and nice. More interesting than lunch was talking to him. He was a keen observer with a fine sense of perception.

When the University reopened, Abha met Lin for the first time in days in class.

'So Lin how are you? Not been around much.'

'Well you know I found a guy. It just happened. He is married, so it is safe.'

'Meaning?'

'Well no hassles you know. No expectations from each other. Both know what the whole thing is about and how it is going to end. It makes things much simpler.'

There is a certain stage in life when all one wants is simplicity—no chase, no thrills—a sense of calm and the idea that an exit is available. Maybe what Lin said was true. Right or wrong? Abha had stopped thinking of life in those terms long ago. Life *is*. That is all. Abha was now free. Absolutely free—no husband, no child, no boyfriend tucked away in India. Just herself with a slice of time entirely her own. Maybe, she needed to start looking at the men around. Evenings here were worse than when she had been newly divorced. When the door of the apartment shut, it was as if she were shut off from the outside world. Often, Abha would go for long walks, bicycle rides and try to keep her morale high. Living far away from the campus meant that she missed out on the community life in the dormitory.

Within a week of the University re-opening, Abha put in a formal request to come back to the dormitory, and was promptly called to the Course Director's room for a meeting. Two other professors were also present. Politely the Course Director told her that it was impossible to give her a room in the University hostel that year, but for the next academic year, they would try.

'Why "try" Sensei? Next year I should be assured of a room at the start of the academic session.'

Something in his expression told her that he did not like her insistence. She simply looked back at him and sensed that a feeling of unease had enveloped the room. Without another word it was clear that the meeting had ended.

Murai sensei called for her the same day. 'Abha san, why were you so impolite with the Course Director? He was very unhappy.'

'But I was not impolite. Why could he not say that next year he would give me a room instead of saying he would *try*. Providing a room is part of the University's commitment to students of our programme. We are not regular students Sensei.'

'This is Japan Abha san. Let me tell you something. When the academic advisors were being allotted, no one picked you up. Since I was the youngest professor, you were assigned to me. I was very tense about our first meeting. But I relaxed when I found that you are not as aggressive as you appear to be. There is such defiance in your eyes. Japanese men are used to submissive women and no one asks so many questions here. It is considered impolite and going against the code of harmony.'

Abha was stunned. Defiance in her eyes? Asking questions? Impolite? She had just been defending her interest and demanding what was her right. Why was that held against her?

'Please apologize to the Course Director.'

'I will not. I did not do anything wrong.'

'I would advise it. It will make your life simpler.'

Abha listened to him quietly, then left the room. Inside she was fuming. What is it about these men—Indian, Japanese or any of them for that matter? Why can't they deal with a woman on an even footing? Why do they feel challenged and insecure by simply a look! It exasperated her.

Abha was still angry when she went to Mr. Murthy's for dinner that night. The First Secretary's house was big. It had a nice drawing room and three bedrooms. In the heart of Tokyo, it was pure luxury. Government of India did take care of its diplomats as was quite apparent.

It felt good to eat home-cooked food with *pooris*. Abha had nearly forgotten the taste of these things!

'You seem to be angry about something?' Diwakar was asking her. Half the people she had met at his exhibition were there for the dinner, as she had guessed.

'Yes I am. It's about the thing we discussed the other day ... ,' she told him about the issue being made of her demand for hostel accomodation.

'I would go by your supervisor's advice. For your Course Director it is now a question of saving face. Even if he wants to help you, he cannot until this issue is sorted out appropriately for him. Seek an appointment with him. For the others it would mean you are going to apologize. See how the meeting turns out, then act accordingly. For the Japanese, honour still counts. Don't you know about *hara kiri*? It is still very much a part of their psyche.'

'But I wasn't impolite. How can he hold the look in my eyes against me? And he actually tells my supervisor that! This is sheer madness.'

He just said quietly, 'Don't drag this matter.'

Abha mulled over things for the next two days. Then paying some heed to Diwakar and Murai sensei's advice, she sought an appointment with the Course Director, and went to meet him without any intention of offering an apology.

'Abha san, how are you? Murai sensei was saying that you have chosen foreign direct investment as your thesis topic. That should be useful with economic liberalization underway in your country. But you may have trouble finding data here?'

Diwakar had been right. For the Course Director the fact that she came to see him was enough. He really did not expect or need a formal apology. This seemed to be the key. Maintain harmony and hierarchy at all costs, at least on the surface.

Abha went to the nearest public phone booth after the meeting and called Diwakar's office.

'Thanks for your advice. It worked out just the way you had said it would. Anyway I had decided not to apologize for something I had not done, but he did not mention the other day at all.'

Before she knew, she had run out of the damn coins. The conversation was cut off midstream. She decided to call him from Tokyo the next day when she went for the internship. It would be cheaper.

The internship lectures were over and the group that came from different universities around Tokyo was moving towards the station. Angelo, a Mexican from another University, caught up with Abha.

'I have been meaning to ask you for sometime now. Will you have dinner with me this Friday evening Abha? We can meet at Sakuragicho station at 8 pm.'

Abha knew she had to decide in a split second. With the open, direct approach of a Westerner, he could sportingly take a 'no' as well. But why not? She had all the time and space in the world to experiment with a date. He was good looking despite a ponytail and could speak English.

'Okay will do. But we go *betsu betsu* right?'

'Hey I am not Japanese. This one is on me.' The Japanese tradition of splitting costs on all occasions was something they now well understood.

'We will see.' They parted ways at the station. Abha spotted a phone booth and remembered the aborted conversation of the previous day.

'Sorry about yesterday Diwakar. I ran out of coins.'

'That is why it is important to have a phone.'

'What were you saying yesterday when we got disconnected.'

'I don't remember. I will be going to Yokohama sometime middle of next week for a meeting. I can buy you a cup of coffee if you are free around 5 pm on Tuesday evening.'

'I will call you on Monday and we can decide.'

Married men had propositioned Abha many times in India; somehow this did not sound the same. In fact, Diwakar did not give that impression on any occasion. Anyway, Monday was far away. On Friday she had a date.

On Friday, Abha found herself smiling as she caught the train to Sakuragicho from Yokohama station. Angelo was waiting on the platform itself. They both punched out and walked towards the waterfront.

'There is a nice Indian restaurant in the shopping mall behind the waterfront. It's called "Maharaja". Would you like to go there?'

'Angelo, it is expensive and I know you get the same scholarship as I do, so forget it. Let us go somewhere more affordable.'

After dinner at a small café, they walked to the waterfront, sat on the steps and watched the lights. Abha felt strange. She had never gone on a date like this before. Here she was, thirty-three years old with a five-year-old daughter back home, dating a Mexican guy on a Japanese shore. It sounded crazy.

They chatted about their countries, cultures, homes and families. They had only exchanged pleasantries during the internship; Abha found that beyond a point it was difficult to talk at length to a foreigner in a personal setting. But Angelo did try hard. Music, movies, Japanese, food, weather—almost every subject under the sky was covered.

'You are the prettiest girl in the course. I am sure you are aware of that.'

'First, I am not a girl, I am a woman. Second, thanks for the compliment. Now it is getting rather late and we should be heading back.'

'It is so relaxing here. Let's sit for some more time.'

Abha knew instinctively that he would try to kiss her. In a way, she waited to see what would happen. It was strange to watch herself and the situation as an outsider. Something surreal about it.

And he did. He brought his face closer and lightly brushed her lips with his. In that instant, Abha caught his smell and realized she did not like it at all.

'Sorry Angelo. I really don't think I want to get into all this at all. Let's move.'

'Okay, no fuss.'

They walked back to the station. He took the rebuff in his stride. Soon enough they were talking about the course and both of them knew as they said bye at Sakuragicho station that there would be no second time.

How much was Abha going to learn about herself in this strange land? For the first time she realized that a man's smell mattered to her. Later, as she lay in bed, she wondered what else mattered to her that she did not even know of.

The sound of Nupur's laughter ran out loud and clear from the other room. The house seemed to light up as the melodious cackle of the little girl reverberated around. Shikha was home with her nine month old daughter for a few days.

In the house, normally there was only Amma and Simran. It had come alive with Nupur's arrival.

Simran left the kitchen and went to the room where Shikha, Nupur and Amma were sitting.

'Amma, my stomach is hurting. It must be the food I had yesterday on the train.' Shikha was complaining as Nupur sat on top of her.

'Come Nupur, come and sit on Simran Mausi's stomach instead.' Simran lay on the bed and Nupur clambered on to her. If she had been married, her own children would have been much older by now. Simran thought wistfully as she rocked Nupur. Whenever

Simran held Nupur in her arms something twisted in the pit of her stomach. Where had she gone wrong with Hussein? Simran could still not free herself from that dream. Maybe if he had married, she would have taken steps to move on in life. For a long time she had lived on hope. Now all hopes had receded, but the habit of Hussein was not disappearing. He had passed by Delhi a few weeks ago, and they had met in Ashok Yatri Niwas where he was staying. They had slept together after a long gap.

Once Simran came home, an empty feeling had settled in her being again. Maybe, when she saw Nupur, it was the empty feeling inside that twisted.

Diwakar and Abha were sitting in a café on the rooftop of a store at Yokohama station. It was Tuesday evening and after finishing his work in Yokohama they had met at the station. The city lights seemed far away down below. At eye level, there was only darkness all around. Abha watched as Diwakar placed the order in immaculate Japanese.

'How did you journey from a village near Belgaum to Tokyo—it is a long journey.'

'For me education provided the wings. A government school for meritorious children from the rural areas had opened at the district headquarters. I joined it on a scholarship after an exam in class five. The canvas changed. And it has been changing ever since.'

'So what does a small-town guy feel now after becoming a big-town person?'

'That primarily we were taught to be idealistic. Our school teachers dared us to dream so that we could build a new world order. They never prepared us for the real world.'

Abha looked at the dark outside. In big towns, they were never encouraged to dream about changing the world in school. Dreams were all about individual achievement and competition. With the passage of time, the baggage of cynicism simply grew heavier. That is what she found to be singularly absent in Diwakar's personality. The total absence of cynicism and weariness; instead, there was a childlike appreciation of everything around. Something she herself had lost somewhere along the way.

'I am thinking of doing something on foreign direct investment issues for my thesis topic. I will collect some data when I travel next to India. Do you have anything that you think can be useful for me?'

'I am sure something will be there. When you come to Tokyo next week drop in at my office. By then I would have put together some relevant material. Have you been to Kamakura? It has a beautiful Buddha in the open. Legend has it that if you visit Kamakura once you will always come back to Japan.'

'Yes I have. And, because I learnt of the legend only later, I revisited it with Parul. If I visit this country again it has to be with her.'

'So what do you think of marriage?'

'Well it is good because you can have children.'

'That is one of the most interesting replies I have ever got.'

'Why, do you ask everyone you meet this question?'

'I do ask many people. Just to see what's the first thing that they mention.'

'And you? What is your take on it?'

'I think that any relationship in general follows the theory of fantasy and exposure.'

'That's pretty grim.'

'Not at all. Exposure doesn't mean the end. It can build further fantasies.'

The place was filling up around them. Clouds of cigarette smoke started to swirl around the room, smoking being a favourite activity in Japan across age and gender.

'Slowly this place will become suffocating, so let's move. I will catch the train from the station. That was an interesting cup of coffee. See you next week in Tokyo.'

They came down to the platform entrance and with a wave of the hand, he vanished across into the crowd after punching in with his ticket.

Diwakar was the kind of person who never made a splash at the first meeting. He had a quiet intelligence, and an unobtrusive and reassuring presence. Abha rather liked him, and especially talking with him.

Outside the station, it was cool. The hot and humid summer had made way for the cool autumn breeze. Trees were shedding leaves. Autumn felt no different in Yokohama from Delhi. Abha's mind drifted to a forthcoming trip. The foreign students were to go to Nagano, nestled in the Hida Mountains, which form part of the Japanese Alps. The brilliant hues of the maple leaves in autumn would be the highlight of the trip.

The news had spread in the last few days like wildfire through the good offices of Peter. Nearly seven months in Japan and they were all still struggling with the language, the prices, the food and homesickness. The desire to see Japan beyond the limits of Tokyo and its 'dormitory towns' was strong and this opportunity was greeted with great enthusiasm.

On the appointed day, the bus left Yokohama early morning. As the bus moved away from the bustling Kanto area, the surroundings became soft and green. The roads were smooth; houses with sloping roofs dotted the beautiful countryside. The view from the bus window was like a quaint picture postcard. Abha realized that Japan, outside Tokyo and its surrounding areas, was simply spectacular.

'*Momiji-gari* or maple-leaf viewing is a traditional Japanese passion and people travel long distances to see the autumn colours,' speaking into a mike, Yori sensei, the accompanying faculty member on the trip explained to the cacophonous bunch in the bus. The miles rolled past and soon the bus started moving higher and higher. The bright afternoon sun was at its peak and with the passing hours a lull had descended in the bus. The road gradually turned, and spread out in front were the mountains. The slopes were splashed with colours—vivid patches of flaming red, bright orange, yellow, bluish-green and even grey, like the palette of some celestial painter.

As if in a trance, Abha watched this celebration of life. Even Peter had slumped into silence as the fading sunlight frolicked on the mountain slopes.

After a night spent sleeping on *futons* in a *ryokan*, a traditional inn, the next day was spent seeing the colourful leaves at close quarters while walking on designated trails in the mountains. During the day, the group visited a rural house meant to enable visitors to observe traditional Japanese living. Flaming red, a resplendent maple tree stood in the neatly laid out garden in the backyard. When the wind stirred the flames, some leaves fluttered to the ground and added to the red carpet spread out below the tree. The vivid colourful image of that tree stayed with Abha all the way as they journeyed back to Yokohama in the evening.

Autumn had always evoked melancholic images of fading colours and falling leaves back home. But in Japan, Abha understood how beautiful, vivid and inspiring it could be.

Night had fallen by the time they wound their way uphill to the campus of the University in Yokohama. When Abha shut her eyes, the beautiful, colourful hills flashed past.

Nature teaches that change is a certainty, an essential part of the celebration of life. Then why do we resent and fear change … .

The Day Lingers

When Nana and Mausi returned in the late afternoon, Parul remained cloistered in her room. She had neither eaten her food nor changed her clothes. Mausi is knocking at the door. Parul knows she has to open it. She realizes that their return meant Ma was married, and had gone to his house. She hates everyone at that moment.

'Parul let us have lunch and then you can go and spend the afternoon with Nani.'

Parul does not want to meet or speak with anyone. She stretches in her bed and remembers the time when only three months were left for Ma's return from Japan. She was nearly six and often wondered why her Papa had white hair while all her friends had fathers who had black hair. There was some thing which she did not follow, but she did not know. She had asked Nani about Papa's hair colour and Nani told her that many people dyed their hair while her Papa did not.

Deep inside, Parul knewn something was amiss in this reply, but at six, so many other things claimed attention. Then, she went to Bina Mausi's house and chanced upon a photograph. Her mother dressed like a bride and a man next to her. Parul had instinctively known that this was a key to the gap. She had rushed to Bina Mausi and asked her about it.

'Parul this photo was taken when your Ma was participating in a play some time ago.' Mausi had looked unsure, but her voice carried no hesitation. Parul had accepted the reply, but decided to question Nani when she reached Delhi.

When she asked Nani, she received the same response. She knew that they were all lying. She decided to probe further.

'Nani what play was this? When did Ma do it? Who is this man with her?'

'Parul your Ma will be here in some time. Why don't you ask her? I don't remember the details.'

Parul realized that the key to the gap in her mind lay only with Ma. She had been waiting for her return anyway, but now the wait became all the more impatient. She now waited with the burden of unanswered questions in her heart.

Then Ma came, just as she had promised, on her birthday. They had organized a small party for her friends. The whole day passed in chatter, cake cutting and opening of Ma's suitcases. It was only at around midnight that she had Ma to herself. The moment they lay down in bed she asked the question she had spent months forming in her mind.

'Ma were you ever married?'

'Yes.'

Parul remembers the relief that had swept over her body.

'Thank god, you did not lie to me.'

She had hugged her mother and then over the days she had understood difficult words like 'divorce', 'custody' and 'single parent'. She had been relieved; the gaps in her mind had filled up.

Then Parul had gone back to her life of toys, friends and school. Now again she is expected to understand new words like 'remarriage' and 'new father'.

Parul gets up and opens the door. She sits with Nana and Mausi and gobbles some food while Reena Didi fusses around her.

After food, she leaves with Nana for the hospital. Parul knows Nani will try to explain to her all over again, the same things she has been repeating for the last few months. She understands the reality at the surface, even accepts it, but it hurts for some reason Parul cannot comprehend.

When she walks in Nani spreads out her arms and Parul runs into her embrace. There is so much comfort in her arms—Parul sought them so often when Ma was away in Japan. She even found a trace of Ma's smell in Nani. She plays with Nani, tells her things that often she does not share with Ma. Especially these days.

'Parul did you eat something?'

'Yes Nani.'

'Tomorrow there is a small party in the evening for friends and relatives.'

'I know Nani, and then we are all going to Goa—all three of us. Then we will go to his hometown.'

Parul still does not have any name for him. Until sometime ago, she had called him 'uncle', but she knows it has to change.

All of a sudden all her pent up frustration pours out in a torrent of tears. As she weeps inconsolably, Nani hugs her and lets her cry.

'You know him Parul. For quite sometime now. You have spent time with him. So you don't have to worry.'

'It's not him Nani. He is okay. I cannot bear the idea that my mother is getting married. Now I will have to share her with him all the time. Until sometime ago, it was only for a part of the day, now all the time there will be someone else. Now he will be with her in our room and I will have to shift.'

Aarti Devi knows that she has no platitudes for these fears. Time would bring its own solutions. Time the eternal healer.

'I hate her Nani. I will never love her again.'

Even as she says it, Parul knows, as well as Nani, it is not true. Parul knows that Ma did not say 'yes' till Parul agreed to the marriage. Ma is always there for her—she knows. And he is considerate too, never imposing, just letting her be. Maybe it will turn out well. Somewhere amidst all her confusion, Parul prays that it will.

Yokohama, Unveiled

When Abha visited Diwakar's office for the first time, she saw that the window had only other buildings as a view. There were bright lights, and innumerable computer screens with people hunched over them. The whole ambience had a kind of dehumanized feel. People interacted more with their computer than with other people. This was the future?

Diwakar's cabin, tucked in a corner, had all the gadgets an office could ever need. Abha remembered her office in India. They were like two different universes. There was a long way to go before Government became paperless and computer driven in a real sense.

Diwakar heaped some material on the desk.

'Thanks, I will have a look. If you come across anything else, keep it. I will pass by and pick it up.'

'How will I tell you Abha? You still don't have a phone.'

'I am planning to buy one by the end of this week. Parul will be coming in next month. I am so happy.'

'We must have you over then.'

'I have been to so many of these Indian community dinners now. How do you sustain it? This constant meeting and eating with the same people. Conversations are often limited and the same things are repeated.'

'Come on Abha. You want to know where there is a sale, where you can buy cheap cloth, shoes, etc. The Indian community is the best guide. They know all about that.'

'You know what I mean. On a personal level, people are much better. Jyoti and I met up for lunch twice and had great fun.'

'Once here you cannot isolate yourself from the community. The family needs it.'

They left his office and Abha accepted his offer to drop her to the nearest station. On the way to Meguro station, he drove through Ginza, Tokyo's high fashion avenue, full of bright neon lights that hid the stars above.

'Look at Ginza from the back glass of the car. It has a different and interesting look.'

She peeped behind. The receding lights made her feel as if life was being left behind somewhere.

'Let me know your number as soon as you get the phone,' Diwakar said as Abha got off the car. Abha nodded, waved and was lost in the teeming crowds.

Once back at Yokohama station, Abha took a bus to the University. The idea of shutting herself behind the door of her apartment depressed her. In the dormitory there would be some life. That evening her coursemates had decided to dine together bringing in what each had cooked. Abha bought ice cream and they all gathered round the table.

The table was loaded with strange and unfamiliar food. After the meal, they sang songs from their respective countries, and sat there remembering home, family and friends. Whatever the country, culture or religion one came from—what hurt or gave happiness was pretty much the same. And women—their problems were much the same. The degree, intensity and format of the problem may change, but the struggle and agitation was essentially similar and familiar.

Abha installed a phone in her room. It made a great difference to her life. She could speak to Parul whenever she wanted. One night Parul called to say that she had lost her first tooth. Abha felt miserable. She was not there when something so momentous had happened to her daughter. It was past midnight, but she had dialled Mary's number and cried. Mary consoled her and helped her through it. In the morning sunshine, Abha found her own behaviour inexplicable!

At times, the phone would ring in the morning.

'Today there is some interesting news on the Net about Indian elections. Want to know?'

Diwakar would call her whenever there was some interesting news on the internet.

'Thanks but I am running for class. Will call you when I get back.'

'You give me a call and then I will call you back. That way you save on the bill.'

Sometimes he could be thoughtful, actually most of the time.

The human mind is much like a mathematical equation; take out one variable and the entire function changes. Once Parul's stay in India was decided, time started flying. University, internship, cooking, walking, meeting people—life's pace at times made Abha breathless. Autumn had given way to winter and it had become cold. Abha waited impatiently for it to snow. She had never seen snow in reality, only in movies. Parul was coming to Japan for her holidays, and Abha's apartment again started taking on the hues of a home. She collected movies, toys and chocolates in anticipation of Parul's arrival.

Abha was worried, as she would be left with some classes even after Parul's arrival.

After the lesson that the accomodation issue gave about the Japanese, Abha found things were not so bad. The University had not provided her accommodation, but the professors were kind enough to allow her five-year old to sit in the classroom. Parul sat in one corner of the lecture room, playing with her dolls, while Abha attended the last few classes before winter break. With a quiet understanding, Parul cooperated wholeheartedly in the strange arrangement.

Abha was sitting in Murai sensei's room that continued to be a heap of books, while Parul played on the floor, when Abha noticed them. The small flakes drifting from the sky.

'It is snowing. Parul look its snowing! Murai sensei just look out of the window.'

Soft flaky snow was drifting outside the window.

'It comes every year Abha san. And when it lasts for many days it becomes slushy, dirty and quite depressing.'

'But Sensei it is beautiful. Just breathtaking. When you see something like this for the first time it completely overwhelms.'

After the meeting, Parul and Abha walked towards the bus stop with snowflakes swirling around.

'Ma it is so soft. You don't feel it at all. Just look at you—you seem to be under a shower of cotton.'

It was magical to walk in the snow for the first time. The world seemed covered under a white sheet. As if a curtain had fallen on all things. It snowed intermittently the whole night.

The next morning, when Abha and Parul ventured out, the entire city was covered with snow. Trees had snow-laden branches, cars had become heaps of snow, and the roads were trying to peep out from beneath the white sheet. Murai sensei had been right; it had become quite slippery and slushy. It remained the same for the next few days. It snowed intermittently and the whole city became white. After the initial euphoria, the bleak and colourless white became rather monotonous.

'Ma when will this white go and things become normal and colourful again?'

'We are actually going to see more snow in Hokkaido in the north of Japan for two days, so you had better get used to it Parul.'

The phone began to ring. 'So how is the snow going in Yokohama? In Tokyo we are buried under snow.'

'Same here. How are things with you Diwakar? Parul is here for a month and we are having a great time.'

'I actually called about that. I wanted to invite you both to dinner at my place next week on Friday.'

'But we are going to Hokkaido for three days. The foreign students have organized a group tour at reasonable rates so we joined in. Sorry, not this time.'

'Call me when you are back and take lots of things to keep warm. It is much colder over there. Hope you both will be there to attend the New Year party at Murthy's house.'

'Yes we will. See you.'

The New Year party at Mr. Murthy's was an all-Indian affair. The room was full. The men sat in one group while the women in another. Abha watched as the children played some games. Another year had crept in.

Looking back, it was unimaginable that just a couple of years ago she was doing the rounds of dreary courts and lawyers. It already seemed like a bad dream. Then it had overwhelmed her, but the distance from it had grown rapidly. How her life had changed. She had never imagined that at thirty-three she would be in Japan, a single mother, studying and rediscovering her own sense of curiosity.

'At last I get to meet the young lady I have heard so much about. She is really cute.'

'Thanks. Is this how the whole evening will go? The men and women in separate groups, with the men drinking and the women chatting and going to the kitchen alternately. You don't drink Diwakar?'

'Small town *sanskar* you can say. I have not yet started is how I put it.'

'So you leave some scope for the future? Why don't we organize some games or something? Better still tell me what do the Japanese do on New Year?'

'They go to shrines in or around their neighbourhoods, light candles and pray to their ancestors or gods.'

'Sounds beautiful.'

'You want to go and see?'

'Oh yes. It would be interesting'

At midnight, the whole room had reverberated with wishes of 'Happy New Year'. Then the food appeared on the table, the most attractive part of the evening.

While Abha was gorging on the delicious Indian meal, Diwakar informed her, 'After food, a group will walk down to a shrine nearby. Join in.'

A motley group of about seven from the gathering set out for the shrine. The night was clear and there was a chill in the breeze. Some distance from the apartment block, tucked away, was a small Shinto shrine. There was a long queue outside. People of all ages stood with candles in their hands and waited for their turn. Abha discovered it was much like visiting a temple back home. At the entrance, they first washed their hands, and then lit incense sticks. Then the candles were placed on the ground before the sanctum and they had to clap. The long line of flickering candles cast a benign and mysterious shadow inside the temple.

Abha stood there with Parul, hands clasped and eyes closed. What to pray for? She could think of nothing that she actively wished for anymore. A sense of equanimity had taken hold—was it a blessing not to have anything to wish for or was it the death of dreams? She could not decide.

As the group walked back to Mr. Murthy's house, Diwakar asked, 'You seem pensive after going to the shrine Abha.'

'I found that I had nothing to pray or wish for fervently. Just asked God to bless us.'

'How can you stop dreaming? I believe that a person is as big as his or her dreams. The essence of life is the capacity to see new dreams everyday.'

'You poets—all the time talking about dreams. Life is all about reality.'

'There is no duality between the two—dreams build realities.'

'Please it's New Year. I want to begin it on a simple and happy note.'

'Then start dreaming.'

'Let me begin it by thanking you for organizing this visit. It was serene and refreshing. I never thought the Japanese were religious. I had asked Murai sensei about religion, and he had said that Japanese are born Buddhists, marry according to Christian rites and are buried as per Shinto tradition. Quite an interesting explanation I thought.'

'Wishes and dreams have nothing to do with religion. All the people at the shrine were lighting candles to reinforce their own dreams, to themselves, at the dawn of the New Year.'

Parul had returned to India. At the airport Abha had wept, and her little daughter had put her arms around her and advised her. 'Ma you don't cry. Here you are alone, there I have Papa and Nani. Okay?'

When Abha returned to her apartment, she could hear the phone ringing inside as she turned the key.

'She left? Why don't you come down to Tokyo for a cup of coffee now? It will make you feel better.'

'Diwakar that is really thoughtful of you, but Tokyo is really far and I am tired. Tomorrow I am coming for the internship. I will drop in to your office later, if that is alright with you.'

'Sure, do that. I also have some more papers that may help in your study.'

The stillness of the room seemed to overpower Abha. Parul's things were strewn around the bed. The utensils were in the sink and a half-finished drawing was on the floor. Abha felt utterly lonely. She called Mary and Lin, but both were out. To escape the confines of the room, she embarked on one of her long and solitary walks. A long, rambling and aimless walk.

When Abha returned to her apartment, the phone was ringing again. She leapt at it.

'Hi lady what's new?' Rekha. The eternal interviewer.

'So you remembered me. You never replied to my emails. I had given up on you.'

'I have called you now, isn't it? It's far better. How does an email matter? So how are things, what's new? Found someone? I hope you are having some good sex.'

'I tried, but it doesn't work that way for me Rekha.'

'You really know how to waste time. In college you spent time hanging around waiting for that guy from St. Stephens. And now I don't know what you are waiting for.'

'Wish I knew myself.'

'I called to tell you that I will be in India in Feb or March. Will you be coming then? Let me know your dates so that we can synchronize and meet up.'

'Will do. How is the man in your life? You still with him? Any long term plans?'

'Not yet. I am comfortable with this arrangement. Abha I am away from India and its tangles, so I can afford to live the way I want.'

'What about him?'

'Frankly that is not my problem. I am only concerned about what I want. Gotta go now. Tell me your programme on mail. Bye.'

The phone was still in Abha's hand when the line went dead. Was that what life was all about—knowing what one wants and then doing just that? On that count, she had not fared too badly. She had actually done what she wanted most of the time and had willingly paid the price too. Had Ujjwal been a waste of time? Definitely not. It was more than a decade since they knew each other. They had different lives, had grown older but still remained on each other's horizon. Their interaction had never followed any set pattern. Ever.

Abha went outside and put clothes in the washing machine in the corridor, and came in and started cleaning the room. She missed Simran suddenly. It was always like this; the urge to reach out to Simran caught her unawares. She wondered what Simran was doing these days. It had been a long time since she had heard from her. Life was unfair at times. Of the three of them, Simran was the one most suitable for marriage. She was the ideal wife material, but she had never actually got around to it at all.

They had come far from college days. To a life totally distinct and different from the one they had imagined for themselves. Was this the sum of life? After every few years, on looking back, you find yourself standing on a strange and unknown road, awaiting the next milestone.

The evening had deepened and the neon signs around Shibuya station were slowly coming to life. From where Abha stood outside the station, a huge screen played advertisements. She scanned the crowds for any sign of Diwakar. They had decided to meet at Shibuya station, since Diwakar had come for a meeting nearby. Once the correct exit was identified, there was little chance of missing each other at a station. Abha wanted to collect the papers he had found for her thesis work.

Abha watched the young girls milling around. There were hordes of schoolgirls, or at least girls dressed like schoolgirls, around, looking unreal and make-believe. Perhaps she was growing old, but the style of dressing and make-up displayed was definitely not her sense of beauty.

Love hotel signs twinkled all around the periphery of the station. Initially Abha had found the idea dreadful. These were places that one could hire for a short duration—even hours. Over time, she had realized they were practical. Instead of having couples harassed in public parks by the police as it happened in Delhi, or have them do it behind bushes—this made sense. It was a typical Japanese way of order and method—providing facilities for what is needed. Diwakar was late. Abha decided to move after waiting for another ten minutes. Hectic activity was going on around the station. Couples were getting together and disappearing into the lanes of Shibuya. The department stores, advertisements, people, fashion—the glitter and glaze of it was blinding. She had begun to move towards the station entrance when he had arrived.

'Sorry Abha, the meeting went on longer than I expected. Let us go to an Indian restaurant nearby.'

Abha was irritated. Her patience was limited and she hated waiting.

'Actually I can take the papers and move from here itself.'

'If that is what you want. However, it would be more practical for you to eat something; it will take you nearly one and half hours to reach your place.'

He did always manage to soothe her ruffled nerves with quiet, calm and sensible statements. Quietly they walked towards the restaurant, and once inside Abha realized that she was famished.

'This academic year will be ending in a few months. Do you have plans to go to India during the break or you are planning to call Parul here?'

'No, I think I will try and go. Depending on the ticket I can get. Don't you go home sometimes?'

'I will go at the end of the year. My family will go in summer.'

'The food here is good. It has been ages since I ate roti. I have become a veteran rice eater. Diwakar, I even enjoy the sticky Japanese rice now. The way a place grows on you.'

'Much like people.'

'People also grow out and away. I now feel life is a procession of people that one picks up along the way and then slowly discards as time passes. There are just a few who actually do the whole journey together. I have maybe two to three people, apart from my family, I can see knowing and caring about to the very end.'

'You are lucky Abha. I have no one I can claim that for. The people of my childhood and college got lost somewhere during the journey I made, and later you rarely build those kinds of bonds.'

'I think this discussion is getting too dismal, let us shift to something more cheerful.'

Diwakar smiled. He looked around at the brightly lit restaurant and said, 'Agreed. So let me tell you that whenever I look into your eyes I can never forget I am a man.'

Abha burst out laughing. 'I can't believe it Diwakar, you are trying to flirt with me? I think we passed that stage long ago.'

'Absolutely not. I am just telling you a fact. That is all. Now it is time to move or you will miss the last bus from Yokohama station to your place.'

He walked with her to the station entrance and then moved towards his car. Abha punched in and stood in the queue at the platform. It was late and most of the men in the queue had faces flushed from beer. However, she felt no sense of fear or insecurity.

The interaction with Diwakar had undergone a kind of subtle change with his comment. Was she blind that she never saw it coming? They spoke to each other nearly everyday. They met up quite often. Moreover, it had been an individual connection—no social or family thing. The train rolled in and Abha boarded it. She would think about it later, if the need arose.

They sat in complete silence. The green and brown stark interiors were not at all aesthetic. There was no clock in the room, but somehow Abha felt that time was ticking away somewhere. What was she doing in the love hotel with Diwakar? Well she was an adult and so was he—they were both there by consent for a specific purpose. But she sat like stone on a chair while he sat on the bed. Over the last month, ever since the fateful day in the Indian restaurant in Shibuya, things had changed. They called each other often, and tried to meet up as frequently as possible. Abha had let it happen. Maybe somewhere Lin's logic about married men being safer had appealed to her. The time in Japan was a slice of life that belonged totally to her, and she decided to do just what she wanted. So, she found herself in the love hotel ready for what was to follow.

But it had turned out different. Perhaps it was her middle class upbringing. The strangeness of the love hotel, the idea that there were two hours and then the phone would ring to ask if the time was to be extended, or it was the man in front of her—it simply froze her. She felt stupid and a prude, but could do nothing to overcome it.

'Sorry Diwakar.'

'For what? There is nothing to be sorry about. Let's go.'

Once outside the hotel, Abha felt relieved. Now what? Where does this leave them? She had wanted to ask, but could not. A sense of complete foolishness enveloped her. In silence they made their way to Shinagawa station in Diwakar's car. Not a word was exchanged.

'I will call you tomorrow.' He said, as he dropped her at Shinagawa station.

As she saw his car drive off Abha wondered if both of them would speak to each other ever again.

The next morning as she was leaving for the University the phone rang.

'Abha it is now Sakura season. Next week when you come to Tokyo take some time out and we will go to Yoyogi Park to see the Sakura. Now I know you are running late. So give me a call when you have time.'

He had called her and somehow as she spoke to him the memory of the debacle last evening seemed to fade. Did it really matter so much? Maybe it was better this way.

During the day, Abha had her weekly meeting with Murai sensei. After finishing the discussion he said, 'I am giving a flute recital in Kawasaki on Saturday. I wish to invite you to it and for a dinner afterwards.'

'Sensei that is wonderful. I would love to come. Please tell me where I should meet you.'

'At Kawasaki station, on the platform where trains come in from the Tokyo side. I will be coming from Tokyo. Be there at 5.30 pm.' On Saturday, they met at the appointed place and walked to the venue. The recital was in a small auditorium. Murai sensei played the flute rather well. At the end, after a lot of incessant bowing, they left the auditorium.

'We will go to Yokohama station and have a Japanese meal in traditional style. There is a good restaurant I know there.'

In half-an-hour, Abha found herself seated on the floor across a low table from Murai sensei. Abha wondered fleetingly at the cost distribution the meal would entail, but decided to enjoy the new place. She had started loving tempura, but had not developed a taste for sushi yet.

'I should have taken you out for a traditional meal much earlier as your academic advisor, but I have been rather busy.'

That explained the impetus for the outing. The food Murai sensei ordered was tasty and was served in an artistic manner.

'In summer you should try and climb Fuji san. The sunrise from there is beautiful. It is like a pilgrimage for most Japanese.'

'Have you done it Sensei?'

'Twice. It is quite a tough climb you know. How do you like the internship?'

As the evening progressed, the restaurant became full. Most of the patrons were men. As usual, smoke started filling up the room. Thankfully, Murai sensei did not smoke, but as was usual with the Japanese, after two beers his face had become beetroot red.

'Have you been to a karaoke joint Abha san?'

'No Sensei, I do know that it is the national pastime here, along with pachinko of course!'

'Pachinko is boring. You just put your money in the slots and turn the machine. Quite passive. I enjoy karaoke much more. Let us go to a karaoke place nearby. For this meal, you pay only five hundred yen as you are a student. The karaoke will be on me.'

It was Abha's first trip to a karaoke lounge. Murai sensei paid some money and he was given a TV with a mike. He selected songs and began to sing along with the music.Most of the patrons at the karaoke were young couples. They slouched around the place and sang along. Murai sensei seemed to enjoy himself immensely. He chose an English song and asked Abha to sing too. Abha joined in, but she found the whole thing quite boring. By the time they came out of the karaoke lounge, it was time for his last train and her last bus.

'*Domo arigato* Sensei. That was really nice.'

Automatically they both bowed to each other and left. Just some months ago, Abha had found the bowing strange. She did it now as if she had been bowing all her life! A gentle spring breeze was blowing at the bus stop as she waited. The Sakura season had begun and before one could drink its ephemeral beauty, the blossoms would wither away.

The cherry blossoms or Sakura were in full bloom. Yoyogi Park was blooming and laden with Sakura trees glistening in the spring sunlight. Groups of people sat under the trees, picnickers enjoying the gorgeous view. Delicate white blooms with a pink hue shrouded the dark brown branches. It seemed like nature's own symphony expressing the union of yin and yang. The flowering Sakura trees were a sight to behold.

They had met after the Shibuya debacle for the first time, and Abha had thought the meeting would be stilted and awkward.

'Cherry blossom viewing is a national celebration here. People go to famous parks to watch this beautiful spectacle.'

'It is absolutely delicate and fragile Diwakar. No wonder it doesn't last long.'

'Things that don't last long also have an impact.'

'How come you always have a view that is diametrically opposite to mine?'

'Because you and I see things in a different way. But that is what makes it interesting.'

They strolled around the park and watched the people milling about. It had not turned out to be awkward or odd as Abha had thought it would be.

'Have you climbed Mount Fuji?' Abha asked.

'Not yet. Never got down to doing it. Abha, will you climb with me this summer?'

He had said it so simply. There was an innocence in him that belied his age and exposure.

'Yes.'

Parul was sitting in her lap; Mummy was reclining in the bed, with a cup of steaming tea, while Papa was busy with some papers. Abha had come for twenty days at the end of the academic year and was enjoying every minute of it.

'So what do you like most about Japan?'

'Mummy that it is safe and there is total anonymity.'

'And the people?'

'They are polite, but not spontaneous. Somehow they all seem programmed to be polite, but there is a lack of warmth.'

The phone was ringing as it had been since the two days she had arrived. Bina di was planning to come for a few days with her children. Simran was planning a day off and Rekha was arriving over the weekend. The days at home for the small vacation held the promise of a nice time.

'Hi. How are you?'—Ujjwal—the only missing link.

'Hi Ujjwal. I am fine. Hope this time you are going to be around. Are you in Bombay?'

'I moved to Delhi about three months ago. I did mention it in my mail.'

'I know. But you travel a great deal.'

'Let us have lunch next week. On Tuesday?'

'That is fine. Will catch you then.'

The days in Delhi raced by. Simran had not been able to take a day off, so Abha visited her in her office. They walked down to the Udipi restaurant and lunched over steaming idlis and a cup each of South Indian coffee.

'Imagine Simran, life has changed so much, but this joint hasn't changed at all. The same guy sits behind the counter with the photos of all the gods behind him. Even the food tastes the same.'

Abha sensed a strange sadness in Simran, a quiet desperation of sorts. In fact, she could not recall when she had last seen Simran happy or smiling. A kind of melancholy had become part of Simran's personality.

'What's up Simran? Is there something?'

'I don't know Abha, these past few months I have been feeling such a sense of vacuum. I can't pinpoint the exact reason.'

Maybe, because emotionally and actually you are stuck in a situation that is not going anywhere. It is just static, Abha wanted to say, but kept quiet. This journey towards something more conclusive, Simran had to undertake on her own.

'You know Abha I will always love Hussein, but … .' For the first time, in all the years Simran had mentioned a 'but'. 'Abha till sometime ago, just the fact that he was there in my life, in any manner was enough. But now, something inside has changed. I really don't know how to deal with it.'

A great distance has to be traversed before we can finally 'see' ourselves from a distance. And, till we see it ourselves, nothing in the world can do it for us.

'This is part of the process called life, Simran. Somewhere along the way we need to cut the ropes to find ourselves. Maybe you need to find a new equilibrium within yourself, in your relationships.'

'Like Ujjwal and you?'

Ujjwal? The lunch had been great. They had caught up on their lives, on work, children and parents. Was that what it was—a different equilibrium between them, nurtured over the years? Abha wondered.

'Maybe. I have never sat and analysed it like this for myself before,' Abha answered.

'You found someone in Japan?'

Abha sat pondering over the question. Had she found someone? Did Diwakar fit the 'finding' bill? Had she been actively 'finding' someone really?

'Not really Simran. Life is so different there. When I am there, I am like a different person. Very selfish, self-centred and thinking only about myself.'

'I feel now it is important to be like that at times.'

Outside the restaurant, the spring evening of Delhi was struggling with the summer that was threatening to drown its very existence. Tilak Road was full of traffic and people were rushing to catch the DTC buses on their way home. Nothing had changed and yet everything had changed. For them.

Rekha looked good and confident as usual. She had not spread out as Punjabi girls often did. She was in terrific shape, dressed in designer wear, looking as if she had stepped out of a fashion magazine. In the midst of chaotic Connaught Place, at the serene and quiet Imperial Hotel, courtesy Rekha's expense account, Abha and she were at lunch again. The two of them sat there ensconced in piped music, hushed ambience and good food.

'So tell me what's new?'

'Rekha when will you stop expecting something new each time we speak?'

'But if there is nothing new, life becomes so boring!'

'You tell me, what is new in your life?'

'I am into the fold of a Buddhist guru out there. I find so much peace in chanting the mantras he has given me. The job and the guy are going great guns. I travel a lot too.'

Abha was astounded. This was something she had never associated with Rekha.

'You into a guru? What has gone wrong with you? Religion was the last thing on your mind.'

'You know Abha, at times I feel so empty. Then chanting the mantras gives me real peace.'

'I think Rekha, we are all going through a mid-life crisis. Even Simran was talking about this kind of thing the other day. We are all in our mid-thirties, nearly, and it probably has hit us.'

'Maybe. But you at least have a daughter.'

Rekha had said it in a matter of fact manner, but a tinge of wistfulness seemed to hover around the sentence. It caught Abha by surprise. Parul—was it because she was there that Abha never felt empty? She did feel alone and lonely at times, but not empty. Was the great fable of motherhood being the prime fulfiller actually true?

'Nothing stops you from having a kid Rekha—if that is what you want.'

'That is what I do not want Abha, it is too great a responsibility. What I meant was that I increasingly feel these days that beyond a certain age you want to live for something other than yourself—it can be a kid, a cause … .'

'A guru? Please Rekha don't get into it like that. And why I am at the other end—I want to just live for myself for sometime. On my own terms.'

'It's a cycle. You've done one part of it, now you want the other. We are the middle generation Abha. Our mothers always lived for others, we are oscillating in between. Maybe your daughter's generation will be able to live just for themselves the way men do—without guilt, without sanction.'

Living without guilt, without sanction—the dream of generations of women. To break the two chains that bound them under the guise of religion, duty, motherhood and everything else for centuries.

As she drove back home after the lunch, Abha noticed that the flowers in the roundabouts in Delhi had started to wilt under the scorching sun. Soon the temperatures would rise, coolers would start whirring, load shedding would begin, water would be short, the Amaltas would bloom with the flaming Gulmohar and Delhi would be drenched in its glorious summer. But Abha wouldn't be there to see it as in a week's time she would be back in faraway Japan.

Once Abha returned to Japan, the hard work expected in the final year completely swallowed her up. Preparations for the internship presentation, assignments, thesis writing and chasing the University authorities for accommodation took up all her time. They had not yet relented, and Abha had not given up either. A harmonious tug of war on the accommodation issue carried on.

Nearly three weeks after her return, Abha waited for Diwakar outside Meguro station. The breeze in Tokyo was still cool and many of the commuters rushing back and forth were clad in light sweaters and shawls. Delhi would be sweltering in the month of May. For Abha, Delhi was the benchmark, to understand and relate to any other place. Like a constant canvas, the city stretched across her mind's landscape. The evening was darkening and the rush hour of the commuters in

Tokyo had begun. A sea of surging humanity passed her by. Diwakar had pulled up on the other side and was flashing the car lights to attract her attention. She crossed the road and got into the car.

'How was Delhi?'

'Good. I met everyone who mattered.'

'I thought as much. You look happy.'

Diwakar always commented on her mood, never on her looks.

'And you? How have things been here?'

'Tokyo missed you.'

'When I am there, this city seems unreal, but when I am here Delhi never fades from my consciousness.'

'You love Delhi. Any one or anything you love remains a part of your consciousness even if they are not around. They become a part of your stream of consciousness, so there is never a disconnect.'

They reached O'Daiba pier, and sat in a small restaurant for coffee. The water in front and the shiplights floating on it, gave the place a sense of detachment from the hectic pace of Tokyo.

'I am planning a trip to Mount Fuji in the second week of June, hope you will join me.'

Abha remembered seeing the mystical mountain closely on the way to Nagano. The bus had turned a corner and they had seen Mount Fuji, glistening in the autumn sun. Clad in glittering snow, it rose to meet the sky in all its pristine glory, absolutely alone. Was it so mesmerizing because it stood alone and distinct in that landscape? That solitary splendour created a haunting image.

'I will.'

'Wear sturdy shoes, cover up and be prepared for an arduous walk. We will start in the evening and try to catch the sunrise at the summit.'

'Do you like hiking generally?'

'No. But this is different. It is a journey of the mind too.'

Abha watched him as the breeze caught his hair while he looked out into the darkness of the water. He was looking good. Maybe it was true, beauty does lie in the eyes of the beholder.

'What are you writing these days?'

'Some poetry about my hometown Belgaum. How it was so long ago. When I think about it, I feel I am still stuck mentally in Belgaum. All my writing is centred around it.'

'How come? Doesn't Japan figure anywhere in your writing?'

'It does, but more as a comparison, a counterpoint. The longing and yearning is for the life left behind.'

'Probably because it is the place you grew up in. Like I have discovered how much I love Delhi only after I left it so far behind.'

'It is interesting; I have never lived in Delhi, only passed by. I found it big and isolating. These days I feel I must move beyond the bonds of Belgaum. There is an urge to broaden the creative horizon.'

The lights at O'Daiba pier were bright and beautiful. The stillness of the water nearby and the sounds of Tokyo could both be heard clearly.

'I always thought the 'poet-types' were quite insufferable. Although I am an avid reader, poetry is one thing that never catches my attention. When I see poetry in a magazine, I just skip the pages. I am much more a prose person.'

'Prose is also poetry. Anything that is an expression of love for life is poetry. It is not something distinct from life or compartmentalized. Even a bright smile is poetry.'

'Really Diwakar, sometimes I am amazed. How do you have such an abiding passion for life?'

'What is life without passion Abha? You think you don't have a passion for life? All your rebellion stems from the fact that you have an incredible passion for the beauty of life.'

'Me and rebel? I belong to the conforming type. You have seen it.'

'We all have both streaks in us. It just depends where the balance tilts. Check it out within yourself.'

Why had she never thought of herself as rebellious? As the train raced to Yokohama station, Abha wondered what rebellion actually meant.

Under the able and enthusiastic leadership of Peter, the group in class had planned a hike up Mount Fuji for the foreign students.

'Peter I cannot climb. I am now an old woman. Just keep me out.'

'Hey Aunty Mary this is not good. You are still young and you will enjoy it. Imagine staying two years in Japan and not climbing Mount Fuji! There is just no excuse.'

'Well I have promised to go with some Indian friends. So count me out.'

'Abha ditch your Indian friends. You can go elsewhere with them. This trip all of us are going for together.'

As the hectic planning progressed, Abha knew with whom she was going to climb the mystical mountain.

In the car, a soulful ghazal by Lata Mangeshkar played, while outside, the wide, smooth highway raced by. The landscape beyond the highway was hidden behind huge walls that separated the road from the area it passed through. It was a bright sunny morning as Abha and Diwakar drove towards Mount Fuji.

'When will we ever have roads like this in India? I wonder.'

'I am optimistic it will happen sooner rather than later. Already we are all talking of infrastructure, etc. I got something packed from an Indian restaurant for us. When you have a lot of work to do, it is only our own kind of food that is filling enough.'

'Diwakar do you know cooking?'

'No. It was never the thing expected from us when we grew up. And I never got down to learning later on.'

'The typically pampered Indian male, a woman always around to look after these things!'

'That is not a fair statement to make. I acknowledge that it stems from my upbringing, but I do not believe it is right.'

'So what do you believe?'

'All of us should be capable of looking after ourselves and both men and women should have the opportunity to explore their potential.'

'That sounds a lot like some UN jargon.'

'Nothing gives you the right to berate what I said I believe.'

Abha looked at him with surprise. His jaw had set in a particular manner and his face looked smaller. Was he hurt or angry?

'No offence meant.'

Mohammad Rafi had joined them with his melodious voice in one of the lilting duets of the olden days.

'Hope you have brought a lot of warm clothing. We are going to start the climb from the fifth station so as to catch the sunrise at the eighth station. I am told it is very cold at the summit in the early hours of the morning.'

'We seem to be slowly gaining height Diwakar.'

'Yes we have now left the highway so you can also see the scenery in the light of the setting sun.'

As they moved up, the whistling of the wind could be heard. Smoky clouds raced towards the car and danced on all sides.

'Look at Mount Fuji, Diwakar, it seems like a cake with an icing of clouds around it.'

The top of the mountain was swathed in a layer of clouds while on the road the sunlight could still be seen.

'The weather seems to be rough on top.'

When they reached the fifth station and stepped out, the wind nearly blew them off their feet. The sun had melted away and it was cold, damp and dark.

'You feel up to taking on this weather Abha?'

'Yes I will. I might never get the opportunity to climb again. I will not be here the next climbing season.'

They set out with a bag containing food and water, wrapped in jackets and caps with torches in their hands. It was pitch dark all around, only torchlights, in hands or foreheads, bobbed up and down along the path. Groups of people were walking up in the darkness. 'It is so dark Diwakar. If the torchlight fails, one can easily fall off the cliff.'

'That is why they recommend carrying spares and walking in groups.'

'Why are so many people coming back?'

Just before they reached the sixth station they were informed that Mount Fuji was in the grip of a typhoon and climbing had been suspended for that day.

Something colder than the wind around her clamped Abha's heart. She stood there, stock-still. Unbidden tears clouded her eyes.

'Its okay Abha we can do it another time.'

The disappointment made her speechless. Abha knew it was her last summer in Japan. The University group had already done the trek, and it was not easy for Diwakar to find time. In that solitary moment, she realized how much she wanted to fulfil the journey. Like a robot she turned back, but could not start walking. She stood frozen on the edge of the mountain.

'That is the end of my dream of climbing Mount Fuji.'

'Why do you think so? Anyway they always say—you must leave something for the next time.' Diwakar tried to cajole her into moving, as she stood on the edge of the mountain.

Abha stood near the edge of a cliff, facing never-ending darkness; it felt as if the earth ended on that ledge. Another gust of howling wind screeched past and, suddenly, the sea of darkness parted like a curtain to reveal below the twinkling lights of a Japanese town. The inky space was transformed in a flash into a jewel-bedecked sheet—full of life, gloriously beautiful. Then the clouds came back and all was black again.

'You know I think I came for this sight. It was magical, just like a dream Diwakar. It was so beautiful.'

'Those were the lights of Kawaguchi town.'

In a flash, her sense of disappointment had diminished. So what if the mystical mountain had shut its gate on her, standing on the edge of nothingness she had seen light, beauty and hope.

With a lighter step, Abha made her way back to the car. It had started to rain making the drive down treacherous and slow.

'Are you hungry? It is nearly 10 pm. We can stop and eat in one of the resting places on the highway.'

'It is pouring Diwakar, let us try and get back.'

'I will drop you to your place. By the time we reach any station your last bus would have left.'

After a lot of searching and taking wrong turns, they managed to reach her place by midnight. It had not rained in Yokohama.

They were still damp from the rain. A strange smell of rain and food wafted across the small room. Abha stood at the counter that served as her kitchen heating the food. Diwakar had put out plates on the floor near the bed.

'It is really small isn't it? Sometimes I wonder how I have managed to live here for whole one year.'

'Homes are small here. That is why people invite you to restaurants and rarely to their homes.'

'I never realized I was so hungry. Now I am famished. Your idea of getting an Indian meal packed was great. Imagine eating a burger or a sandwich now.'

As they ate, he talked. About his life and his dreams, much like a longtime childhood friend. His damp cream shirt had dried, but the blue denim jeans still had deep patches of blue where the rain of Mount Fuji had seeped in.

All of a sudden, Abha was acutely aware of his presence in the small room. He was talking about making another go at Mount Fuji in the next week, or the next week … . Was he thinking the same thing while he talked endlessly? He leaned on the wall and in a careless manner looked out at the moon that was bright and clear in the sky of Yokohama.

'The sky must be erupting around Mount Fuji, and see what a tranquil moon is keeping us company here. Just some distance and everything changes.'

As Abha bent down to pick up the remnants of the meal, the whiff of a clean male smell mixed with rain enveloped her. His presence disturbed her, pulling her in a compelling manner. She was surprised at the raw urge that grasped her insides. She went and sat on the bed. It was the only place in the room that allowed them to sit facing each other.

'Come and sit on the ground and see the moon. Isn't it like a friend looking in for a chat?'

Abha went and sat next to him. To her the moon seemed simply a blob of light thousands of miles away. She was conscious only of his presence next to her. The feeling was delicious and in a way entirely new. He turned around and his lips were on hers. A gentle touch full of anticipation and hope. Then they had looked at each other and smiled. The kind of smile only two lovers could exchange. They held each other and he quietly showered kisses on her forehead, eyelids, nose, hair and ear lobes. A sweet drowsiness had overtaken Abha. His face was between her breasts and he whispered something in her ears. 'Yes' she said without hearing what he said.

She was crushed under her own overwhelming desire leaping all over her. He was all over her, inside, outside and for a moment, everything froze. It was a triumph of bodies with no conquests and no defeats—just a rhythm and music that is eternal and innocent. The abandoned quest for Mount Fuji had reached a sweet climax. Something that had happened to her for the first time.

The summer was over and autumn had crept in. At the University, the group had been busy trying to cook up a thesis that would be acceptable.

'You need more data Abha san. I have printed out these articles for you in English from the internet. Maybe they will help you.'

'Thank you Sensei.' Why was time flying at this breakneck speed? Life had taken on wings and there was never enough time.

'I wanted to inform that in December you can shift back to the University dormitory.'

'December Sensei? With just three months to go for the course to end? That is unfair.' She could be candid with Murai sensei; they had developed an equation free of the constant Japanese expectations of harmony.

'December it is. Take it. At least for three months you will save some money.'

Diwakar said the same thing to her when she told him over the phone that day. 'I am travelling to Kita Kyushu next week. Will you come? On the way we will go to Hiroshima too.'

Sometimes life moved at such a pace and was so wonderful that it seemed foolish to sit back, stop and think. Their relationship had taken wings. Two people could have so much to share, explore and discover—it was unbelievable. From the delight of the body to the intimacy of the soul, they were locked in one endless dialogue. All lovers feel that theirs is the most incredibly beautiful and unique relationship, while countless others have been down that road before. But it is true—between two individuals, the universal interaction finds its own exclusive and matchless rhythm and pace. When the interaction sweeps across the entire being and consciousness, it becomes irrelevant and futile to think about other things.

'Let me know the dates. I will try. I am also busy with my thesis.'

When Abha had put the phone down, it had rung again.

'Ma, how are you? I am missing you and waiting to come to Japan in winter.'

From the distance, Abha could hear the longing in her child's voice. 'I am also waiting for your visit,' she replied.

Abha put the phone down and looked outside at the autumn night. It was silent and dark. Japan had given her a valuable gift—

the ability to live with herself. Silences and solitude did not trouble her anymore. There was no urge to surround herself with people, things or sounds. Was it because Diwakar was there in her life? Their interaction was full of spaces in between. Obviously, it was not just that. The isolation of the apartment, distance from the University, the solitude—all had worked out as a blessing in disguise. Perhaps life takes on an interesting hue when it is lived fully, one piece at a time. Nothing knocked at the doors of the mind from behind and nothing that awaited mattered. The piece of life at hand waited looking for colours, shape and form. There was so much peace in the realization that the journey itself is the destination.

Rekha was strolling in the duty free shops at Changi airport. She had spent the weekend with friends in Singapore, and was on her way to London. She picked up a few lipsticks and made her way back to the lounge to wait for her flight. With a glass of wine in her hand, and the *Economist* she stretched on an empty sofa.

There was something about her new employer, Citibank, in the magazine. Rekha read it with interest. She was very happy, her career as an investment banker was moving up in the right direction. She was moving to Citibank in London, which she was confident would lead to the financial capital of the world, New York. It was only a matter of time.

As soon as the offer had come in her mail, Rekha had wrapped up her life in Hong Kong in a week. She needed the move to beat the feeling of ennui that gripped her at times. Her guru had given her the coordinates of their group in London. Rekha was not sure she wanted to remain in that circle. The charm had somewhat worn off, although she still chanted the mantras to relax.

Her cell phone beeped. There was a message, 'Hope you are doing fine. Am hoping to find something in London and join you soon. Miss you in Hong Kong already.' Rekha did not know how to respond. She messaged back 'Sounds good. See you.' She was leaving behind everything in Hong Kong. A new life and journey beckoned.

Suddenly Rekha remembered that in her hurry to leave Hong Kong she had not told Papaji about her move to London. She dialled the home number. Papaji and Biji lived on the ground floor in their own home in Model Town now. Bubble, her younger brother, had moved to the US two years ago with his family. His wife was a simple homemaker who had produced the obligatory son within the first year of their marriage.

'Rekha, *kahan si* (from where)? Why have you called after so long?' Papaji sounded old on the line.

'Papaji, I am moving on to a new job to London. Am on my way. When I reach and settle there I will let you know the new address and number. How is Biji?'

There was silence on the line.

'Papaji can you hear me?' Rekha nearly shouted. Others in the lounge looked her way. She got up and stepped outside to speak.

'Yes. I can. Biji *theek hai* (is fine). You should have passed by Delhi. Rekha why don't you find a job in India? *Udhar bilkul akeli hai* (You are all alone there).'

'Hey Papaji, you don't mean that. This is the good time for me. My career is on the upswing. I'll call you guys to London when I settle down. Okay now my flight has been called. Bye.'

Walking towards the departure gate, Rekha felt a surge of excitement at the prospect of a new job, new city, a new life.

'Abha san I would like to invite you for a dinner with some friends next Friday at Sakuragicho.'

'Anything special, Sensei?'

'Not really.' Murai sensei looked secretive as he kept looking at the computer screen as he said that. Abha was sure he was hiding something. However friendly they were, he was her academic guide and some formality remained.

'So I will see you at 8 pm at the gate just outside Sakuragicho station on Friday?'

'Yes Sensei.'

On Friday, Abha was invited for dinner at Jyoti's home. She would need to change that. It had been a long time since Abha had met anyone in the Indian community in Tokyo. She had dropped out of sight—probably unconsciously.

Her only connection to the Indian community was Diwakar. Now as always he had interesting updates for her when they spoke on the phone. 'Did I tell you that Mr. Narayan hosted a dinner and he did not invite the Puri family who are one of the long-standing residents of Tokyo? The fact fuelled dinner conversations for nearly a fortnight.'

'That reminds me, Murai sensei has invited me for this dinner. He did not specify who else will be there or why we are going.'

'Why are you thinking about it? Just go and enjoy yourself. Whatever it is you will know soon enough.'

He made things sound simple and plain. Was that the secret of finding joy in life—seeing it in all its simplicity? Their relationship could have been mired in many complications and tensions, but it was not.

'The amount you call Yokohama, the phone bill will be phenomenal Diwakar!'

'Words are important to life. Remember what you say can never be withdrawn. You can tear up what you write, but not what you say.'

The mystery around Murai sensei's dinner remained. On Thursday, he had discreetly reminded Abha as he had met her on her way to another class. No one else from the class had been invited, so it was clear it was not related to the course. Abha had strolled in to the administrative office of their course, and chatted with Minato san to gather some hint, but none had been forthcoming.

Abha reached Sakuragicho station by quarter to eight, and paced impatiently near the ticket punch. The ferris wheel was turning ever so slowly in the distance and the lights of Yokohama were bright and luminous. At last, Murai sensei had emerged from the station, but there was no one else with him.

'*Kombawa* Sensei.'

'Abha san you are already here. Thank you so much for coming. We will go and wait inside the shopping mall near the Indian restaurant Maharaja for my friends.'

He hurried ahead and she followed him mystified by his secrecy, urgency and excitement which she sensed.

'Do you like Sakuragicho Sensei? I think it is the most beautiful place in Yokohama. My daughter and I came here very often.' She tried to break the silence that had enveloped them as they walked to the mall.

'Hmmm. It is nice.'

It was obvious his mind was elsewhere. They were now inside the glitzy interiors of the mall that buzzed with people and products. At the start of her stay in Japan, the shine and shimmer used to strike Abha, but it was easy to get used to better things.

'Sensei you heard about this course in Sophia University for foreign students? Do you have any news of it?'

'Yes I have the papers with me. I had planned to give them to you, but forgot. Take them from me on Monday.'

Murai sensei kept looking around at the various directions from which a person could come to the Indian restaurant.

'Sensei who are we expecting?'

He was quiet, as if weighing within himself the response to that question.

'Abha san, I have invited a friend for dinner and since I wanted to go to the Indian restaurant I invited you to help us in the ordering.'

Was he seeing someone? Could the books, the hours spent before the computer and his flute leave time to see someone? He could have simply sought her advice on the food. The questions raced across Abha's mind as they waited. Murai sensei had turned out to be an interesting person, dabbling in many things and full of life.

'Abha san, I think I must tell you the truth. I want to get married and after a lot of searching on the internet, I came across someone I wanted to meet. I have invited her today. You will also meet her and give me your views.'

'Sensei, you should have met her first on your own. I am a foreigner, how can I say anything. I do not know much about Japanese marriages and all the expectations that are involved on both sides.'

'You are intelligent and I know after meeting her you will give me a balanced view. Japanese marriages—they are so difficult now-a-days Abha san. It is difficult to find a girl of your choice. I do not want the colleagues at the University to be involved at this stage. But I need another perspective too.'

Across all countries and cultures, the problem was the same. It was difficult to find someone of one's own choice. She was there to help Murai sensei decide his marriage? Nothing could have been more incongruous, and more interesting.

'What does she do?'

'Kyoko is a doctor. She works in a hospital in Tokyo and lives there. She is ready to move to Yokohama. We will have to find a suitable house and if all goes well we will get married in April.'

'You have discussed all this without meeting each other?'

'Yes we have to know if our basic parameters match before we meet. She too needs to find time in April. See—my diary—it is full until March. So many meetings, conferences, papers to finish.'

Most of the Japanese carried these diaries, in which they wrote the smallest engagement that was to cross their path. Marriage also had to find a place in the appointment diary!

'There she is.'

Murai sensei hurried across to meet a petite, pretty-looking woman coming across. They bowed to each other, shook hands and came over to her. Once seated inside the restaurant, Abha took charge of ordering the food. As she did so, she did a mental calculation of the bill, knowing well that she would end up paying some part as her share.

Kyoko appeared nice and composed. Abha could not speak to her much as their language skills did not match. Abha was poor in Japanese and Kyoko in English.

After dinner when the bill came, Murai sensei paid up and they walked out. 'Abha san your share is two thousand yen and Kyoko san your share four thousand yen.'

Abha could not believe it. Even in a meeting for marriage purposes, the costs had to be *betsu-betsu*. However, it had not surprised Kyoko. The three of them walked back to the station and Kyoko took a train towards Tokyo.

'Sensei we could have gone on a train together. The train would have stopped at Yokohama too.'

'No it is better this way. So what do you think?'

'She is nice and seems keen on the alliance too. That is always a plus.'

'I think so too. I will write to her how I feel tomorrow. Maybe she has a different opinion.'

Murai sensei and Abha boarded the next train to Yokohama. Murai sensei took out a newspaper and began to read. Abha looked out at the lights. It was so different and yet so similar. The settings and manners change, but the quest for a suitable partner was universal.

Outside the sights were a blur, inside the train it was quiet, comfortable and the styrofoam glass on the table in front was not shaking.

'How can the train not shake at such speed?' Abha demanded of her drowsy co-passenger.

'That is why it has changed the concept of space and time in Japan. People travel from Osaka to Tokyo everyday for work. A journey of more than five hundred kilometres is covered in just over two hours. Can you imagine travelling one thousand kilometres everyday in a shaking train? It is not called the bullet train for nothing.'

When the silver grey bullet train thundered down at the Shin-Yokohama station, the gust of wind generated had nearly swept passengers off, although they waited behind a barricade at least two metres from the train. The doors opened and Abha and Diwakar stepped into the luxurious coaches. Abha was excited on her first journey on the legendary 'Shinkansen'.

'And imagine it is on time by the second. In India, we take it for granted that long distance trains will be late. Doesn't it fascinate you Diwakar, the Japanese were also razed to the ground in 1945 and look where they are now and where we are?'

'I am taking a nap now. You think about all these things.'

Abha watched him as he slept. It was difficult to cast him in any role—lover, friend, paramour. He was all that rolled into one. His presence was reassuring, easy going and relaxed her immensely. Rekha's words, uttered long ago rang in her ears, 'Good sex is a good binding force'. Abha had realized the truth in that statement, similar to Rekha's awakening; Abha had understood how fascinating and actually enjoyable the whole thing was. Even more when one could talk endlessly—the way Diwakar and she did. They remained in one long continuous dialogue with each other.

Like the next link in the chain, Simran came to her mind. A few days ago, one of her long letters had arrived. Her younger sister Shikha had been diagnosed with stomach cancer in the last stages. Abha remembered Shikha the way one remembers the younger siblings of good friends—like a shadow that clung to the house. It had a shape and form, but no colour. Shikha's illness had suddenly given her image a clarity. It was difficult to accept the harsh truth—she did not belong to the dying generation. It was unfair and unjust. Simran was looking after Nupur, Shikha's daughter, while the family was fighting a losing battle for her life. Abha had not written to Simran for long. Her days were full, and there was a lot happening in her life. And what could she write? That she was sleeping with a married Indian man in Tokyo. It sounded inane, stupid and incomprehensible. Could she really explain to Simran how it had happened? How it really was? Did she really want to explain this to anybody, even Simran? As she sat in one of the fastest trains in the world, with a man she could not label, a child waiting for her in India, she nevertheless felt happier than she had been in a long while.

Hiroshima is a symbol of destruction and resurrection. At first glance, it was like any other Japanese city—prosperous and busy. It could have been Tokyo, Yokohama or Osaka. Skyscrapers loomed large, and neon signs lit up the skyline. There was no sign of the tremendous devastation of 1945. Abha and Diwakar had stopped for a few hours on the way to Kita Kyushu.

'Have you been here before Diwakar?'

'No. Hiroshima was on my "to do" list for a long time now. I am glad I came with you.'

He often said the most sentimental things in a matter of fact way. 'How did they do this Diwakar? Rebuilt it so well.'

'I call it national character. Something we in India have yet to identify and feel proud of.'

They walked through the Peace Museum. There were burnt shoes, tiffin boxes, clothes and a watch that had stopped at 8.32 am. The images were countless, merciless and haunting. It was unimaginable to think that most of the people died due to intense heat—literally melting to death—children, women and men who were going about like any other day in their lives. The aftermath of the first nuclear bombing in human history was disturbing.

'Why are we seeing it? It is so grotesque and frightening.'

'Abha, one needs to see the truth to be able to see things in their correct perspective.'

Kita Kyushu is a bustling town near the sea. While Diwakar attended to his work, Abha walked around the place. It was an interesting mix of old world charm and present day hustle-bustle.

In the darkening evening, together, they walked the lanes of the small town. The lit-up Kokura palace, atop a hill, with the night sky in the background was beautiful. Without warning, it began to rain and they took shelter in a small area and ate steaming *udon*, the Japanese noodles.

'While I was walking around I saw that *Titanic* is running here. Let us go and see it. I love watching movies.'

'I haven't seen a movie in a theatre for years now. Somehow, fell out of the habit of watching movies. I think I have missed a whole generation of Bollywood heroines. As far as English movies go, I can't follow the accent. Remember I am a small town boy who studied in Kannada medium!'

'Well I will fill in for you. You just might enjoy it. It is supposed to be a really good movie.'

They had walked to the nearest theatre and watched the movie. The next day they were on their return journey to Tokyo in the bullet train. Outside, the scenery was hazy; inside it was calm and serene. 'So did you like the experience of watching a movie again after a long time?'

'Yes. The movie was well made. But it was much like a Hindi movie wasn't it? Class differences, a villain and a hero and of course a winsome girl in between.'

'That is true when you put it like this.'

They were in the bullet train bound back for Tokyo. 'Abha what are your plans on your return?' He asked.

'I better get into my thesis with full fervour. Also, I am planning to take up that course in Sophia. It will be interesting.'

'No I meant when you go back to India.'

'Diwakar it is still far away. I have so much to do here before that even comes into my perspective. I will get back to my job in good old Government of India of course.'

He remained quiet and started looking out of the window on the other side of the aisle.

'I was talking about other aspects of life.'

'You mean marriage?'

'Maybe, one of the things.'

'Well I will think about it seriously. You know, once I go back Diwakar, it will be as if the life I had left on hold will take over.'

'Tell me about this course you are planning to take up in Sophia University.'

They talked as the hours and the miles flew past. Abha started feeling drowsy.

'Diwakar while on the way here you slept and now you have just been talking all the way. I want to sleep for sometime now.'

'When we were coming I knew that we will be together for the next two days. Now I know we will catch different trains from Tokyo station.'

The course at Sophia University was free, but entailed travel to Tokyo thrice in a week in the evenings. Abha convinced Mary that despite the expense, it was a good learning opportunity, and together they started on the new venture.

The course was interesting with many foreign students from other universities participating. Since the University was in Tokyo, it gave Abha a chance to meet Diwakar more often. On the third visit as Mary and Abha walked out of class, Mary had spotted Diwakar.

'There is an Indian looking guy at the gate.'

'Yes he has come to meet me. You carry on, I will come later.' Abha caught up with Diwakar and they walked to a small garden near the University and sat on a bench. The evening sun had set and a luminous glow was spread over the lawns.

'Diwakar this is like romancing in college. After class you roam hand in hand in the University garden.'

'Did you romance someone in college?'

'I did want to, but it never worked out.' After a long time Abha remembered Ujjwal in Japan. Like this.

'Have you decided something about shifting to the dormitory in December?'

'Yes I have taken it up. When Parul comes, I will simply smuggle her in for the fifteen days that she is here. Now I can do it. The authorities will look the other way, as it is only a temporary thing.'

'I am planning to go home to Belgaum in December.'

'Alone? Why now? Go after March.'

'No there is something that has come up about the land records. My father needs me to be there. And why do you think of things in this capsule like thing. It is not as if after March we will not meet.' Abha kept quiet. To her mind, life was like a set of sentences. When the full stop came the next one began. Each drew meaning from the one before, but also had its own independent existence.

Diwakar walked to Ichigaya station to see her off and then bought a ticket too.

'Where are you going?'

'I will go in the train with you to Yokohama and then come back without punching out. It will be nice.'

As they stood lurching in the train, Abha watched him. They had come a long way since the first day they had met in the Indian

Embassy in Tokyo. Their different backgrounds, language, kind of people they had grown up with, nothing had come in the way. As her course neared conclusion, time had begun to make its presence felt. It had crept in like an unwanted third element in their space. It was always there watching, at times sniggering, at times sympathetic, but always there. And Abha had accepted long ago that time was the ultimate winner, the final arbiter.

New Year eve had come again. Parul had come to Japan and they were in the University dormitory. Parul was by now on first name terms with Abha's classmates. They doted on her, as she was the only child amongst adults who all had children waiting for them. Cake, wine, beer, plenty of food, music and chatter mingled with a deep sense of sadness in the group.

'Abha I am waiting for your beautiful daughter to grow up, then I will marry her,' Peter proclaimed his not so honourable intentions yet again, and the whole group burst out laughing.

'I bet by next year this time only a few of us would be in touch with each other.'

'Aunty Mary, why are you always so pessimistic? Don't you know about email?'

'But she is right Peter. Many of us may not have access to the internet easily in our home country. Abha, when I want to come on a Buddhist pilgrimage to India I will write to you. Do remember me then.'

'Of course Amrut. You must get in touch.'

'And Abha, when you marry you must invite me. You must get married. It is a waste of womanhood.'

'Peter when will you stop speaking like an overbearing African male?'

'Never, Aunty Mary, because I will always be African and a male, hopefully!'

The easy bantering born of the closeness of the past year and half had gone on. They were all different and yet so much the same. Peter and Amrut danced to some Mongolian music, looking like two cute kids. It is life that keeps reminding us about age, especially when children grow up. Parul had gained height in between their last meeting. She sat there swinging her legs to the music. Abha felt her heart in her mouth. The tenderness and love that a child could inspire still caught her by surprise at times.

As the New Year dawned, Abha wondered what Diwakar was doing in his hometown. Since he had gone, a strange silence had descended. She had shifted back to the University dormitory and Parul had arrived. Yet there was a strange quiet. Perhaps the incessant phone calls, the never-ending dialogue had suddenly paused. Often, when she passed a public phone booth while on the move, she would want to call him only to realize he was not there. Abha was not yet prepared to admit to herself that she missed him.

'What is your New Year resolution Abha? Mine is to go back to Namibia and marry. I am growing old and soon enough my son will never let me. I know God will help me.'

'Well I have not thought about that yet Mary. In my case, I feel that when I do decide to marry I will manage to take Parul along with me. I have tried very hard to build a relationship of trust and openness with her.'

'The Indian system is good. A man can have only one wife by law. In our part of the world this doesn't exist.'

'Maybe you should marry an Indian man Mary!!'

'Oh you Indians, you rarely marry outside your community. Even after generations, you still marry within. I have seen it in Africa.'

'Lin what about you?'

'I am looking for a PhD programme if possible. I want to stay some more time.'

'Of course our Lin has grown roots here!' Peter winked at the group. There was something sad and desperate about Lin at that moment. She tried to smile however.

After some more songs and dance, the party broke up. Parul and Abha sat on the steps of the dormitory.

'Ma I will never come to Japan again?'

'Why do you say that? You may come again on your own.'

'No I mean now. You will come back and then we will never come here again.'

'That is true Parul.' The end of a certain way of life is painful, especially when it had been happy and contented.

'Ma when will you come? Tell me the date. I will then mark the date in our calendar and strike off each day before it after I go back to India.'

'I will come back by your sixth birthday. That means in the first week of April.'

'Promise Ma?'

'Promise.'

As the New Year moon shone on them on that cold night in Yokohama, Abha could clearly see the impending closure of many things in her life.

It had been snowing all night. Abha sat in Murai sensei's room while he went over his observations on her thesis. His remarks were in red in the margins in Japanese. He painstakingly explained to Abha the additions and deletions needed.

'You will have to present this thesis to a panel and defend it. So think of that too.'

'Sensei if I may ask, what did you and Kyoko san decide?'

'We are still finalizing things. In principle, we have agreed to marry in April. Our parents have also consented. Now she wants to find a job in this part of the country. She doesn't want to commute long distances after marriage.'

'Congratulations Sensei. It is very good news.'

'But by then you all would have gone to your respective countries. You will not be able to attend the wedding. Neither of us is free before the third week of April.'

The snow was falling in sheets outside the window and the buildings in the distance had already become white.

'How is your course at Sophia going? When do you finish?'

'In the next fortnight Sensei. I have to make a presentation there also. Lots of work. It is snowing so badly today I do not think I can go to Sophia today.'

'It is good that you decided to do the course. You must mention it in the thesis presentation in some way.'

Murai sensei sounded somewhat proud of her. The kind of pride that seeps into a teacher whose student had done better than expected. Abha looked around his room. It had not changed much. Books remained scattered all over the place, including his crowded table. She had learnt a lot from him, about his culture and society. He had become a friend.

'Abha san I do want to tell you that I have really enjoyed being your advisor. In the beginning, I had misgivings. I thought you were very aggressive and loud, but then I realized it is only your sense of curiosity. It has been refreshing to work with you. I hope we will stay in touch even when you go back.'

'Why Sensei, you are saying farewell already? We will keep meeting in the next two months also.'

'This time will fly. It is going to be a busy time.'

Abha walked back to the dormitory and started working on the thesis corrections. Outside the room window, night had fallen and the swirling snow lit up occasionally in the lights of a passing car. Abha had started counting the days like Parul. Everyone was slowly saying goodbye. All of them deciding at the last minute what to buy, what to sell, what to throw away. She had decided to give her TV and VCR to Vivek. He was moving to a job in Tokyo and needed to set up home.

The ring of the phone broke the quiet.

'Abha hi. What's new?'

Rekha, the eternal interloper. She surfaced at the most unexpected moments. In fact, that had become a hallmark of her consistency.

'Nothing. Packing up from here. Back in India in two months. And you? You have called after months.'

'You know I call you whenever there is some change in my life. Maybe when I am going through a change I reach out to you because you are a link to my youth. The fact that you are there gives me a kind of stability.'

'What's up Rekha? You sound sentimental. It's so unlike you. Is everything alright?'

'I moved to London sometime ago. I joined Citibank here.'

'Alone?'

'Yes, at the moment. If he feels like it, and can find something here he may also move.'

Even across the thousands of miles, Abha could sense a strange sense of confusion in Rekha's voice. Outside the window, the snow came down in sheets, determined to drown the world.

'I don't want this anymore Abha. Somehow, this moving all around the globe, working, travelling, cooking, washing—it has tired me. I don't want this life anymore.'

'What is it that you want?'

'That I do not know as yet. I just know that this is not the life I want anymore.'

'You know Rekha, I think our problem has been we always know what we do not want, but never know what we want.'

'Abha don't confuse me further. Knowing what we don't want is important; it may lead to knowing what we do. Anyway, you are supposed to cheer me up, make me feel better. Whenever I call you and speak to you, I feel a sense of hope. So don't disappoint me, okay. Tell me did you find someone?'

In that moment, Abha found herself telling Rekha about Diwakar. It was a relief.

'Abha it's the limit. Even in Japan, you went and found a married Indian guy to lay? You must be nuts. Anyway I hope it has been good.'

'Rekha you are incorrigible. Is that all you think of?'

'You better not think of anything else too. Pack your bags and get out of there. He is married remember.'

Rekha, the great leveller. Always putting things in their most prosaic perspective.

'I do.'

'Good. Will catch you again soon. Been on the line long.'

Abha put the phone down and wondered what Simran was doing at that moment. Her sister was in the last stages, and Simran was busy coping. It seemed unreal that Simran's younger sister was actually dying. May be when Abha visited Simran next, Shikha would be lounging around the house with her little daughter Nupur in tow.

The phone had rung again.

'Hi. Your phone was engaged for long. I just wanted to know if you had got back from Sophia. It is snowing so heavily.'

'Diwakar, I never went today. It was too cold and forbidding. Where are you calling at this hour from?'

'I came out for a walk in the snow and was hanging around the phone booth for the past fifteen minutes waiting to get through.'

'Rekha called. Go back now. It is cold.'

Since he had got back from India both of them had been busy. She with her University assignments, and he with his work. Or, had it been that both of them were trying to loosen up and let go?

Jyoti's house was full of guests from India. A delegation had come from the Agriculture Ministry. Mingling with the guests Abha found someone who knew Kishore ji very well. Another officer knew her ex-boss. She caught up on the gossip in the corridors of North Block. Before she knew it, Abha had slipped into her old hat, and become a bureaucrat. At the dinner, her student life in Yokohama seemed like a dream. The network of India's gigantic bureaucracy is actually quite close-knit, there is always someone known or heard of.

'Jyoti, coming to your house reminded me quite clearly of where I am headed. It was interesting. Thanks a lot for everything while I was here.'

'But Abha you somehow dropped out of sight the last year. I always enjoyed talking to you. It was like a breath of fresh air in the atmosphere. Keep in touch.'

Abha was on the last train to Yokohama. It was full of red-faced men and tired looking women. The commuters stood in their typical stone-faced manner and awaited their destinations. Abha had begun to feel a sense of belonging to the train commuters—an affinity with the impersonal behaviour and sense of anonymity they provided. It was hard to imagine that in a matter of a month the sight of these trains, their commuters, all the glitz and glitter would be a thing of the past—a bunch of memories, which would gather dust and fade away as other realities staked their claim.

'We get to invite one personal friend to the convocation that is being specially organized for the course,' Peter the broadcaster was declaring. They had just finished with their thesis presentations and technically the course was over. Just a few remaining classes, the convocation and then time to return. The airline tickets had been booked.

'What are you doing over the weekend, Abha? Let us have a party in the dormitory and get together again.'

'This weekend I am busy, Mary. How about next weekend?'

'That is too near the last few days. Let us see. We will plan out something in the week.'

It was a blessing that no one asked why she was busy, where she was going. In India, there would never be respite from such questions.

The weekend saw Diwakar and Abha drive to Fujinomiya. A beautiful city at the base of Mount Fuji. It has lakes, gardens, shrines and a drive that leads to the ocean. Quiet, away from the hustle and drenched in nature. However, all the beauty escaped Abha's eyes. There was a palpable sense of doom hanging in the car. Abha felt she could rest her head on the tension that hung across.

'So we visit Mount Fuji again, even if it is at the base. Just look at it.'

Mount Fuji, swathed in fresh snow, majestically adorned the sky.

'It reminds me of the Ganga. You can see it at so many places and everywhere, it inspires a sense of awe and divinity.'

'It comes from the way we look at them, Abha. Otherwise, they are just mountains and rivers.'

They reached a small youth hostel tucked in a green hillock. The caretaker, an elderly Japanese woman warmly welcomed them. The wooden building had traditional Japanese *futons* on the floor and a small warm kitchen. The place promised adventure, solitude and romance.

After a cup of tea, they drove to the shore and sat on a rock. The ocean was gurgling away and waves crashed against the rocks. The sound of the waves filled the silence between them.

'You are stopping in Thailand on your way back? Where will you stay?'

'Am still trying to find someone. I might as well see it; I do not know when I will step outside the borders of India again.'

'I have some friends there, I will ask them to put you up for two days. There should be no problem. What are your immediate plans in India Abha?'

'Well I will go back and join work. The idea itself sounds terrible. Then have to re-open and start my house at Pandara Road. I think Papa needs a thorough check up. There are so many things to do.'

The next day they strolled on the hillside. Early spring flowers bloomed along the path. Mount Fuji had kept a vigil on their walk. It was cool and green. The wind played with Diwakar's hair and threw them gently back. He always looked good when the wind swept his hair away from his forehead.

'All along I always had a dream that I will have an incredibly passionate and involved relationship in my life. Full of intimacy, joy and sharing. Someone I can touch where I want, when I want, I can tell my erotic fantasies or anything else that I want to. Where there are no pretences, no walls—just togetherness.'

'You are basically an idealist and a poet.'

'Why, is there no such thing as unconditional love?'

'Diwakar I do believe in love, but at times just love is not enough.'

During the lunch which comprised hot and steaming *yakisoba*, the caretaker kept them company with her innumerable questions about India. They were her first Indian guests. She had never had Indians in her place before. She wanted to know about the Buddha, Varanasi and Rajgir. Abha had not been to either of the two places, but Diwakar had taken his parents to Varanasi.

In the evening, when their drive back was to begin, it started to pour. The sunny day was lost in the cloudy and dark evening. In the fading light of a grey sky, Mount Fuji seemed like a hulking monster in the distance. As the car turned the corner and the hostel disappeared from view, Abha felt a sharp pang within. The two days, fraught with unspoken tension and grief, had been relaxing and serene too. How could such opposite emotions co-exist?

She watched as Diwakar drove with complete concentration through the sheets of rain that plastered the windscreen. Lata Mangeshkar's voice was keeping them company. The raindrops collided with each other in the headlights.

'Seems like a cosmic dance to me always. The way the leaves twirl in the wind and the rain dances. What about you?'

'You know the difference between you and me Diwakar? You see things in layers, while I see them just as they are. So I see a lot of rain that is treacherous for fast driving, while for you it is a cosmic dance.'

'You see what is most comfortable for you to see. In compartments. That does not mean you are unaware of the other dimensions.'

As they left the hills behind, the rain stopped. The evening light had still not totally disappeared. The car picked up speed and raced towards Tokyo.

'I can move back to India.'

Diwakar's statement remained suspended on the tension wire that had not disappeared.

'India is not Tokyo, Diwakar. The anonymity, the freedom that I have had here, does not exist in India. There I am answerable for all my movements. And most of all, in the long term, this kind of relationship does not work for me. We will only end up hating each other.'

Abha had said it. Once said it sounded plain and logical. So completely understandable. Could he not see it? Diwakar smiled and then a small tear trickled down his cheeks. He concentrated on the road, and Abha looked out of the window. It was pitch dark outside. The walls on the sides of the highway kept out the lights of the neighbouring habitation.

'Diwakar, I would be happy if you came for my convocation next week. It is in the forenoon. Will it be possible for you?'

'I will make it possible. I have never seen Yokohama National University. It will give me a chance to see it and meet all the friends you talk about.'

It had to be done this way. The present had to take over the impending future. There was no other way.

The convocation ceremony ended with a small reception. The professors wished them luck. All of them exchanged bear hugs, made last minute promises to keep in touch through permanent contact details. It was an emotional moment. Abha was quite sentimental as she accompanied Diwakar to Yokohama Station.

'How are you going to the airport, Abha?'

'I will take the train. There is no problem.'

'No I will come and pick you up at Shinagawa and from there drive you down to the airport.'

'Diwakar I don't want that. I hate goodbyes.'

'But I do want to do that.' She could not argue when he said it that way.

The last night in the dormitory was strange. Mary had left in the morning; Lin had failed to find any other course and left in the afternoon. They had all cried together. The men had started leaving too. Abha's room was bare. Most of her things had been distributed or thrown away.

Two years had gone by. Two years of learning and healing for her. As Abha lay in bed, she tried to look ahead, and not at what she was leaving behind. She thought of Parul—how she must be waiting for her Ma. She thought of work, of her house, of her parents. The moment Japan appeared in her stream of consciousness Diwakar also appeared and she wanted to deal with that only when she was far away. So Abha did not think about Japan at all. The last night in Yokohama was spent thinking about all that was awaiting her in India.

They were on the way to the airport. Tokyo was receding in the window of the car with every passing mile. Tokyo Tower was left behind, as were the high-rise buildings and market places.

'This is the address and number of my friend Mr. Dubey. He will come and meet you at Bangkok airport. He will be carrying a name placard for you. So look out for him at Bangkok airport.'

'Thanks a lot. I will go around on my own after taking some guidance from him.'

'That is alright. You can ask them for any assistance you need. When you reach Delhi give me a call that you have reached safely.'

Abha kept quiet. She would think later. It would be simpler to deal with. As the airport came into view, Abha felt the landscape looked blurred. She did not realize when she had begun to cry. She was leaving behind so much in the fabled city. She cried silently for it all, while Diwakar drove towards the airport.

When she had checked in her things and it was time to move in for the security check, he hugged her. As his smell enveloped her, Abha suddenly recognized all that she was taking with her from this fabled city. It made her feel better.

She turned around and after waving to him, walked into the waiting lounge of the airport. She did turn one last time, but Diwakar was already walking back.

In anticipation, Thursday

Outside the hotel window, the calm waters are sapphire blue. The beach, carpeted with sand, is inviting. The sea breeze laps at the palm fronds gently. It is tranquil and quiet. Mauritius is like paradise. Since her arrival two days ago, Rekha has seen innumerable rainbows across the clear skies. As she connects her laptop to the internet, the date suddenly crosses her mind. Abha is getting married today. Again. Rekha looks at her watch; it must be noon in Delhi. She wonders what is going on in faraway Delhi.

Abha ultimately took the plunge. It needed some guts to get into the marriage thing all over again. Rekha remembers Abha as always having a strange combination of rebellion and conformity. She constantly leapt towards one while staying tied to the other. It is probably the curse of their generation of women.

Lounging on the hotel bed with the gorgeous view outside, it is easy to recollect the long distance they have traversed in their lives. In fact, it seems like yesterday when they dreamt and planned their lives in the SRCC canteen. Rekha remembers the innumerable cups of tea in the canteen over which they thought of career, marriage, kids and the whole gamut of life. Nothing had seemed unachievable or out of reach then. Over time, they realized how life quietly snatched from their grasp many things they had taken for granted.

Love was found and lost, marriage vows were made and broken, jobs were struggled for and then given up. So many choices, so many different routes.

Rekha herself had branched out. From her marriage, her job and from her long-time companion too. Why is it that the things that one strives so hard to achieve also become a burden at times? Then, along the way, one does find something or someone worthwhile, a passionate driving force.

Abha has done it ultimately, after quite a long journey. It must have been difficult, perhaps frightening even, to decide to marry again. Especially when there are children. Rekha knows well the uncertainty and endless arguments that must have gone on in Abha's head for months. Convincing parents and the child, it must have been a long and difficult haul.

Is it life that makes us so practical? Why was Abha not swept away in a passionate desire to go ahead? Why do women always have so many questions and issues to confront and decide on when thinking of something for themselves? Why can it not be like the men? 'I want, so I will.'

Rekha dials Abha's home number, but it rings endlessly. They must still be busy. She decides not to ring on the mobile. Rekha thinks about Parul. Rekha knows the little girl is undergoing her own trauma in the situation. She oscillates between mature acceptance and in-built resistance to this change.

But, everyone has a right to live for himself or herself. Rekha hopes that it will work out for Abha this time. It seems like a good decision from all points of view.

All through the years, Rekha always reached out to Abha when there was something going on in her own life. Abha has a core that remains unchanged whatever her personal situation. She has always given Rekha a sense of hope and continuity.

They are in their late thirties now—quite unbelievable. But perhaps there is there some truth in what is said—that mentally we never grow beyond our twenties.

Rekha wonders what Abha is wearing to court. It is strange to imagine that she is getting married in court. Rekha has never attended a court wedding. A wedding means bright lights, flowers, food and the sacred *pheras* around the fire. Rekha would have been there for Abha's marriage, but Abha had announced the date only ten days ago. By then she was committed to this conference in Mauritius. So now, she is sitting in Mauritius, instead of attending the wedding in Delhi.

It is time to go to the conference. While she will be making a power point presentation to a room full of people, Abha will be saying 'I do' or whatever it is they make you say in court. Thousands of miles away.

It is thousands of miles away so what if the cities are in the same country. Mumbai and Delhi are thousands of miles from each other, and in the furnace that is Delhi Abha is getting married. Today. Simran sits in the stuffy office with reams of paper strewn in front of her. She is in the middle of a branch audit, but is mentally in Delhi. A cup of tea lies cold on her desk.

Simran cannot understand why she is stuck in this audit team. The letter landed on her desk just a week ago, asking her to leave immediately for Mumbai. She tried to wriggle out of it, but to no avail. Simran wanted to be present at Abha's marriage, but it was not to be. Just two days before the date she flew out to Mumbai. Her mobile rings. It is her mother.

'Simran I hope you are coming back on Sunday. I am tired and I think I am going to fall ill.'

'Yes Amma I will. You take care.'

She looks at the time. It is nearly noon. She wonders what Nupur was doing at school. She dials Abha's number, but no one picks up the telephone at her home. They must be busy.

Simran remembers Parul. She is having an understandably tough time. However, Parul was sensible and sensitive. She will overcome, and then her Nani is there to hold her hand. Simran's heart goes out to the little girl. She is not worried about Abha. Her friend always had a knack of taking care of herself.

Simran looks back at the years Abha and she have been friends. They never thought that life would turn out like this. They had made wrong choices, suffered the consequences and learnt to accept each other despite everything. They had exchanged many hot words over Hussein. They had not spoken to each other for months thereafter, but then slowly veered around to each other again. Now that Hussein has receded into the background, Simran understands Abha's anger better. No one can make you see such things until you see them for yourself.

What is love? Simran wonders. Was it the beautiful feeling she felt for Hussein all those years? If so, then how did it start agitating her over time? Does it last only if you come together? Or is it ever changing? Is it just the object of love that changes and the feelings shift focus on the new one? Like it happened with her.

Is Abha marrying for love? Somehow, it is difficult to understand her in these things. She thinks of so many other things while taking these decisions. Always. Maybe it is because Abha has been through a marriage and has a child. Maybe their world views were always different.

Someone comes, dumps some more papers on her desk and disappears. Simran has never completely adjusted to being a working-woman. However, over time she has begun to appreciate the independence work has lent to her life. It makes so many things possible. Though she did not seek it, Simran now values financial independence. She wonders if she would have been happier running a home full time, bringing up kids and waiting for her husband to come home. Maybe.

Our dreams never really die. We just take bits and pieces from them and try to get them to be real in our lives. Just like she has done. Is Abha doing the same? Is she living her dream or just a part of it? Either way it is not a bad deal.

At least they have the time. Shikha did not enjoy this luxury. Her death changed things for Simran. As she watched her younger sister die, Simran had seen the way Shikha looked at Nupur from the hospital bed. In her tired eyes were all the dreams she would never see turn real. Her death had suddenly woken up Simran to the fact that life is short and abrupt.

Both Abha and she have taken vital decisions for their lives in the past few years, aimed at moving on in life. She thought, perhaps, Abha had already signed on the register as a married woman by then.

Delhi, Change Beckons

The summer had passed and monsoon showers were threatening Delhi. Dark clouds hid the sun and trembled to break out. The humidity and moisture were palpable. Abha stood at the window of her first floor flat in Pandara Road, and looked out at the deserted streets. Suitably threatened by the monsoon, people were tucked indoors. Suddenly lightning seared the sky, and with the clap of thunder rain came pouring down. In sheets. Just the way she remembered it. It was nice to be back in the Delhi rains.

'Didi should I make some tea and pakoras? This is the weather for it.' Reena, the faithful maid, was back with her. She was always thinking of something to feed her. Much like a mother.

'Okay. Where is Parul?'

'Watching TV, Didi.'

'Reena this cable TV is a curse. The child doesn't play or anything. Only watches TV.'

Reena scuttled out of the room. Since her arrival, Abha had discovered that cable TV had exploded in Delhi. Countless movie channels, entertainment channels and the like were available 24 x 7.

Many other things had also changed. Most of all Parul. She had insisted on shifting to their home at Pandara Road, and asserted in clear terms her ownership of her mother and their life.

They had crossed the hurdle of the divorce issue the day Abha returned. After the initial revelation, Parul had asked questions intermittently over the next few months. 'Did my father want my custody also?' 'Do I have grandparents on that side?'

Abha had tried to answer all her questions truthfully. Slowly the questions had petered out. Then Parul had begun to possessively assert their identity—Ma and Parul. Probably a phase that would soon find its own resolution.

'Parul let us sit in the balcony and have some pakoras. It is pouring. It is so beautiful.'

Very reluctantly, Parul left the TV and came into the balcony. The rain was pelting away. The neem tree in front was looking like a drenched woman; a sweet strong smell of wet earth wafted through the window.

'Ma let us go to the terrace and get wet. Please.'

It was easy to forget such small pleasures. Children ensured their revival. Maybe that is why children are necessary.

'Come let us go.'

Mother and daughter ran up the stairs and played in the rain. Drenched and exhilarated.

Delhi and everyday life had caught up at a frantic pace since Abha's return from Japan. Within a week, she felt as if she had never been away. Only when Diwakar called to enquire about her welfare, she felt a whiff of Tokyo around her.

'How was your stay in Bangkok?'

'It was good. Your friend was nice. How are things at your end?'

'Fine.'

They had both kept quiet. The distance on the line had stretched endlessly.

'Okay. Send me an email soon.'

'Will do. You take care.'

Why did it become so difficult to talk to him, when it had always been so easy? Had they built walls around themselves or had time and distance constructed their own spaces? University life, the perfection of Japan—everything seemed so far away. As if it had happened in another lifetime.

Office had taken up most of Abha's time and consciousness. Her office was in Nirman Bhawan—a huge sprawling building on the side of Raj Path. A matchbox structure, with endless rows of rooms on either side of the corridor. Unlike North Block with its grand exteriors, verandahs, spiral staircases and intricate ceilings. After two years spent in relative leisure, as a student, the discipline of having to sit in the same room from nine to five was extremely trying. Abha would often tire of sitting on the chair and would pace up and down in the room. Like a caged animal.

'Madam, you have enjoyed yourself in a foreign country for two years. You should not complain about anything.'

When Abha asked for a more comfortable chair, the person in charge had remarked. She realized that she had to contend with this strange sense of jealousy of the people around her.

'Sharmaji, I stayed away from my daughter. It was not an English speaking country. So I think I do deserve a better chair. Don't you think so?'

'Madam, I was just saying it like that. But it must be a beautiful country. Different from us right?'

Japan different? It was like a different world altogether. When Abha had seen the run down corridors, the dust, the innumerable papers that swamped her office she had felt that the impeccable order of Japan could not actually exist.

However, things had changed even in the maze of the government. There was a gleaming computer in every officer's room. Abha had opened the computer in her room eagerly, and discovered to her utter delight that it was connected to the internet. It was like a breath of fresh air. Often circulars landed on her desk, which had also been sent via email. The system was dealing with both the paper and cyber world simultaneously. Even personal assistants were typing the official notes on the computer. The old ubiquitous typewriter, the trademark of government offices, was being consigned to history. There was a slow and steady transition.

The phone on her desk was ringing. Often she picked it up without waiting for the PA's assistance. She had seen a slight glint of disapproval in the eyes of Mr. Rawat, her greying PA, one in the old mould. Officers were not supposed to attend their own calls.

'Ma, it is already 6 pm. Why are you not at home? Don't you remember we have to go to Nani's house today? It is Friday.'

It had escaped her mind. Her household had fallen back onto the same pattern. The weekends were spent with Mummy and Papa. The drive had however worsened. Crossing the bridge on the Yamuna River was a nightmare; it was full of traffic and pollution. Below the bridge, the river was a dull line of grey. It looked sad, pathetic and forlorn. People honked, crossed the road in the midst of traffic and all kinds of vehicles from cycles, auto-rickshaws, buses and scooters to cars swarmed the bridge. Just the thought of that drive made Abha feel tired.

Abha watched as her parents had another of their interminable arguments. Was it possible to remain like this over a lifetime? It seemed an incredibly sad waste of time. Especially for her mother. Her father had his work, his friends, his life, but Mummy—she was the one who had lost a sense of purpose in this endless bickering. It was impossible to play peacemaker. So Abha watched TV, Parul played outside with some friends and her parents argued.

That night as she lay reading a book, her mother came and lay down beside her. Automatically Abha put her arm around her and continued reading.

'Abha there is a proposal referred by Usha aunty.'

Even if some things are expected all the time, their actual occurence can be disorienting.

'Mummy not now. I am reading.'

'Listen at least. The boy is also divorced. His twelve-year-old son lives with his mother. He is in a good job in Chennai and is from our community. The family is also good.'

Parul was sleeping soundly, heedless to the discussion that would have a momentous impact on her life.

'Say something, Beti. I feel you must think about these things at the right time. When the child grows older it will be tougher on her.'

What could she say? Her conservative parents were pursuing a second marriage for her with such vigour. Abha had known this issue would come up. Sooner rather than later. She had to contend with it, decide and then act.

'Mummy, I heard you. Let me think about it. We will discuss it next week.'

'Alright. Tell me what book you are reading.'

'Mummy it is a beautiful book called The *Alchemist* by Paulo Coelho. It is so inspiring.'

'Tell me the story in brief.'

Abha told the story to her mother. It is comforting at any age to bond with one's mother. Abha understood her own parents much better since she had become one herself. With the passing years, she had begun to view them as individuals, not just as parents.

Her parents had grown older; it was discernible and palpable now. Still they worried about her. For them their single daughter was an unfulfilled responsibility. Abha had this strong urge to speak to Diwakar, but banished the thought even as it was taking form. There was no melancholy in the banishment. It simply was.

She decided to call Simran the next day.

Simran was looking haggard and drawn when they met at the same Udipi café. In a flash, hot steaming South Indian coffee and idlis were before them. The food smelt the same.

'How is Shikha doing Simran?' One look at her and Abha understood Simran had no room for her troubles.

'She is sinking everyday. Abha, she is in so much agony. We all now want her agony to end. It is terrible to watch a life being snuffed out like this. It is worse for Nupur. She is only one and a half years old. Imagine she will never have a mother all her life.'

Abha had not gone to see Shikha, because Shikha did not want to meet people.

'You keep up your spirits and health. You are going to need all your resources now. Office, home, hospital—so much to take care of, Simran, take good care of yourself.'

'I am trying my best. Shikha's husband and in-laws are also very good and supportive, but what can anyone do?'

Outside it was raining again. The drops of rain managed to drench commuters waiting for buses. Inside, the café managed to remain untouched and unchanged. The coffee cups in their hands were the same too; only they themselves had changed so much.

'Are you still in touch with Hussein?'

'Actually Abha, I really don't know. He has called many times. He is ready to come to Delhi, just to be with me. As if that is what I need. I wish he could be by my side while I go through this. But now I have stopped feeling hurt by my own desires.'

Abha looked out at the dripping rain. What Simran said was true; often our own desires are what cause all the pain.

'Abha, can you imagine Shikha is dying. She will disappear from the face of the earth. She is five years younger than me.'

Outside the downpour had stopped as suddenly as it had begun. The rainy season was giving way to the cool autumn. Simran was crying silently into her coffee as Abha sat there wondering what life was all about.

The watch on Abha's wrist read 6.15 pm. The meeting did not seem to end. The handful of people in the confined room in North Block fidgeted and collected their papers, but the meeting continued. Outside it was already pitch dark. In winter, when Abha came to work in the morning there was daylight, by the time she finished it was pitch dark. The days felt inordinately long.

Parul would be fretting. Abha could nearly hear the insistent ring of the phone in her room in Nirman Bhawan. The moment the clock went past 6.30 pm, Parul would start calling her. It was as if she was programmed to expect her mother back by then. If she needed to stay longer, Abha had to keep Parul informed.

Abha had not yet told Parul that she had agreed to meet the person suggested by Usha aunty. What could she tell the child? That Mummy was thinking of getting married? It was difficult and absurd at the same time. Maybe it was premature to talk to Parul. It was all confusing and incredibly tough.

The meeting ended abruptly, and a collective sigh of relief went around the room. Just as they were going to walk out, one of the officers stopped them.

'Please let me look outside to see if there are any monkeys.'

Abha remembered the monkeys which would be seen strolling in the North Block corridors after office hours, but it had never been a matter of concern. The officer opened the door, looked out and then closed it again hurriedly.

'Sir, we need to call the security people.'

Abha cautiously peeped out. The sight outside was terrifying to say the least. Hordes of monkeys of all ages were roaming the North Block corridors, screeching and whimpering. They walked as if they owned the place. The sight was scary. They waited for being rescued from the predicament. The monkeys of North Block had multiplied and now become a menace. Some things did change in the labyrinth of the government all the time!

'I don't understand why we cannot get rid of these creatures through some kind of operation.'

'I am told there is some instruction in some file that the monkeys are not to be disturbed.'

'So, we can be disturbed, but not the monkeys.'

The room had been full of views and counterviews. Apparently, it had become a daily occurrence. Whenever officers stayed late in the office they had to first peep out to see if monkeys were around. After office hours, once North Block was empty of its inhabitants, the monkeys came to claim it. They roamed the corridors and the verandahs with great aplomb. Consequently, all windows were meshed and all doors locked, to keep the monkeys away from the Government's precious files and papers.

'Do you know there is something called "monkey disposal". If the monkeys get hold of a file and as a consequence a few pages are missing it is officially noted that the monkeys got it!'

Some things never ceased to amaze. One of them was the absurdity of the way the Government functioned on certain issues. That it worked, nevertheless, was the other amazement.

Outside the door could be heard sounds of sticks beating on the ground. Thereafter, there was a knock at the door. Cautiously, they all stepped out. Escorted by security people, busy beating sticks on the floor, they made their way out of the building.

Abha had given a lift to a colleague who resided in Pandara Road.

'How come it has come to this? When I was here more than two years ago it was not such a menace.'

'Abha ji, their population has probably grown faster than ours. Then there are people who feed them on Tuesdays for religious purposes. All in all it has become a mess.'

'It is dangerous too. Imagine if they attacked someone.'

'It is said in North Block that these monkeys are the souls of the officers who did not get the promotions they wanted. They come back and haunt the rooms they think they should have sat in!'

At home, Parul was busy watching TV. The moment Abha entered, she said 'Ma I want to go to Gauri's house to play. I was waiting to ask you. Reena Didi said I can go only if you say so. Can I go?'

'Okay go. But come back by eight.'

Gauri lived in the block across the square. They could see her house from their window. Parul had gone out and Abha was all alone. Her little girl was slowly on her way to creating her own world, her own friends and her own ways of spending time.

The small restaurant at Triveni Kala Sangam was slowly filling up. It was a nice winter afternoon with the sun shining bright. The kind of day when the sun invited people to embrace its warmth. Abha watched the crowd around her as she waited for Ujjwal. They had decided to meet for lunch at Triveni because he wanted to stroll around the small art gallery later. Since she had come back from Japan this was only the second time they were meeting. Life had such a way of claiming all attention

She watched as Ujjwal walked in, talking animatedly on his mobile. He had begun to grey and had filled out. It was interesting to watch someone like this from a distance. It was like seeing them anew. He looked assured and confident, someone who knew his place in the world. Once he sat down in front of her, the accumulated experience of life kind of wore off, and he was like always. Known and familiar. They had known each other long before any of the people who were now intrinsic to their lives had entered.

'Sorry for being late. I was caught up in something.'

'That's alright. It is such a nice day. Nice and sunny. I love it like this.'

His mobile had begun to ring again. The mobile phone's intrusion in life irritated Abha. It was everywhere. At office, home, restaurants everywhere. As if the instrument had an equal hold on life. She had resisted taking a mobile. Why would anyone want to be approachable at all times, was beyond her understanding. However, the mobile was a technological leap from which there was no escape. Eventually it would catch up with her, she knew.

'I am planning to buy some paintings. You know it is a good investment and the Indian art scene is booming. Are you interested?'

'You and I belong to a different economic league Ujjwal. Anyways, paintings don't move me. Maybe the static does not inspire me. I am much more a books, movies and theatre person.'

'I must say, ever since you came back from Japan you are a much more relaxed person. A kind of quiet has descended on you. You met someone there?'

In a flash, Diwakar was sitting in front of her. Abha felt a smile inside. When she had hugged him at Narita airport nearly nine months ago, she had realized she was always going to be happy when she thought of him, because she had been so happy with him. She had become free in a way she had never been before.

'Maybe myself. I think I really got to know myself much better there.'

'That is a difficult task. Most of us spend our lives running away from our own selves.'

The food arrived and in between phone calls, they got down to the business of eating.

'How are things after a break of two years?'

'So much has changed, and yet it remains the same. All the expectations of the life left behind are just waiting to be fulfilled.'

'What is it that you want?'

'You always ask me that Ujjwal. As if it is easy to know what one wants.'

'But you do need to know Abha. Often we never think of what we want really seriously. We just assume we know. That assumption often turns out to be totally incorrect. '

'True Ujjwal. Someone else also told me sometime ago "What is life without passion?" How is life with you?'

'Well I feel very tired at times. Bored too. In the private sector you have got to slog.' Both of them were now in completely different orbits, yet somewhere there remained a convergence. A sense of ease and comfort that overcame all that had become different. Abha never felt he was a stranger, despite the years and the gaps.

'What is it that you want Ujjwal?'

'I really wish I knew. Am looking for a change from my current job. Maybe I will also try my hand at teaching part time. How is Parul? Not met her for a long time.'

'She is fine. Growing up. Next time I will bring her too.'

After lunch, they strolled in the art gallery, as Ujjwal went on making enquiries about the pictures.

Back in office, Abha accessed her email. A New Year greeting was there for Parul and herself from Diwakar. He had mailed her after a long time. Already, Tokyo and all its associations seemed like a dream. It was a nice chatty mail. He had finished his poetry collection and it was likely to be published soon.

The New Year was around the corner, and Abha had not even noticed. Even after such a long gap, his mail seemed to be the continuation of a conversation left off somewhere … .

Despite the weekend, the Yamuna bridge was crowded. It was a test of endurance to navigate the traffic towards East Delhi. The Metro was increasingly awaited in Delhi.

Parul was humming away to the song playing in the car. She was nearly seven, and Abha could clearly discern a distinct personality taking shape. She kept her things meticulously, had outgrown cartoons and loved Indian pop music and Maths. It was fascinating to watch one's child grow up.

'Ma we have not gone anywhere outside Delhi since you came back from Japan.'

'That is true. Where do you think we should go?'

'Let us go to Lucknow to Bina Mausi's house. I love it there. I went there twice with Nani-Papa while you were away.'

'Not a bad idea. Let me see how I can arrange my leave and then we can go for a few days.'

Abha's mind had been on other things. She had agreed to meet 'the man from Chennai' that evening. It was inevitable.

At home, Mummy was on edge. The whole house seemed to be engaged in some kind of hectic activity centred around cleaning and decoration. The best tea set was out, along with a fresh coat of polish on the brass lamp.

'Mummy I think you are getting unnecessarily bothered. He is only someone coming to meet us. For heaven's sake!'

'Let me do things I want, Beti. I have found out everything from Usha. The boy is good, his family is well placed. He is from our caste. If it works out, it will be a good thing.'

How come when it came to marriage, the parameters of suitability remained the same for parents? Each time. As if the mantra would work at the end. Was that what really mattered in a good marriage?

The 'man from Chennai' was sitting on the sofa. He was ordinary looking but there was a quiet about him, which bordered on rigidity. Abha did not want to judge him harshly. Over tea, they talked.

'I have also been through a divorce and so I know that it is never easy to explain why it happened. I just hope that you have really put it behind you the way I have.'

Abha appreciated his clear and direct approach. 'I agree and I think I have. If you don't mind my asking I would like to know what is the commitment regarding your ex-wife and son?'

Abha could not believe she had asked such a question. From where had this brutal and yet necessary question come into her mind? He looked a bit taken aback, but it was important to get the basics right.

'Well I have paid the alimony in lump sum. My son visits me in the holidays and we have a joint custody over him. I will remain responsible for his welfare like any father should be.'

Then the discussion had moved on to jobs, interests and the like. Papa and Mummy had come, met him, talked to him and then quietly left the room again.

They had fallen silent. The way two people often do when conversation seems to run out. Parul came charging in from outside breaking the silence. She stopped short when she saw a stranger. Instinctively she came and clung to her mother's side.

'This is my daughter Parul. She is in the third standard and is seven years old. Parul say "*Namaste*".'

Parul quietly folded her hands in obedience. Then, as if to escape further commands, she ran out of the room.

'She is very pretty.'

'Thanks.'

'I am sure if we do decide to get together we can look for a good residential school for her to stay. She can visit us in the holidays.'

Suddenly the windows and doors of Abha's mind clamped shut.

'Actually, in my scheme of things she stays with me.' There would never be any bargaining on this issue in her life.

'Of course we can discuss this. I just said it by way of suggestion,' he said.

After the man from Chennai had left, Papa and Mummy huddled around Abha and tried to counsel her about all the good things in the match. Parul watched TV obliviously in another room.

'Mummy how could he just decide Parul's fate in such a decisive manner. He should have asked my opinion. Anyway, for the time being, I want to leave it at this.'

Papa interjected 'Let us see what they say, and then we will think about this further.'

The matter was left hanging, like these things often are.

On Sunday when Abha and Parul entered their apartment in Pandara Road, the phone was ringing.

'Hi girl, what's new with you?'

Rekha had this knack of catching Abha just when she required to ventilate.

'Nothing much. I met this Mr. Suitable and he really got on my nerves with his approach to Parul.'

'Relax Abha. You should expect these things. Don't you know in our system the woman is supposed to be just grateful that someone is ready to marry her at all? Especially when she has a so-called past and baggage too. Come on, you have a marriage in the past, and a kid too!'

'Well so does he. Anyway, I see your point. Tell me what is up at your end? How is London going? Are you still there?'

'Yes. Although I am now in Greece. Came on a holiday. Abha I really want to quit this banking thing, this staying away from India. Everything. It is strange, but now I feel like coming home. Doing something there. In a way, contributing.'

'Why do we all think that at thirty-five we can begin our lives anew? Why do we have such unrealistic expectations? Look at you. Good job, travelling around the world, a lover—and yet you crib.'

'It all seems so empty and pointless from where I am. Ever since Biji died, I have started feeling it even more. I wish you could see it.'

'Tell you what, Rekha, come down for a few days here.'

'I have also been thinking about it. Okay, catch you later. Bye.'

Abha opened the locks to the rooms, while Reena and Parul opened the windows. The phone started ringing again.

'Abha she died this afternoon. The cremation is tomorrow at Lodhi crematorium at 11 am. Bye.' Simran sobbed as she put the phone down.

Shikha's journey was over. Like a film, the years that Shikha had flitted around in their childhood seemed to replay in her mind. How was it that when someone died, even insignificant memories assumed a clarity and significance not there before?

Shikha's cremation was quiet and quick next day, because they decided to use the electric crematorium instead of the traditional fire. All the people connected to her life were present, except her little daughter who was at home.

Simran wept inconsolably, while Shikha's husband kept a stoic silence. Shikha dissolved in the smoke that emanated from the chimney of the electric furnace.

Soon there was an email from the 'man from Chennai'. He seemed to be keen to get the alliance going. Abha sat and stared at his message. In her mind, his presumptuous statement echoed whenever she thought of him. She sent him a short reply about meeting him when he was in Delhi next.

Outside, spring had arrived. The roundabouts were full of flowers and the birds chirped loudly on their way home. Simran and Nupur were coming over in the evening to spend a few days with them. It had been over a month since Shikha had gone.

At home, Parul had already taken Nupur under her wing. Simran—her dear friend, older and wiser was sipping a cup of hot tea. Abha joined her in the balcony. It was a long time since they had sat together in a relaxed setting.

'How is your mum Simran? How is she coping with the tragedy? Its still unreal.'

'She has totally immersed herself in Nupur. That is her way of dealing with it.'

Nupur was busy playing with the dolls Parul had pulled out from her cupboard and strewn before her.

'How is she doing Simran?'

'Do you know ever since Nupur's father has gone, he calls often and speaks to her, but he never asks us to send her over.'

'Do you want to send her there?'

'Actually no. She is too small. Who will look after her there? His parents are also in a different town. But he should at least say it.'

'Simran thank your stars that he is not asking. Then you would be wondering how to keep her with you. Be reasonable, maybe he is thinking the same thing and so not saying anything about it.'

The evening sun had gathered the last rays to leave them for the day. Abha glanced at Simran reclining in the chair. She looked tired and drawn. She had the fatigue that long illness and eventual loss of a loved one bring to the living.

The two girls were playing hide and seek. The house was full of sounds of laughter and chirping. As they ran around the house, hope seemed to flicker in the gloomy evening.

'Tell me Abha, what has been going on with you. We have not had a chance to catch up since you came back from Japan.'

Abha had not been able to share much with Simran. There had been no time. The moment Simran spoke about Japan, Abha remembered Diwakar. It was as if he was synonymous with Japan. She had thought of telling Simran about him, but what was there to say?

'My parents are actively looking out for a match for me. I met a guy also some time ago. There was another proposal also from some NRI. But I don't want to go abroad leaving my job and all.'

'Do you want to get married Abha?'

'Actually yes. Simran, I had never thought of living my life alone. Ever. I like the company of a man. I miss having a physical relationship and I see marriage as the best way of getting what I want.'

'That is one of the most candid statements you ever made to me. If that is what you want, you must seriously go for it.'

'But Simran I also don't want to marry for the sake of being married. It has to be a considered choice and my life after that has to be better than it is, as of now. There is a certain equilibrium in my life now; it has to move to a higher one if I do decide to get married.'

'Somehow it sounds very calculated Abha. But I guess it is right and practical.'

'The man from Chennai' had sent emails and called Abha too. His pursuit seemed to be that of the proverbial Indian male who could not accept that a woman could even think of turning him down.

Abha had a lurking suspicion that Papa had run a newspaper matrimonial advertisement. He would pop suggestions all the time. On her next weekend visit, Abha asked him outright; the haste with which he said 'no' confirmed her suspicion. Years ago, this would have led to a full-scale battle, but they had mellowed over time. They had learnt to accept each other.

Abha and Parul returned on Sunday evening. Parul fidgeted in bed for a long time before asking, 'Ma, what do Nani and Papa keep talking to you? When I come in the room you all keep quiet.'

Parul had noticed. Her self-preservation instinct did not let things go unnoticed easily, being rather pronounced.

'They want me to get married.'

'But you were already married. Nobody marries again.'

'They do Beta. Marriage is supposed to be a lifetime thing, but if it doesn't work you can think of marrying again.'

'But why do you want to marry?'

'So that when you grow up, I will have someone and will not be alone.' Why had she said such traditional things to her daughter? Did every generation say it to the next because it was the easiest justification or because at the end it was the truth?

'But Ma you have me. You don't need anybody else. When I grow up we will stay together like Simran aunty and her mother.'

Was it possible to discuss these things in detail with a seven-year-old? In their minds, everything about life is simple and straightforward.

'Ma, has my father also married again?'

'Yes, he did Parul. Many years ago now.'

Parul was quiet. The issue acquired a different hue now. Abha let it be. This would be a long haul. Parul had fallen asleep. The sound of her even breathing relaxed Abha. The moon far away in the sky tried to peep in and share the warmth of the mother and the child. Abha lay awake for a long time.

Had mid-life blues caught up with all of them? Rekha was restless in London, Simran was struggling with her emotions and she was contemplating marriage in an extremely bland and practical manner. Had she lost her capacity to dream? Was it possible to dream when there were so many issues to consider, especially an innocent seven-year-old who slept next to her with the abandon only children have.

It was a bank holiday and Simran was at home. Amma had given Nupur a bath, and was busy cooking in the kitchen. Nupur came, opened her colouring book and sat next to Simran. Her freshly bathed smell enveloped Simran. Feeling a rush of affection, Simran picked her up and hugged her.

Nupur struggled and freed herself, and continued with the colouring. Simran opened the cupboard that had Nupur's clothes. It was a mess. She began putting it in order. Amma came and sat down on the bed, and started praying. Since Shikha's death, Amma had turned to religion in a big way. After Amma finished they moved to the dining table for lunch.

Simran was busy chasing Nupur around the table with a chapatti roll. The doorbell rang just as Nupur took her third bite.

Amma opened the door to find Nupur's father on the steps. She welcomed him warmly. Nupur ran to him and hugged his legs. He picked her up and swung her in the air. Simran watched the utter delight on Nupur's face and felt a strange pull at her insides. The sudden arrival of Nupur's father made her inexplicably nervous.

He joined them for lunch, and they remembered Shikha. He obviously had come to say something. Simran could sense it. Had he come to take Nupur? Suddenly Simran realized she was not mentally prepared for such an eventuality.

'Amma ji, I have taken leave for a month and am going to be with my parents. I thought I should take Nupur with me.'

'*Haan haan* (Yes, yes). Yes of course Nupur must spend time with you and her grandparents.' Amma readily agreed to the proposal.

Simran felt her throat go dry. She waited for Amma to ask about his plans for Nupur after the month was over. However, Amma was busy chopping fruits for her son-in-law. She could not bear the uncertainty and asked, 'Are you going to drop Nupur back at the end of your leave?'

Amma shot her a disapproving look, but Simran had to know.

'Yes, Amma ji, I feel it is better if Nupur is with you people for sometime. I hope it does not inconvenience you both.'

Simran felt a wave of relief. The knots within her untied one by one. She felt light and began smiling again. Amma reassured him about Nupur being welcome in her house.

Nupur's father left in the evening for a two-day work trip to Agra. He would take her on his return. As soon as the door shut on him, Amma said gently, 'Nupur is his daughter Simran. You must remember that.'

Did it give him the right to take Nupur away from her life? Simran wondered. Not after Nupur had been with them for over a year. Or did it?

Simran pushed back the disturbing thoughts and started packing Nupur's things for the coming month. She had just closed the suitcase when her phone beeped. She checked the message; it was from Hussein. Simran was surprised. It had been a long time since they had been in touch. 'Am in Delhi day after tomorrow. Can we meet?' Her first instinct was to agree, but then Simran remembered that Nupur would be leaving the day after tomorrow. For a month.

Nupur was sleeping. A light of innocence. Simran sat near her pillow and gently stroked her forehead. The child frowned in her sleep and turned over.

Simran's sms read 'Can't make it.'

'I got a good offer in India and next month I am moving to Bangalore. It will be close to home. It is always easier to think about things in one's own country.'

When Abha read the mail, a strange wave of apprehension washed over her. Diwakar would henceforth not be in far away Tokyo, but in Bangalore. More than a year after her return, he had also decided to move back.

The insistent buzz of the intercom drew Abha back to work. A Parliament Question landed on her desk and she got lost in the maze these instruments of democracy tend to create in government offices. A Parliament Question elicits a step-by-step approach. When it first makes its appearance, the effort is to pass it on to some other division or desk. 'This doesn't pertain to us' is the first line of defence. Once that fails, if it is an unstarred question it does not pose a problem. It requires only a written reply. However, a starred question means the beginning of a long period of grind. Long hours would be spent trying to visualize what supplementary oral questions could be linked to the basic question. Reams of statistics, information and notes were prepared. Ministers were briefed and more notes prepared. After all this effort, if the question was listed lower down in the Question Hour of Parliament it might not come up at all. Then the file would be packed up, to be retrieved only when a similar question came up. It often did, in the next session of Parliament.

Luck had favoured Abha, so she had to contend only with an unstarred question. However, it kept her in the office till about 8 pm. When she reached home, she found Simran there. Alone.

'Hey where is Nupur?'

'Gone for a month with her father.' Simran sounded lonesome when she said that. Abha gave her a quick hug and said, 'It's alright Simran. He is her father. He will take care of her.'

Abha checked Parul's bag for the next day at school and scolded her for not completing her homework. After dinner, once Parul had gone to bed, Simran and Abha sat in the small balcony.

Simran said, 'Abha don't you find it difficult to manage her all alone? Doesn't the feeling of responsibility scare you at times?'

Abha was quiet. She had never asked herself this. When she looked within, the answer was unambiguous and clear.

'No, Simran, to the latter question. She is my child. Period. As to the first one, managing is tough at times due to work pressure, but that is a problem all working mothers face.'

Moonlight was streaming in through one of the windows. In that light, Simran looked rather tired and drawn. Simran broke the silence.

'Abha did I tell you I called Hussein and told him to stop calling me and move out of my life completely some time back. Not that he was there, but I felt the need for a formal closure.'

Abha saw the truth in the statement. Each one needs to find their own resolution.

'Shikha's death changed my outlook on life. It is too short, Abha. I must move on in my life in every sense.'

Death was the final arbiter. Hindu philosophy extols *shamshan vairagya*—a sense of detachment born after a cremation. That death could also provide an impetus to life was often overlooked.

'What did he say?'

'Nothing much. Just "Okay, if that is how you want it." You know Abha, I must say that grudgingly I respect the guy for not giving me false hopes. Ever.'

'We all have had a long day Simran. Let us go to bed now.'

Abha lay down next to Parul and snuggling up to her sleeping form fell asleep in minutes. Simran lay awake for sometime wondering what Nupur was doing.

Abha and Aarti Devi sat in the small balcony in the Pandara Road house. She would come and stay with Abha for a change. Age was creeping down her whole system, and she kept unwell.

'Abha you don't seem to like anyone that we come across. Age is going against you now Beti. If you want to get married, compromise on some things and go for it. Parul will resist more as she grows older.'

'Mummy of course I am ready to compromise, but it cannot be something as basic as Parul or my job you know. And really Mummy I don't want to marry just because I have to.'

'Sometimes, I wonder where I went wrong with you. Bina is so well settled in her life.'

The question would have made Abha feel guilty some years ago. But it was not so any more.

'Mummy, why is it so important to always lay the blame at some quarter. Can you not accept that things often just happen? I am well settled. I can take care of myself and my daughter.'

Abha had learnt long ago that as long as you do what you are supposed to do well, the rest falls into place.

'That is not what I meant. Just that … .'

Abha knew how she felt. Her incredibly brave and intelligent mother had tried to instil confidence and independence in her two daughters. Why had she not realized that change always had a price? The price was not always harsh. Her mother had done her bit for the generational struggle of women. There was just this far each generation could actually go, before the baton was handed over.

'How are all your friends?'

'Simran is alright. These days she is missing Nupur as she has gone to her father. Rekha may come next month for a few days to India. Her father now lives in Hoshiarpur, their hometown.'

'Neither of them is married.'

'No Mummy. Does it matter? Being married is not the be all and end all of life.'

'I know. But there has to be something other than yourself. When you come to a certain stage in life, you need something more than yourself to live for. You have Parul.'

Was that the truth of life? That at the end you need something other than yourself to live for?

Abha loved the days when Aarti Devi would come to stay. The three of them would go for long drives, have masala dosa at a good South Indian restaurant and chat. Life was idyllic and Abha often wondered if she was disturbing this harmony by thinking of marriage again.

Rekha had hired a car to whisk her straight from the Delhi airport to Chandigarh. Her cousin would join her there and together they would go to Hoshiarpur. Rekha was going to Hoshiarpur after nearly a lifetime. Papaji had settled there after Biji's death. Her memories of the ancestral home remained clear. They were happy and cheerful memories. Childhood memories of the hustle-bustle of the house seemed to envelop her in the lonely ride.

Delhi had changed a lot. As the taxi whizzed past the flyover under construction, the entire city seemed to be undergoing an overhaul. Rekha observed with interest as swanky shopping malls, hoardings and logos of international brands flashed by. India had changed. It was different from the place in her memory. She had returned after nearly half a decade. She had not come after Biji's death; instead, she had called Papaji to London to live with her.

He had come, tried to build a life in the damp and cloudy climes of London. After six months, he had decided to return and settle in Hoshiarpur. 'I want to die at home Rekha.' She hated such maudlin talk, but understood the feeling behind his decision.

Rekha dialled Abha's number from her mobile. It was still early and Abha's voice was groggy with sleep.

'Abha am on my way to Hoshiarpur. Will be back next week and will meet you on my way back to London. Keep yourself free on Friday night. Okay girl?'

'Hey Rekha what the hell. You land up and call like this. Stay with me for a few days on your return.'

'Girl, be thankful I am meeting you! Jokes apart. Next time I will stay with you. Okay? See you. This is the international phone. Bye.'

The taxi had left Delhi and Rekha looked outside the window. It was different from London, Hong Kong or all the other places she had been to. She always remembered being irritated by the dirt, crowd, the unkempt look of the place. Today she felt a sense of relief. Had the perfection and order of London set in a sense of ennui? Was she simply missing the sun?

Rekha had received an email from a prestigious investment bank a few weeks ago. A positive job offer from the city of her dreams—

New York. She had been looking forward to this move for many years. As Rekha stared at the computer screen she had felt nothing. Simply nothing. No happiness or joy. Only a deep sense of fatigue.

She had decided to plan a trip to India. Maybe it would put things in a better perspective. Maybe her sense of inertia would disappear and she would be recharged about her life and career.

The taxi jumped on a pothole, and Rekha nearly banged her head against the roof of the car.

'Slowly please,' she instructed the driver and reclined against the seat. Hindi film music was playing inside. It sounded good. She had forgotten the pure joy of a full-throated Bollywood hit.

London seemed far away. Remote and distant. Hoshiarpur seemed dear and familiar. Hardayal Tayaji must be quite old now. Rekha felt glad about her decision to visit them. She was dreaming about her ancestral home as the taxi sped towards Chandigarh.

Abha had known that Diwakar would call her once he settled down in Bangalore. When she heard his voice after more than a year it had felt wonderful. The reassurance and warmth of an old friend. They had chatted for a while about the highlights of the year gone by.

'My poetry book is getting released next week in Belgaum. The local Member of Parliament has agreed to release it. Come for the function.'

'That is impressive. Its too far you know. Anyway all the best.'

After she put down the phone, Abha felt it was a blessing that Bangalore was so far away. She looked out of her office window. The sight was depressing as no trees could be seen. Only a vast expanse of sky. When the window was open, she could hear the traffic of Maulana Azad Road rushing past.

Rekha was back from Hoshiarpur to catch the flight to London the next morning. Abha left office at the stroke of 5.30 pm to spend some time with her. When the doorbell rang, Abha ran to the door. Impulsively she gave Rekha a hug. It felt good to meet her after a long time. Rekha was smarter, looked good and happening. The angularities of her Punjabi personality had smoothened and she had matured into a global woman.

'How do you manage to look so good, Rekha? You are one of the few people who have grown better with age. You don't have a single grey hair.'

'I colour it you know. You should also give up henna and start using a good colour. So tell me what's new?'

Abha burst out laughing. Some things never changed and what a blessing that they did not. Life was the sum of all that one could count on.

They sat around the simple meal Reena had prepared. Parul seemed awed by this new entrant in their house. Rekha ruffled her hair and said, 'You look like your mom! I got some chocolates for you. Take them from my bag.' Parul scampered off.

Abha told Rekha about Diwakar's move to Bangalore.

'For you he is still in Tokyo alright. Don't waste any more of your time okay?' Rekha's nonchalant comments made a lot of sense, most of the time. Her somewhat cynical wisdom often had more than its share of hidden truth. Despite her self–obsessed demeanour, Rekha managed to see things from an extremely neutral perspective.

'So what's up with you? Your companion moved to London?'

'No. Maybe it's better this way. Who knows? You tell me what's up with Simran?' Abha briefed her on the happenings in Simran's life. 'Simran should stop being a nanny to that little girl. If she wants to do something good for Nupur and herself, she should gather her guts and adopt her. Her dad would probably be happy. Girls are not wanted you know that—don't you?'

Rekha had spent the last few days in Hoshiarpur, in the heart of Punjab. She had always known that the birth of a girl child was not welcomed in her ancestral place. The rituals announcing the birth of a male child were different. On this trip what she had seen had frightened her.

'No house seemed to have any young girl Abha. There were only boys. As if young female children did not exist.'

The walls in the remote villages of Punjab were plastered with slogans that brutally said, 'Why spend two lakhs later? Spend two thousand today'. Advertisements announced the cheap and easy availability of ultrasound machines for sex determination of unborn foetuses. If it turned out to be female, it was aborted.

'Abha, we always thought that economic development made things better. But look at my home state. Punjab is one of the richest States in India and it is there that the ultrasound has invaded every village to eliminate girls. Technology is assisting the murder of thousands of girl children.'

After a long time Rekha had felt passionately about something. The scenario had shaken her.

'How come this big social and demographic disaster is happening Abha and no one is doing anything about it?'

'Rekha there is a law that I have heard of. But like many others, it is not being implemented.'

The entire evening the issue of the girl child dominated the conversation. Rekha, the global woman, independent to the core, had found something that moved her in far away Hoshiarpur. It drove her as if she was possessed. They talked late into the night, and before they realized the taxi was there at the door to take her to the airport.

'When will you come again Rekha? What happened to your plan to move back? It would be good to have you around. It is only when I meet you that I realize that I actually miss you in the long intervening gaps after which we meet each other.'

'Soon, girl. I have a strong intuition that I will be back sooner than you think.'

And she had gone into the night with a wave of her neatly manicured hand.

Bangalore was far, but in the changing face of India it was another city from which people travelled back and forth all the time. The city had become the icon of emerging India, full of hope and energy. Creating a confidence that had been elusive for centuries.

Diwakar had come to Delhi for a seminar, and Abha waited for him in the lobby of Maurya Sheraton. On his suggestion, she had invited him for tea at home. The lobby was full of people coming and going. Abha wondered how she would feel on seeing him after such a long time, in a different setting altogether. Maybe when she saw him she would wonder what she had been doing. Maybe he would be a total stranger, as often people tend to become; maybe this meeting would be the real end.

The elevator door opened and Diwakar walked out. Abha saw him before he did. He looked just the same. Plain, dark with intelligent eyes. But those eyes were behind spectacles that had not been there earlier. Diwakar smiled in a way that lit up his whole face when he saw her. There was nothing remotely strange or distant about him. The warmth of his smile covered the long space after which they were meeting.

'When did you start wearing specs?'

'Since the past two months. I am past forty Abha, five years older than you.'

They sat in her car and moved towards her house.

'It is good to be driven for a change. Role reversal you may say. Delhi traffic is really chaotic isn't it? Bangalore is not much better in terms of roads, but it has an energetic pulse now. It is India's global face and identity. Its a good time to be back in India. Do you see the palpable change that is happening in our country Abha?'

All through the drive, they had talked. About how he observed India's changes. He had come back after a long time. Coming back home after a few years abroad was akin to meeting a child after a span of time. There was the desire to absorb the changes, coupled with hope that they were for the better. There was unconditional acceptance, nevertheless.

'What is really clear, Abha, is the sense of hope and confidence that is there in even the common person. It is amazing. This did not exist some time ago.'

She wondered what he was thinking as he watched the traffic of Delhi pass by. The conversation was on two levels—one that was going on and one that was flowing beneath. Does the tang of past intimacy float around all future interactions?

They reached her home. Abha's mother was also there for the week. Parul recognized him immediately as someone whom she had met in Tokyo. He had brought photographs of the launch of his poetry collection. In one of them his parents were on stage. An elderly rural couple, nothing urban had touched their personality. He had indeed come a long way from his roots.

Parul joined them in the car when Abha went to drop him back.

'So has the marriage decision been taken?'

Diwakar asked in a soft tone making sure that Parul would not hear.

'Not yet. Nothing has been finalized yet. How is your family?'

'Udayan is fine. He is now eleven. He has settled down in his school. I am encouraging my wife to take up a job. Parul what do you miss about Tokyo the most?'

'The trains . They were so good. And you, what do you miss?'

'All the pretty Japanese girls.'

They reached the hotel. He stood at the foyer of the hotel until he vanished from their view. Once again, Abha thought it was good that Bangalore was thousands of miles away.

'Send me a copy of the law and rules related to pre-natal diagnostics techniques. Am looking for it on the internet, but it is not there.

Cheers

Rekha'

Ever since Rekha had gone back, she bombarded Abha with emails seeking information on various aspects of what she had seen in Hoshiarpur. She unearthed names of NGOs and individuals on the internet and asked Abha to locate them, get their addresses and numbers. Abha used all her clout, professional and personal, to get answers to Rekha's various questions.

The 2001 census data analysis had begun to come in. What Rekha had witnessed in Hoshiarpur was backed by data. The disproportionate sex ratio of children in the age group between 0 to 6 years in the country was shocking. The worst revelation was that the richer states like Gujarat, Punjab and Maharashtra were the most affected. The richer and better off in India were using technology to kill their female children before they were born.

It had been a revelation for Abha too. The impunity with which female foetuses were being killed belied belief. Something had gone extremely wrong with where the nation was headed.

Her office window was open to the cool autumn breeze; Abha was busy trying to finish some work. The intercom buzzed. The reception sought her permission to allow Simran to come and meet her. Abha always felt that the security installed managed to grow more walls between the public servants and the public meant to be served.

Simran walked in after sometime and flopped on the chair in front. It was one of her rare visits to Abha's office. They were both busy and kept in touch more on the phone. Much the way Diwakar did. Over the last two months, he had called her often, just to chat. He also emailed her any interesting things he came across on the internet. 'Call for some tea. I am exhausted. I hate government buildings in Delhi now. You have to spend half an hour just to gain entry Abha. It is such a waste of time.'

'I know. But we live in dangerous times Simran. That is what they want us to believe. Maybe it is true, but I don't know if this much policing will ward off anything in an eventuality.'

Simran was silent and looked around. The years that they had spent together did not necessitate a constant stream of conversation. Only when Abha raised her head from work Simran said, 'Nupur's dad wants to get married.'

'It's alright Simran. He is young. He must have become alone the day Shikha was diagnosed with cancer.'

'What about Nupur? She will have to adjust to a new person in her life.'

Abha's mind was on the note before her. From somewhere within her, Rekha's remark had burst forth.

'Why don't you adopt her Simran?'

'Adopt as in? She is staying with me since Shikha's death. She can continue to do so. I have no problem.'

'And you have no right either. Simran, as a simple caretaker you have no right on the child. You love her, want her to be with you—then adopt her, legally become her mother.'

Simran remained quiet. She seemed drawn and tired. The thought was a challenge to her current way of life. She had probably not thought of the responsibilities of parenthood. There had been no need. Perhaps it had been unfair to burden her with the thought.

'I just said it Simran, you don't have to get so serious. Rekha had mentioned it to me the last time she was here, I just repeated it. Forget it.'

The tea came and quietly looking out of the darkening window, they sat in silence again.

'Is it possible Abha?'

'You mean legally? I do know that it is possible for a single Hindu female to adopt a child. If you want, we can contact a lawyer. But I think you really need to think it out before you even venture on fact-finding. It is a lifetime thing—parenthood. We can divorce our spouses, but not our children.'

'I understand that much Abha. I was just asking.' They left Abha's office together. Abha dropped Simran to the station from where she would catch the local train to Ghaziabad. They talked of other things on the way, but the possibility that the conversation had opened up hung around them like a cloak. That is what words do—the train of thought they initiate can never be halted.

The next day was a bad one at work. The boss was cranky as the support staff had all left early for the day. It was Friday and in government offices, Friday meant a licence to leave early. Abha wound up for the day, and before leaving for home decided to check her mail. There was among others, a mail from Diwakar.

'I have decided to opt out of my marriage. The decision has come after a lot of thought and preparation. Since the last fortnight, I am in Hyderabad. I have shifted base here. Udayan and his mother are in Bangalore. All in the family know my decision. The only thing I want to say is that I have always had the courage and conviction to follow my dreams.'

The words hit Abha like a sledgehammer. In a few lines, he had disposed off such a grave matter. Abha suddenly felt as if her head would burst. This sensation of sheer tension and fear had not gripped her since her divorce had been sorted out. It was like a jolt. Abha put her head down on the keyboard to orient herself. She left the office and drove down to the nearest long distance phone booth. She had to speak with him. Only the anonymity of the phone booth could temper the chaos inside her. Why was it that when faced with a difficult situation we only think of ourselves? Was it an evolutionary thing?

'Diwakar why are you doing this?'

'Because that is what I want to do.'

'You have a son.'

'I know. I don't need you to tell me that.'

'I want to tell you that if you feel that I will marry you at the end of it, please do not assume any such thing. I have never thought of you in terms of marriage.'

'I don't think I have said that I expect such a thing from you. I am doing this for myself Abha. Go home now. We will speak later.'

When Abha reached home, Parul was out cycling with her friends. Even in her turmoil, Abha fleetingly wondered if she was wearing something warm to ward off the autumn evening chill. Abha sat with a cup of tea in the small balcony and let the cloud of fear take over.

When we are children, we fear the unknown—the dark shadows on the wall, the wind whistling outside in a storm. As we grow older, the fears get sharper. They acquire clarity and character. She had been through these phases of fear and despair innumerable times. This was like watching her own thought process from a distance. And waiting for it to tire itself out.

The wedding date was fixed. Two months later Nupur's father would be a married man again. Simran sat in her office with papers strewn all around. Somehow, the news made her simmer with anger. They were all forgetting Shikha so quickly. Amma and she had got lost in Nupur, now her husband was also taking a step forward in his life. At one level, Simran accepted it as the right thing, but it did not stop her from being hurt.

Her mobile rang. It was Nupur's father. Each time he called, Simran felt a cold feeling grip the bottom of her stomach. Did he want Nupur to go and live with him? The possibility made her nervous and dread his calls.

'Sorry to disturb you in office, Simran di, but I wanted to come over on the weekend to Delhi to discuss something. Is it okay if I come home at around 5 pm on Saturday? You will be back from the bank by then.'

Simran felt breathless. Her nightmare seemed to be coming true. A recurrent dream stepping out and becoming a reality. She was struck dumb.

'Simran di, can you hear me?'

'If I want to legally adopt Nupur, how would you feel about it?' Simran felt someone else had said it. Then slowly a sense of relief began to seep into her bones. At last Simran was free. She had done the right thing by bringing it out in the open. The thought was chasing her since the day she had been to Abha's office. She had to explore the possibility, before she let Nupur go out of her life. Simran felt a calm descend on her being.

'Simran di we can discuss when I see you,' he said quietly.

The demons of fear plaguing her disappeared. Simran had taken the leap; the courage to carry on would also come.

Abha had turned to work. She immersed herself totally into it. She organized a batch lunch in her room after a long time. Eight of her colleagues were clustered around their lunch boxes. All of them older, wiser and full of cynicism.

'Did you hear about that fellow in the IAS who resigned because of the Gujarat riots? It was on the ground that the communal strife had "sickened" his heart.'

'Come on, he had a job with this international NGO, so he could afford to quit.'

What had happened in Gujarat since the burning of a Sabarmati Express coach was simply mayhem. Its aftermath had been a churning in ideas, thoughts and ideologies.

'Give him some credit. I do think that the killing in Gujarat was disgraceful.'

'What about those burnt alive in the train?'

It was possible for people from similar environments, similar background and similar expectations from life to sit on diametrically opposite sides of the fence. The debate was endless and stretched the national fabric at two ends.

It was probably the burden of the middle class—to bear the load of conscience as passive onlookers, armchair rebels and be pulled in opposite directions. Maybe it stemmed from the web of expectations that surrounded the individual. Life was never one's own; it was answerable to so many others, Abha thought as the debate overtook the lunch and became rather bitter.

When Abha reached home in the evening, Reena told her that her mother had asked her to call home immediately on return from office.

'Abha that man Diwakar I met that day, how long is it that you know him?'

'Mummy I know him since all the two years I was in Japan.'

There was a silence on the line as if Mummy expected her to add something. Abha's mind was in a whirl. Why was her mother questioning her in this manner? At that moment, she was not a thirty-seven year old woman with a nine-year-old daughter. She had become a frightened child wondering what had made her mother so mad.

'His wife says he is leaving home because of you.'

Abha was filled with so many questions in response to that one statement that she became speechless. Diwakar's wife had called her parents? Why should she? What had he said to her? What in the world was going on?

'Mummy this is crap. Why are you entertaining such conversations at all?'

'Did you have a physical relationship with him?'

There was something extremely painful in that moment. Her relationship with her mother had never crossed this threshold. Like most women of her generation, for Aarti Devi, the physical was never to be discussed, talked about or acknowledged. The question was a watershed between them. A bridge crossed. The tension and anger of her old mother had flown down the phone line. Abha's long silence indicated the nod of assent it was meant to be.

'So it is true. How could you Abha?' And her mother put the phone down.

Abha stood there with the phone in her hand. Was it as simple as that? Could one actually draw the graph of relationships—whether of their cementing or breaking? Could there be an axis of causes and results in this arena of life? In her experience, relationships were seamless, they charted their own course.

Just then the doorbell rang, and Simran walked in. One look at Abha's face and she knew something was amiss. At long last, after all the years, Abha told her everything.

'Why did you never share this with me? So much happening in your life and not a word?'

'You were tied up in so many things Simran. It just never came up.'

'So what are you going to do?'

'Me? What is there for me to do? Mummy has to understand that this has nothing to do with her.'

After a few days Abha called Diwakar.

'What have you said to your family? Why is this happening?'

'Abha all of us resist change. This is part of the process that has to be gone through for this to end.'

'You can sit there so calmly and say it because it doesn't affect you.'

'How do you know what is happening to me? This is my problem, I will solve it. I can only say I am sorry for your parents being dragged into this.'

'What about your parents?' Abha remembered their photograph. This kind of thing was not part of their life.

'My parents respect my capacity to take decisions about my own life and they know that I am alone responsible for them.'

'Do you know that in our legal system, as a man asking for a divorce you can spend a lifetime struggling for it? I have seen court cases that have dragged on for decades.'

'You know something Abha. What is difficult is the process of deciding. Once you know what you want the rest doesn't really matter.'

Abha had nothing to say to that. It was an echo of her own determination during her messy divorce. Who was she to try and preach to him? She remembered hating all those who had advised her as if they knew what was better for her.

Simran called her often those days. Her life had moved ahead. Both Amma and Nupur's father had agreed to her proposal to adopt Nupur. Simran was gathering courage to embark on the road of parenthood. When motherhood happens as part of life, the courage, patience and wisdom needed comes along with it. In Simran's case, it was a considered decision, and she would have to bring up Nupur alone. But for once, Simran was not afraid.

Abha had been surprised when Simran thought about adoption seriously. But Simran had always been like that. Something had to appeal to her soul, then she would traverse any terrain to try and achieve it.

Winter had set in. Daylight disappeared quickly and the long dark nights were depressing. Abha had emailed Rekha many times, even tried to call her. However, Rekha had vanished. As she often did.

Rekha sat in the lounge at Heathrow airport. In her bag, was a one-way ticket back to Delhi. Her years abroad had shrunk and fit into two large suitcases. Life had a knack of coming around in circles. Rekha sipped her red wine and awaited the call for her flight. She had not told anyone in India of her decision to return home.

The door to the lounge opened and someone who looked very familiar walked in. Rekha could not place him immediately. Then he saw her and smiled tentatively. In a flash Rekha remembered. Ujjwal. She smiled back and he came and sat next to her.

'My god Ujjwal, we are meeting after donkey's years. How are you? Where are you going?'

'I am on my way to the US for work and you?'

'Well. I am going back to India. For good.'

Rekha had never imagined that the first person she would share this with would be Ujjwal. It felt good when she said it aloud like that.

'Really? Why? What happened?' Ujjwal sounded concerned.

'Oh nothing to worry about. I am joining an NGO that works against female foeticide back home.'

Ujjwal absorbed her statement. He walked to the counter, took a can of beer and came back.

'How did you take such a tough decision Rekha? It must have been really difficult. Giving up a life built through years of hard work for something totally different.'

Had the journey to this point been difficult? Her nebulous restlessness had begun years ago. It had nibbled at Rekha's insides as she went around the globe doing what she wanted to do. The gap had grown in size and begun to occupy a large part of her psyche. Then on the trip to Hardayal Tayaji's home she had found something that moved her, agitated her and pushed her. It made her feel passionate about something. Thereafter, the journey to this moment at Heathrow had become inevitable.

'Ujjwal what we want changes over time. I gave my best to investment banking. I enjoyed it while it lasted, but once I realized what now ignited my passion, I had to follow it. It is all about being able to identify the "what", the rest simply follows.'

The beer was over. Ujjwal was deep in thought when Rekha's flight was announced.

'Okay Ujjwal. I am off. Will see you in Delhi. You must be in touch with Abha. I will catch up with you through her.'

'Yes I am. See you. All the best.'

Ujjwal was still sitting clutching the empty beer can in his hand, when Rekha swept out of the door to the flight that was taking her home.

Adoption was not an easy process. There was a lot of paperwork to be done, many visits to courts and lawyers had to be made before the task could be accomplished. A thorough and detailed process had to be undergone to ensure the best for the child. The process that was supposed to take about three to four months was taking time in her case, as Simran was a single woman. Rekha came back and immersed herself in the fight against female foeticide. She made frequent visits to Punjab and managed to meet Papaji often. At last, her nebulous longings had found root. Her prism of life had broadened.

A few months after Rekha's return Simran legally became Nupur's mother. A milestone in both their lives. An act of courage and love. It transformed Simran's life.

They were sitting in the Gulati restaurant in Pandara Road market, digging into succulent butter chicken and naan. Abha, Rekha and

Simran had got together after a long time. While the kids played at Abha's house, the three of them celebrated life. Just the three of them. Rekha turned over the pretty ashtray sitting in the middle of the restaurant table.

'Made in China. Just as I thought. The way these guys are manufacturing and exporting their goods. We are all drowning in them. It is a conquest through products.'

'They don't make saris as yet, do they?'

'Simran that's not the point. We gotta wake up to China, sooner rather than later.'

Abha remembered growing up with memories of the failed 'Hindi-Chini' bhai-bhai slogan. Later, China had come to mean Chinese food or endless debates on the single-child policy. All that had changed now. Everywhere, like two siblings India and China were compared and contrasted continuously.

'We have woken up Rekha. The media is full these days of India versus China, and speculations about which country is going to be the next economic powerhouse.'

'I keep wondering. What is the point of this "India Shining" business when we still kill our girls, even before they are born.'

'Rekha do you think this trend will come down?'

'You want to know the truth Abha. This damn thing may never change—laws will change, technology will change faster. The only thing that doesn't change is the craze for male children in our system.'

It sounded dismal, but so did many other things that happened all around them. Yet there were many positive things happening in the country. Perhaps all times in history were similar in a way—the good and bad occurred together.

'Basically I don't understand why people want sons. Look at Ravi, he has all the rights, but no responsibility. At some level, this is also changing. Some of the people I met in the adoption process told me many urban couples wanted to adopt girls as against boys.'

The place was filling up for lunch. The restaurant square of Pandara Road in the midst of New Delhi had grown from a place full of eating joints where men would come in at odd hours with drinks masquerading as colas, into a nice up-market area. There was a fountain, it remained well-lit and people of a wide cross-section frequented it. The food remained as fabulous as ever.

'Do you remember this place in college Rekha?'

'Abha I don't remember it. I only remember Nirula's and that too in Connaught Place. Now they have branches all over the city.'

'Rekha, Parul only wants to go to McDonalds. It has been ages since I went to Nirula's.'

'That's true. Nupur also wants only to go to McDonalds.'

'You both better start thinking for yourselves. Not what the kids want all the time. You think that these kids are going to be around when we are old. No way. Life and opportunity is going to take them off soon.'

As usual Rekha had spoken what was most apparent. Choices for careers and vocations of different kinds were exploding all around. The other day, a friend's daughter had opted to be a wine taster and another one opted for event management. Their children would have a new world full of diverse and original choices.

'Who has seen a good movie lately?'

'When you say good what do you have in mind Rekha?'

'A true blue-blooded Bollywood extravaganza. Where there are beautiful people in designer clothes, living in palatial houses who keep breaking out into song and dance. Something to relax the mind because you really don't have to use it for the three hours.'

'I think *Kal ho na ho* fits the bill. Let us pick the kids and Reena and go.'

They bundled into two cars and went to the movie. Spending three hours in the air-conditioned precincts of a dark movie theatre was a wonderful idea.

The same Thursday

The day is just like any other. It is hot and the sun is shining even at 7 am with a ferocity that is blinding. The only difference is Parul's glum and stubborn face as she gets ready for school. Abha stands at the balcony window and waits for Parul to look up as usual and wave. But the straight back with which her daughter goes off towards the bus stop brings a lump to Abha's throat. It is a difficult day. Abha sits in the balcony. Wide awake. Whereas normally she would have hit the bed again after waving to Parul. Papa is sleeping in the other room. Mummy is in hospital with a broken leg and Bina di is attending to her. Abha looks at the henna on her hands. It has become a deep maroon overnight. The intricate patterns proclaim loud and clear that she is getting married. Today.

Why did Mummy fall down just a week ago in the bathroom? Why is Parul so sad and angry? Why are there so many conflicting emotions when it is meant to be a happy occasion? Are these things always so difficult?

The bell rings and Bina di walks in. She comes and gives Abha a nice, big hug. 'Abha you haven't bathed yet? It is already eight-thirty.

You know we have to reach the office by 10 am. Wow, the *mehndi* is really looking nice.' Suddenly Bina di brings a wave of cheer to the room. Seeing her bustling around the flat, getting things organized makes Abha feel that everything will turn out fine at the end.

When Abha finally decided on getting married again, she had first sought Parul's consent.

'Why do you want to marry anyone, Ma? I am there for your old age.' Her nine year old tried to answer all the arguments in one sentence. Closing all doors for future negotiations and discussions. The discussions had been followed by days of sullen silence and strange behaviour. Abha had waited, but Parul consistently refused to talk about it with her.

'You have already decided Ma. So you cannot understand how I feel. You anyway think that what you are doing is right.'

How could she tell her child that her mother was capable of dividing her perspective? She could see things from both their sides. And that she was the only person capable of bridging the gap between the way the two of them viewed the situation.

'Parul do you want to speak to your school counsellor about this? Talk to Simran Aunty. Someone. This way we are not going to solve the issue at all.'

'You will not talk about this in my school. I don't want everyone to laugh at me. Simran Aunty is your friend.' So the silences continued like a blank wall.

'Parul you know him also now. It is not as if I am getting married to a total stranger.'

'But why do you need to marry at all? You have me.'

'Abha the sari is not ironed properly. You are planning to wear the deep purple one you bought in Chennai recently?' Bina di, bless her, gets the house going at times of need. Papa is awake and is reading the newspaper. A steaming cup of tea is in his hand.

'It is going to be very hot today. Let us hope we can finish the whole thing in the forenoon itself.' Papa is the only person who is relaxed. In a way, he is relieved. His daughter is getting married. For him, that is all that matters.

The struggle with Parul had continued. Abha was amazed to discover an endless well of patience within her. Was this the power of love for one's child?

'Parul, till you say "go ahead" I will not proceed with this. I really want you to understand and accept. This is going to bring a big change in our lives, and till you are ready, there is no point in moving forward.'

Parul had responded with total silence. However, she became happier—the bad news had turned out to be false.

After a lapse of a few months, Parul one day said to her 'Ma I think you should go ahead with the marriage.'

'Are you sure?' Abha did not know what brought about the change. Parul did not seem pressured or tense after the announcement. It had opened the door for Abha to start thinking seriously. Some more months later, when Parul had seemed adjusted to the idea, Abha had asked her, 'What made you say "yes" Parul?'

'You really want to marry him Ma. I understand that much.' Her ten-year-old daughter told her. Calmly and in a matter of fact manner.

'Is there some major issue or worry that you have Parul? We can talk about it.'

'Ma you will love him more than me.'

'Parul the love which a parent feels for a child is absolutely different from any other kind of love. There is simply no comparison.' Even as she said it, Abha knew it would be many years before Parul understood. The battlefront then opened at home with her parents.

'We don't know anything about him, his family, and his parents. They are so different from us in language, food, culture … .'

Reservations and objections that were not baseless but for which Abha did not have satisfactory answers. Mummy's only concern had been Parul.

'What is the decision about Parul? Where will she stay? Have you discussed it?'

'Mummy she will stay with me. That is decided.'

Slowly the walls had crumbled down. Abha then decided on a date, and within two days, Mummy slipped and landed up in hospital. Had Mummy been tense about the impending marriage? It made Abha feel somewhat responsible for her fall. However, Mummy insisted that they should stick to the date.

'There is no question of postponing the marriage. Just go ahead with it.'

As the wedding date neared, Parul's resentment to the marriage had resurfaced. It was painful to see her struggle with the impending change. On some days, she would cheerfully discuss the forthcoming trip to Goa and on others, simply cry. Abha felt quite helpless. Thankfully Gaurav and Bina di were there to take Parul under their wings.

'Mummy is very keen that you go to the hospital and visit her as soon as the ceremony is over.' Bina di is keeping the tempo in the house going.

Abha wears her sari, combs her hair and sees her reflection in the mirror. She looks just the same. Who can say she is going to her own wedding?

They get ready to go to the Additional District Magistrate's office for the marriage ceremony. Papa takes out his new shirt. The phone rings. Kishore ji from Lucknow to wish her luck. He did not manage to get leave to come to Delhi.

'You should keep your hair open Abha. You look so nice.' Bina di addresses Abha, as she preens herself in front of the mirror..

'Bina di it is so hot. The silk is anyway making me sweat already. If I keep my hair open, I will just melt away. Let me put it up in a bun.'

Reena set the breakfast on the table.

'Didi eat something before you go. It can take a long time.'

'Of course I will Reena. I am hungry.'

All three of them sit at the small dining table. There is a contemplative silence on the table. Each one of them is with their own thoughts. Papa, Bina and Abha.

Of all the things, Abha remembers her office. The date for the ceremony was decided after taking into account both their commitments at work. Abha needed to finish a lot of work before the fifteen days' leave was sanctioned to her. Abha had remembered Murai sensei's appointment diary. He had also consulted his appointment diary to fix his marriage date. The same had happened with her. Not a pundit, but other commitments had decided the date.

Abha later discovered that everyone else who mattered had prior commitments too. Rekha was busy in a gender conference in

Mauritius, while Simran was busy with an audit in Mumbai. It was sad. She was going to miss them.

Ujjwal was also out of the country. A fortnight ago, Ujjwal had called to say that he was going to be out for the whole month. Abha decided to tell him about the marriage once he was back.

'Abha have your tickets to Goa been confirmed?'

'Yes Papa. We leave day after tomorrow in the afternoon.'

'Abha you don't have to take Parul with you. I can take her with Gaurav and me to Lucknow.'

'It is fine Bina di. We both feel that if we leave her behind now then she will never get over her feeling of alienation. She should also meet his side. They must get to know her too.'

After breakfast, Abha begins to collect all the papers needed for the ceremony. Her divorce decree, the notice from the marriage office and an affidavit about her intention to marry. All the legal papers needed for the social institution of marriage. Papa, being the bride's father, had insisted on holding a small reception the next day to inform the world about the marriage. Only public acknowledgment provides marriage the required legitimacy.

'Abha, from the office you will come here again or go to his place? Should I put the overnight bag I packed for you in the car?'

She is going to her marriage with an overnight case. It is all so different and bizarre.

'Yes Bina di. We will visit Mummy after the ceremony. Then you all come for the lunch at his place. I will come in here again tomorrow morning.' A married woman. After such a long gap, it will take some time to get used to all over again.

'Abha, I think you should take your official identity card with you. Sometimes these things help in government offices.'

'I always carry it in my bag Papa.' All the things required for the ceremony are on the dining table. Two marigold garlands and a box of sweets. Other than the papers, they were the only requirements for a court marriage.

Reena peeps out intermittently from the balcony window. She calls out excitedly, 'They are here Didi. Sir is waiting in his car downstairs.'

Abha goes to the window to say that she is coming down. She sees him standing near the car door. On his forehead is a red tilak. The only mark of ceremony. It looks rather nice on him. Traditional and bright. He looks up, waves and smiles.

'You had said to me that you never thought of me in terms of marriage. That was then. Now I am single and available and would like you to think about me in terms of marriage.'

When Diwakar had said this to Abha in her office, the day he moved to Delhi some time ago, she had found his approach rather quaint.

'Why would you want to marry me Diwakar? We have already slept together many times. I am only five years younger than you are. I have a daughter. It doesn't make sense. Men past forty marry much younger women the second time around.' When Abha had said this to him, she had actually meant it. It was not a statement meant to elicit a flattering response.

'Because I want to. I had decided sometime ago that this is something I want to do. So here I am.'

Does having a satisfying and intimate affair guarantee a good marriage? Does anything at all guarantee a good marriage? Was she actually prepared to marry him? Questions and conflicting emotions had gone around Abha's head. Days had turned to weeks and weeks to months. He pursued her. Quietly, gently and single-mindedly. This period, more than anything else, cemented the friendship between them. Could friends be spouses? Could lovers become good life partners?

'You know Abha you like the guy. He has a decent job. You have shared physical chemistry with him. You can laugh with him and cry with him. Just go for it.' Rekha, the leveller, had advised her.

'He loves you Abha. And so do you. So just go for it.' Simran the believer in love had been persuasive.

Love? Where did it come in all this? Abha had never stopped to think. Did all that she felt for him add up to that mysterious emotion called love? She had been unable to unravel the nuances of this mysterious feeling. Abha thought of other things; the differences in their backgrounds, compatibility of their jobs, the children. There was simply so much to think about.

One day Diwakar had driven her to the airport as she was going on a tour. The breeze from the car window was blowing his hair back. He had been animatedly telling her something about a new computer programme that had come into his office.

'It's crazy Abha. We are just going to reach a point soon when humans are going to become redundant. A total appendage to that great machine.'

And Abha had decided. Just like that. Some moments in life are decisive because they are so insignificant.

'Come on Abha let us go down. We will go in our car. Theirs is already full.'

'Yes Bina di.'

'Who will drive?'

'Of course me Papa.' Just because she is going to get married does not mean that she cannot drive the car.

As they pass the sitting room, a photograph of Parul and herself framed on the wall catches Abha's eye.

'So is there anything you want to know about me? My health status, my family background, my caste? Financially let me tell you I am at the bottom, as all my savings went in the divorce settlement.'

Diwakar had asked her once they had decided to marry.

'Not really. But there is one thing I want to tell you. Parul will stay with me. She will not go to a hostel or to relatives.'

'Of course. That is something I accepted long ago.'

'I need to put it loud and clear on the table. There will be no negotiations about this in the future.'

'I don't need to repeat the same thing again and again. Udayan will also come and stay with us in his holidays. Do we really need to discuss all these things? Many things fall in place as time goes by Abha.'

Maybe it was easier for men. They did not need to discuss everything, but women did. All their lives women have to negotiate and fight for what is their right. It had been much easier for Diwakar. His parents accepted his decision to marry again without too much debate. He had told Udayan, his son, when he was in Delhi for holidays in spring. His brother had come to meet her parents and now had come with his family for the marriage.

Abha, Bina di and Papa reach downstairs. Diwakar smiles again. It lights up his whole face. Maybe what Simran said is true. This feeling of happiness when she sees him. Maybe this lightness of being is love.

'Abha I will drive ahead. I know the way to Jamnagar House. You can follow our car. '

'Alright. See you at Jamnagar House.'

They get into their separate cars and set off. Abha watches, as Diwakar turns left from the lane.

'That is the longer route to Jamnagar House he is taking Papa.'

'So what? Just go behind. We are all reaching the same place.'

'But I know a shorter route. The building is just across Shahjahan Road.'

Abha turns right from the lane and meanders through the traffic towards Jamnagar House.

Diwakar watches in the rear view mirror as Abha's car turns in the opposite direction. The woman he is going to marry is taking her own way to the destination. He smiles. When he reaches Jamnagar House, she is already there. Smiling and waving to him.

Glossary of Japanese words

Betsu betsu	Separately—paying for oneself
Chhoto matte kudasai	Please give me a minute
Domo arigato	Thank you
Hara kiri	Ritual suicide, usually related to honor
Icho no ki	Name of tree
Karaoke	Singing to taped accompaniment
Koban	Small police box
Konban wa	Good evening
Mizo soup	Japanese style soya soup
Momiji gari	Viewing autumn colors of maple leaves
Pachinko	Japanese pinball gambling on slot machines
Ryokan	Traditional Japanese hotel
Sakura	Cherry blossom
San	Mr, Mrs, Miss or Ms (Suffix)
Sen	Railway line (suffix)
Sensei	Teacher
Shinkanesen	Bullet train
Tsubaki	Name of tree
Udon	Kind of Japanese noodles
Watashi	I am
Yakosoba	Fried Noodles

Glossary of Indian words

achar	pickle
aloo	potato
arre – hey	a kind of address
beta/beti	son/daughter
jaimal	flower garland exchanged at marriage
karah prashad	the offering at Sikh temples
mehndi	henna
namaste	reverential greeting
padmasan	yogic posture
pheras	ritual circling of sacred fire in Hindu marriage
sabzi	vegetable (raw or cooked)
sanskar	inherited or cultivated value

Acknowledgements

I am grateful to

- Mita Kapur, CEO of Siyahi Literary Agency, for believing in me
- Lov Verma, for painstakingly reading the manuscript every time I asked
- Professor Keiichi Yamazaki, for inputs on Japan
- Dnyaneshwar M Mulay, for being who he is
- Pujya, for being the rainbow of my life
- Damascus, the eternal city, for providing the atmosphere to write the first draft
- Life itself!

I would also like to acknowledge,

Mr. Nirmalkanti Bhattacharjee, Ms. Namita Gokhale, Mr Pavan Kumar Verma, Mr. G Gurucharan, Dr. Kumkum Saran, Ms. Faith Mazani, Ms. Sangeeta Verma, Mr. Amod K Kanth, Mr. Prafulla K Prusty, Ms. Shashi Nim, Mr. Harihar Pratap Singh, Ms. Latifah Binti Othman, Mr. Shwetank Verma, Mr. Arshed Bhatti,

Mr. Ashok Sinha, Mr. Deepak Bagla, Ms. Latha Ayyar, Mr. Antony Djokoto, Mr. Pravin Kumar, Mr. Ramgopal Sharma, Ms. Pramila Sharan, Ms. Sudha Iyer, Mr. Abhinav Verma, Mr. R C Govil, Mr. Joshua Landis, Ms. Anjali Bhatia, Ms. Mamta Kumari, Utsav, Agney and the Central Board of Direct Taxes.